Library of
Davidson College

LECTURES

ON THE

GEOGRAPHY OF GREECE

LECTURES

ON THE

GEOGRAPHY OF GREECE

BY

THE REV. HENRY FANSHAWE TOZER,
M.A., F.R.G.S.
TUTOR AND LATE FELLOW OF EXETER COLLEGE, OXFORD, AUTHOR OF
'RESEARCHES IN THE HIGHLANDS OF TURKEY.'

ARES PUBLISHERS INC.
CHICAGO   MCMLXXIV

Unchanged Reprint of the Edition:
London, 1882.
ARES PUBLISHERS INC.
150 E. Huron Street
Chicago, Illinois 60611
Printed in the United States of America
International Standard Book Number:
0-89005-024-4
Library of Congress Catalog Card Number:
74-77868

TO THE VERY REVEREND

ARTHUR PENRHYN STANLEY, D.D.

DEAN OF WESTMINSTER,

WHO HAS DONE MORE THAN ANY LIVING MAN TO

PROMOTE THE INTELLIGENT STUDY OF

HISTORICAL GEOGRAPHY

THIS VOLUME IS INSCRIBED

BY HIS SINCERE FRIEND AND FORMER PUPIL

THE AUTHOR.

PREFACE.

THESE Lectures were delivered at Oxford in Michaelmas Term 1872, as one of a number of courses voluntarily undertaken by members of the University on subjects indirectly connected with the usual studies. On being requested to lecture on Greek Geography, the Author set himself to consider in what way the subject might most profitably be treated; and as the topography had already been given in considerable detail in the excellent articles in Dr. Smith's *Dictionary of Geography*, it appeared best to attempt (1) to enable students to form a more real conception of the country from the impressions of one who at various times has travelled over most of it: (2) to give a brief summary of the principal physical conditions by which the Greeks were influenced: (3) to sketch the connection of the geography and the history, starting from the geographical point of view: (4) to draw attention to one or two subjects, which have hitherto been but slightly noticed.

With regard to the first of these points, Professor Ruskin some time since remarked—"It is to me simply a standing marvel how scholars can endure for all these centuries, during which their chief education has been in the language and policy of Greece, to have only the names of her hills and rivers upon their lips, and never one line of conception of them in their minds' sight. Which of us knows what the valley of Sparta is like, or the great mountain vase of Arcadia? which of us, except in mere airy syllabling of names, knows aught of 'sandy Ladon's lilied banks, or old Lycæus, or Cyllene hoar?'"* It would probably require the Professor's eloquent pen to describe these properly: all that has been attempted here is to furnish the reader with materials, by means of which he may to some extent represent to himself the country generally and its particular features. The second point, that which relates to the physical conditions, was very carefully worked out for a part of Greece many years ago in Kruse's *Hellas;* but as that book is now almost forgotten, and considerable additions have since been made to our information, it seemed worth while to state summarily the influence of the soil, climate, vegetation, etc., on the history and literature. The

* Ruskin's *Lectures on Art*, p. 103.

third may be accomplished by any intelligent student of history, with the aid of a good map; but even here perhaps a guiding hand may be of some service in pointing out the connection. The fourth mainly comprises two points—the connection of the geography and the mythology, and the etymology of Greek names of places: these questions, which may be made to yield considerable results, have been touched upon by various writers, but have hardly as yet attracted the notice they deserve. In the brief space of ten lectures these subjects have of necessity been very superficially treated; the etymologies, in particular, it has been impossible to discuss fully, though references have been given for those who wish to pursue the subject further, and an Etymological Index of names of places has been appended. If mistakes are found in the midst of so many minute details, it is hoped that allowance will be made for them.

The works to which the Author is chiefly indebted are—Dr. E. Curtius' *Peloponnesos,* a book which is distinguished as well by its breadth of view on geographical questions as by its great learning and accuracy of topographical description; this has often been referred to in the notes, and has furnished many suggestions and references besides: Bursian's *Geographie von*

Griechenland, and the excellent articles on Greece in Dr. Smith's *Dictionary of Geography;* together with the numerous books of travel, which have thrown so much light on the country and its antiquities. Nor can he omit to mention the benefit conferred on the English student by the admirable *Biblical and Classical Atlas* now in course of publication by Mr. Murray, under the editorship of Dr. Smith and Mr. Grove, which, both from their scale and their great accuracy, enable the writer on Ancient Geography to feel that his statements may be verified by the reader, even on minute points. The authorities on Etymology that have been most employed, are mentioned at the commencement of Lecture X.

The edition of Strabo that has been referred to, is that of Kramer; the edition of Pausanias, that of L. Dindorf.

As regards orthography, the mode of spelling Greek names that is customary in England has for the most part been followed, for, although it is in many respects unsatisfactory, it seems hardly worth while to relinquish it until a more consistent method, both of writing and pronouncing Greek names, is adopted, than any that has hitherto been proposed; because, while any change is liable to make words look unfamiliar, that system only is valuable for philological purposes, which enables persons to approximate to the sound of the names in ancient times. In the last chapter, however, which deals with the etymology of the names of places, a circumflex has been placed over *u* in terminations, where it stands for the Greek *ου*, and sometimes also over other long vowels, because here the meaning is seriously affected by the distinction.

CONTENTS.

LECTURE I.

POSITION OF GREECE, AND AUTHORITIES ON THE GEOGRAPHY.

Mode of treating the subject—Smallness of the Area of Greece—Its Central Position—Base Line of the Peninsula—Geography of the neighbouring Countries—Asia Minor—The Western Peninsulas of the Mediterranean—Comparison of Italy and Greece—Their relative Position—Geography of the Iliad and Odyssey—The three Basins of the Mediterranean—Africa—Ancient Authorities on the Geography: Strabo; Pausanias—Modern Explorers: William Martin Leake . . . Pages 1-34

LECTURE II.

PRIMARY FEATURES OF THE COUNTRY—MOUNTAINS, COASTS, AND SEA.

The Mountains of Greece—Chains of Northern Greece: of Central Greece: of the Peloponnese—Their general Elevation—Distinguishing Characteristics—Results of their rocky Character—Descriptive Nomenclature of Greek Mountains—Other Sources of Mountain Names—The Sea, the determining Element—Maritime Character of the Greeks—Dangers of the Greek Seas—General Character of the Winds—The Harbours and Islands—Ideas suggested by the Islands—The Islands off the Coast—The Promontories of Greece—Their Influence on the History—Points of contact with Foreigners—Nomenclature of Greek Promontories 35-79

LECTURE III.

SECONDARY FEATURES OF THE COUNTRY: RIVERS, SPRINGS, LAKES, CAVERNS, GORGES.

The Rivers of Greece—Perennial Streams and Torrents—Features of the Larger Rivers—Homeric Descriptions of the Torrents—Character of the Water—Etymologies of Greek River-names—Legends suggested by Rivers—Sacredness of Fountains—Their Appearance in Antiquity—Warm Springs—Legends connected with Fountains—Lakes with no Outlet—Drainage of the Plains—Subterranean Passages or Catavothras—Famous Caverns—Waterfall of the Styx—Gorges—The Acheron—Vale of Tempe.
Pages 80-122

LECTURE IV.

PHYSICAL CONDITIONS OF THE COUNTRY—SOIL AND MINERALS—EARTHQUAKES AND VOLCANIC ACTION—CLIMATE AND WINDS—VEGETATION.

Nature of the Soil—The chief Products—Minerals—Marbles—Earthquakes in Antiquity: in Modern Times—Greece near a Volcanic Centre—Eruptions in Historic Times—Climate of Greece—Contrasts in Different Districts—The Winds in Homer—Their Subsequent Nomenclature—Character of the Several Winds—"Temple of the Winds" at Athens—Distribution of the Vegetation—The Forests—Important Trees in Antiquity—Lesser Growths and Shrubs—Flowers . 123-163

LECTURE V.

APPEARANCE OF THE COUNTRY—EFFECT OF THE CONFORMATION OF GREECE ON THE CHARACTER AND POLITICS OF THE GREEKS.

Appearance of Greece—Classical Character of the Landscape—Symmetry of the Component Parts—Presence of the Sea—Did the Greeks appreciate Scenery?—Indirect Influence of the Aspect

of the Country—The Mountains and the Sea—Their combined Influence—Greek Scenery and the Hellenic Mind—Influence of Soil and Climate—Effect on the Language—Greek Geography and Politics—Individuality of the States—Opposition between Neighbours—Balance of Power—Varied Forms of Civic Life.
Pages 164-198

LECTURE VI.

GEOGRAPHY OF NORTHERN GREECE.

Survey of the several Districts—Macedonia—Pelagonia and Lyncestis—Position of Edessa—Pella—Peninsula of Chalcidice—Thessaly : Character of its Subdivisions ; Effect on its History—Phthiotis—Passes leading into Thessaly—The Western Countries—Site of Dodona 199-220

LECTURE VII.

GEOGRAPHY OF CENTRAL GREECE.

Malis—Pass of Thermopylæ—Northern Locris and Doris—Phocis—Delphi : its Influence ; its remarkable Position; the surrounding Cliffs—Bœotia: its two Basins—Orchomenus—Thebes—Chalcis and the Euripus—The Passes leading South—Megaris—Attica—Seats of the three Political Parties—Athens : its Site ; the Acropolis ; Areiopagus ; Pnyx ; Dionysiac Theatre ; other Sites 221-258

LECTURE VIII.

GEOGRAPHY OF THE PELOPONNESE.

Character of the Peloponnese : its natural Unity—The Isthmus—Corinth—Position of Achaia—Elis : its triple Division—Fertility of the Soil — The Olympian Festival — Description of Olympia—Messenia : its two Plains ; its Climate and Soil—Pylos and Sphacteria—Laconia—The Valley-Plain—Sparta and Taygetus—Arcadia : its elevated Position—Plain of Tegea and Mantineia—Character of the Inhabitants—Argolis—Importance of the Argive Plain—Upland Region of Nemea—Sanctuary of Æsculapius 259-297

LECTURE IX.

ON THE CONNECTION BETWEEN GREEK GEOGRAPHY AND GREEK MYTHOLOGY.

Origin of Greek Myths—Greece suitable for Polytheism—Myths connected with the Geography—Local Myths of Thessaly—Sacred Centres of Mythology—Haunts of Deities—Birthplace of Music—Local Worship of Poseidon—Mythical Genealogies—Descent derived from River Gods—Myths suggested by Water—Myths of the Catavothras—Local Legends of Theseus—Myths of Observation—Etymological Myths—Ancient Legends in Modern Greece—Story of the Copaic Lake . Pages 298-334

LECTURE X.

ON THE ETYMOLOGY OF GREEK NAMES OF PLACES.

Principles of Nomenclature—Names derived from the Vegetation—Names derived from Animals—Caution required—Doubtful Etymologies—Non-Hellenic Names—Vagueness of the Greek Terminations—Peculiarities of Form—Sources of Names: Relative Position; Elevated Position; Enclosed Situation; Maritime Character; Environs, etc.; Water; Pasturage and Tillage; Colour; Resemblances to Men and Animals; Resemblances to Inanimate Objects; Worship of Deities—Names containing Numerals—Names from Occupations, etc.—Political Names—Names evidencing Geographical Changes—Pelasgic and other Names—Phœnician Names—Ancient Names in Modern Greece 335-384

ETYMOLOGICAL INDEX 385

GENERAL INDEX 393

LECTURE I.

POSITION OF GREECE, AND AUTHORITIES ON THE GEOGRAPHY.

Mode of treating the subject—Smallness of the Area of Greece—Its Central Position—Base Line of the Peninsula—Geography of the neighbouring Countries—Asia Minor—The Western Peninsulas of the Mediterranean—Comparison of Italy and Greece—Their relative Position—Geography of the Iliad and Odyssey—The three Basins of the Mediterranean—Africa—Ancient Authorities on the Geography: Strabo; Pausanias—Modern Explorers: William Martin Leake.

IN lecturing on the Geography of Greece it would be possible to give a minute description of all the objects contained in the country, to enumerate the towns which existed in the several districts, and to state what we know of their past and present condition. Of course, a certain amount of such detail is inseparable from every mode of treating the subject, but the method which I have stated would severely try your patience, and at the same time would be, to a great extent, superfluous, because it would add little to the matter contained in Dr. Smith's *Dictionary of Geography*, and, in a collective form, in Bursian's valuable *Geographie von Griechenland*. The object which I propose to myself is rather to describe the physical features of the country, and the works of man upon it, as they appeared to the Greeks themselves, as they

Mode of treating the subject.

influenced their history, and, what is most important of all, as they affected the national character and mind. This may seem at first sight a narrow subject, but in reality is one which it is difficult to restrain within reasonable limits. For, in the first place, the study of geography, being placed, as it were, on the borderland between the physical sciences and those relating to man, holds the most central position of all, and is connected in a variety of ways with many of the others. Climate, vegetation, soil, the composition of the rocks and the metals they contain, the changes in the ground and the influences that have caused them,—and on the other hand the history and mythology of the inhabitants, their art and archæology,—all these subjects, and the sciences which deal with them, claim to be heard, and cannot without injustice be excluded. Even philology, whose province seems the most remote, is now appearing on the scene, and tells us that the nomenclature of a country, which she will help us to investigate, has much to teach with regard both to the places themselves and to those who named them. Fortunately, neither the lecturer on geography nor his hearers are required to be acquainted with anything more than the barest results of the more abstruse of these sciences, otherwise the study of geography would soon come to an end. But in addition to this cause, which belongs to the subject in general, there is a more special reason why Greek geography cannot be confined within narrow limits, arising from the nature of the country and its relation to its inhabitants. For no part of Europe—perhaps it would not be too much to say no part of the world—presents so great a variety of natural features within the same area as Greece; and no country that we are acquainted with has shown so perfect an adaptation to the people who settled in it, and consequently so great power of developing their character and genius. It is this circumstance, if I mistake not, more than any other, which accounts for the pre-eminent greatness of ancient Greece; and for this reason, if for no other, the geography of the country deserves the most careful study.

The first point that strikes us as we look at the map of Greece, is the smallness of the country relatively to the influence it has exercised on the history of the world. The sarcasm that was levelled long ago against Palestine, that a district so limited in size could not have changed the fortunes of mankind, will apply with almost equal force to Greece. The whole length of the country, from the northernmost corner of Thessaly to Cape Matapan in the south, is comprised within 4 degrees of latitude; and not only does it contract in breadth as it advances southwards, but everywhere its area is lessened by the numerous gulfs and bays which encroach upon the land. In particular, the part on which the fame of the country mainly depends—that which lies within Mount Othrys and the mountains of Ætolia—is especially limited in its

Smallness of the area of Greece.

dimensions; and, as a consequence of this, the traveller is surprised by the insignificant distances which separate places of world-wide renown. In two hours he rides at a foot's pace from Chæronea to Orchomenus; in three hours from Corinth to Sicyon; from Athens to Megara is a drive of less than five hours; the sites of Nauplia, Tiryns, Mycenæ, and Argos, can easily be visited in the course of a single day. Similarly, by sea a short run with a favouring wind takes you across from the Piræus to Ægina, and thence to Epidaurus on the coast of Argolis, or from the Isthmus of Corinth to the inmost recesses of the Crissæan gulf under Mount Parnassus. Now, when we inquire into the causes which contributed to give such prominence to so small a district, we find one ready to hand in the position which it occupied in the old world. No other country, in fact, was so central; for, though both Egypt and Palestine might seem at first sight rather to deserve that epithet, in consequence of their lying nearer to the meeting-point of the three great continents, yet there were insuperable difficulties to prevent either of them from assuming the part which was reserved for Greece. Egypt, enclosed in her narrow river-valley, learning a lesson of perpetual dependence from the great river, to which she was indebted for her daily sustenance, and still further enslaved by her minute and cramped civilisation, had neither the power nor the will to influence foreign nations. Had it not been for Greek enterprise, the

Its central position.

culture of Egypt would have remained for ever a sealed book to the rest of the world. And Palestine was reserved for other and greater purposes than to transmit the torch of eastern civilisation to western lands. In her narrow limits, between the desert and the sea, she was the fitting home for a people set apart, among whom the truths of morality and religion were to receive a special and independent development. But the long and almost harbourless shore of Syria was no starting-point for the pioneers of human culture. One solitary exception, that of Tyre, serves to render the contrast more striking; but Tyre, the Venice of antiquity, notwithstanding the wonderful inventions which she transmitted to the Greeks, was too much absorbed in her mercantile gains, and too little occupied by those thoughts and interests which contribute permanently to human advancement, to occupy a really central position. In like manner Alexandria, which the eagle eye of its great founder distinguished as the commercial metropolis of the world, was chosen before its time; it was fitted to be the capital, not of an incipient, but of a full-grown and cosmopolitan civilisation; it required that Africa, as well as Europe and Asia, should be developed before its real importance should be discovered. But Greece occupied in ancient times a position in many respects similar to that of England at the present day: she was the natural point of communication between the old world and the new; all the arts, all the ideas, all the movements, which passed from the east to the west, must necessarily pass through her; she had it in her power to modify and recast whatever was transmitted from the one to the other.

Base line of the Peninsula.   The Hæmus or Balkan mountains, which form the base of the south-eastern European peninsula, are to be regarded as the easternmost link in the great chain, which, under the names of Pyrenees, Alps, and Dinaric Alps, are the line of demarcation between central and southern Europe. But here we must be on our guard against an error, which has only lately been dispelled by geographical research, and affects most of our maps even at the present day—namely, that these mountains form a continuous chain to the north of Greece. The origin of this misconception is to be found in a passage in Strabo, which speaks of the mountains to the north of Macedonia as forming a single line. It runs as follows:—"Macedonia is bounded on the north by what may be conceived of as a straight line formed by Mounts Bertiscus, Scardus, Orbèlus, Rhodope, and Hæmus; for these mountains, commencing from the Adriatic, reach in a straight line as far as the Euxine."[1] This passage is valuable, because it gives us the names of the mountain ranges that form this chain; but it should be observed that it does not come directly from Strabo himself, but from his epitomiser, as the original occurred in the lost part of the seventh book: it ought not therefore to be

---

[1] Strabo, vii. fragm. 10 (Kramer).

interpreted independently of another, though less definite, passage in the text of Strabo, bearing on the same point, in which the statement about the "straight line" is given in a much more qualified manner:—
"The mountains of Illyricum, Pæonia, and Thrace, are, in a certain way, parallel to the Ister, forming, as it were, a single line, which reaches from the Adriatic as far as the Pontus."[2] It was a natural interpretation of these passages, that the country between the Danube and the Ægean was divided in the middle by a lofty range of mountains which formed a continuation of the main chain of the Alps as far as the Euxine, and that the Scardus in particular formed part of this transverse range, and ran from west to east. Now, however, it is known that along one important portion of this supposed line—namely, to the south-east of the modern principality of Servia— the hills do not rise to any considerable elevation, and that the Scardus range ran from north to south.[3] It does not follow from this that Strabo was in error, but the expression "straight line" was certain to mislead, and has caused him to be misinterpreted. The Bertiscus, with which the line commences towards the Adriatic, is the chain of lofty serrated peaks that reaches from the confines of Montenegro to the sources

[2] Strabo, vii. 5, § 1.
[3] This was first pointed out by Grisebach in his *Reise durch Rumelien*, ii. 110, foll., and has since been amply established by Von Hahn in his *Reise von Belgrad nach Salonik*.

of the White Drin; but here the direction changes, and the next link is formed by the Scardus, which still retains its name as the modern Schar, and is a northern continuation of Pindus. In the neighbourhood of Heraclea Lyncestis, the modern Monastir, the mountains again take an easterly direction, and passing the Stena of the Axius, now the Iron Gate of the Vardar, join Mount Orbelus, from which the irregular line of mountains which bore the name of Rhodope leads in a north-easterly direction to the Balkan. The course followed by these chains is sufficiently irregular, but the fact of their having been grouped together is sufficiently accounted for by the temptation which always exists to regard a system of mountains as forming a single line, in order to give completeness and facilitate description: it is thus that we apply that term to the Alps and Pyrenees, though they take very different directions. But, as we have seen, the Hæmus cannot be considered as forming an unbroken continuation of the chain of the Alps, and the interval thus left must be taken into account as partly determining the course of barbarian immigration. At the same time the Hæmus was important as the first of a series of ramparts by which Greece was defended, and as marking out the direction which Greek development was to follow. Being debarred from spreading inland, the inhabitants were forced to take to the sea, and, as we shall subsequently notice, there were other predisposing causes which required them at first to turn their steps towards Asia.

Before proceeding to consider the geography of Greece itself, it may be well for us to notice briefly that of the neighbouring countries, with which it was brought into contact, either in the way of commerce or of colonisation. And first of Asia Minor. That remarkable country, one of the ἀκταί or projecting tracts into which Herodotus divides Western Asia,[4] forming, as it does, a connecting link between the two continents, was of importance to those tribes who ultimately settled in Greece, because, from its natural conformation, it facilitated their onward movement after they had left their early home in the highlands of Central Asia, and at the same time forbade their return. Few countries that we are acquainted with maintain so great a general elevation so near to the sea. At its eastern extremity, where it separates from the mountains of Armenia, it forms a plateau of nearly 4000 feet in height, and though there is a gradual slope towards the west, yet in the centre of the country the great undulating plain which stretches westward from Ancyra is still 3000 feet above the sea-level, and this is only reduced to 2000 when it begins to sink down towards the Ægean. Still more remarkable is the suddenness with which the ground rises both on the southern and the northern coasts; in some places the height of nearly 3000 feet is

[4] Herod. iv. 37, foll.

reached within twelve miles of the Euxine. The central plateau is bounded by two ranges of mountains, which run nearly parallel to one another from east to west—on the north the successive chains which, under the general name of Olympus, pass through Pontus, Galatia, Bithynia, and Mysia; on the south the great Taurus range in Cilicia and Pisidia. Large tracts of the interior are volcanic, in particular the extensive district in Phrygia called Catacecaumene, or the "Burnt Land," which contains a large number of extinct volcanoes, and in the south-east the Mons Argæus, the gigantic cone of which rises to the height of 13,000 feet. The principal rivers that drain it—the Iris, the Sangarius, and especially that which is the most central and far the most important, the Halys—after describing great arcs in their course, and receiving numerous tributaries, make their way through the northern mountains into the Black Sea. So far we have seen nothing in Asia Minor which could lead the Greeks to desire a more intimate acquaintance with it. Their ancestors had passed through it, and some at least of the tribes that remained there were their kindred; but when they had once settled in Europe, there was nothing to induce them to return. And, as a matter of fact, in the most flourishing times of Greece, their knowledge of the interior was very limited. But when from the western edge of the plateau we descend towards the sea, the conditions are all changed. Here, in Mysia,

Lydia, and Caria, we discover all the elements that the Greeks found most attractive—an extensive seaboard, deeply indented with bays and harbours, and fringed with fertile islands, in every way adapted for maritime enterprise; mountains of beautiful form, and thickly clothed with wood; four rivers—the Caicus, the Hermus, the Cayster, and the Mæander—fertilising rich and fruitful valleys; and, above all, a climate which was famed in antiquity as the most delightful in the world. To these natural advantages we must add, what the Greeks never failed to profit by, the remains of an ancient civilisation close at hand, and an extensive tract of country at their back, the produce of which they might transport to other lands.

When we turn from the countries on the eastern side of Greece to those on the western, we find two other great peninsulas projecting into the Mediterranean from the continent of Europe, somewhat in the same manner as Greece itself. Eratosthenes[5] was the first ancient author who drew attention to the points of resemblance in the position of these three territories; and though Strabo finds fault with him for comparing Greece to the Italian and Ligurian peninsulas because of its less uniform character and more numerous projections, yet his criticism is erroneous, in consequence of his mistaken views of the conformation of Greece, and his regarding rather the details than the general

The western Peninsulas of the Mediterranean.

[5] Quoted by Strabo, ii. 1, § 40; and compare E. Curtius, *Peloponnesos*, i. 23.

figure of the continent. Strabo supposed that the promontory of Sunium lay nearly as far south as that of Malea, thus causing the Attic peninsula to advance far too great a distance into the Ægean; and this idea, together with the prominence he assigned to the Thracian Chersonese, prevented him from discovering sufficient unity of form in the Greek continent to allow of its being compared with the other two. In reality, however, it is in the westernmost of the three that the resemblance is the least striking. Spain, which Strabo[6] aptly compares in shape to a bull's hide, the neck-piece being formed by the isthmus that joins it to France, has a marked difference of structure from Italy and Greece in consequence of its massive breadth and the direction of its mountain chains, which run in parallel lines from east to west, distinct from one another, and effectually preventing the country from forming an organic whole. But when we come to compare Italy and Greece, the correspondences are no less striking. We might almost regard the one as a distorted image of the other. In Italy the most salient features are the great northern plain between the Alps and Apennines, shut off from the Ligurian Sea by its barrier of intervening mountains; the long central chain, which forms its backbone, and divides it into two halves, with the numerous lateral spurs that run off from it, either forming inland valleys, or embracing extensive plains

Comparison of Italy and Greece.

---

[6] ii. 5, § 27.

that open on the sea; and finally, the island of Sicily, which is its natural complement, and partakes of the same organisation. We could conceive that by some crushing process the form of this country might be so modified as to resemble very closely the continent of Greece south of the parallel of Mount Olympus. There also we find a great northern plain, that of Thessaly, separated from the western sea by the mountain masses of Epirus; a well-marked backbone of mountains, from which at intervals other chains run off at right angles, though far longer and better articulated than those of Italy; valley-plains, either lying inland or with a maritime aspect; and lastly the Peloponnese, in which the whole country seems to culminate. At the same time the differences of the two countries are not less forcibly marked. The comparatively uniform outline of Italy contrasts strongly with the extraordinary multiplicity of form of the Greek coasts; the islands which stud the seas of Greece, and tended to draw its inhabitants out of themselves, are wanting to Italy; the separate parts of the country are more complete in themselves and more independently developed in the eastern than in the western peninsula; and the limb in which the whole organism terminates has not been severed from the body in the one case, as it has in the other. This last point, slight as it may seem at first sight, was in reality of the greatest importance. When Polybius,[7] in comparing

[7] i. 42.

the Peloponnese with Sicily, remarks that the passage to the one is made by land, to the other by water, he fixes on the distinguishing point of difference between the two. It is another instance of the immense influence of the "little streak of blue water," as in the case of the Hellespont which separates Europe from Asia, and of the channel which gives England her insular position. The "rent" as the Greeks called the Straits of Messina—for this was the origin of the name they gave to the neighbouring town of Rhegium—the rent between Sicily and the mainland effectually prevented that island from occupying a similar position to that which the Peloponnese held in Greece. It is true indeed, as Mommsen has remarked,[8] that in its historical relations Sicily was in earlier times quite as decidedly a part of Italy as that district was of Greece,—an arena for the struggles of the same races, and the seat of a similar superior civilisation; but at a later period this ceased to be the case. And, on the other hand, had the island of Pelops really been an island, it would have lost more than half the advantages of its situation. As it was, the isthmus secured to it all the benefits of an insular position without any of the disadvantages. While it enjoyed the neighbourhood of the sea on every side, a long and varied coast-line, naturally accompanied by a temperate and equable climate, and well-defined boundaries, which promoted the feeling of independence, and kept

---

[8] History of Rome, i. 6 (Eng. Trans.)

injurious influences at a distance, it possessed at the same time a secure and uninterrupted outlet for its commerce, and a bond of connection which could save it from complete isolation, and cause it to participate in the interests and the ideas of the continent to which it was attached.[9]

Before leaving the question of the correspondences and contrasts of Italy and Greece, we should notice one point which materially affected the relations of the two—viz., that these countries stand, as it were, back to back to one another. The outlets of Greece were all towards the east. On the side toward the Ægean the coast is far more indented with bays and inlets, and consequently there is a much larger number of harbours to act as a starting-point for maritime enterprise. The principal maritime plains, especially those of Attica and Argolis, open out in the same direction; and the chains of islands, from one to another of which the sailor might pass without losing sight of land, all suggested to him an easterly course. We cannot, therefore, be surprised, if at an early period the course of Greek colonisation and commerce set almost exclusively towards Asia. But when we turn to the west side of Greece, we find that, with the exception of the bays of Pylus and Methone in the south-west of Messenia, the Peloponnese has hardly a harbour to offer; and farther north, the districts that lay along the sea-

Their relative position.

[9] E. Curtius, *Peloponnesos*, i. 21.

board, Acarnania and Epirus, being irregular masses, composed of confused mountain chains, were too far removed from the civilisation of the rest of Greece to form a link of communication with the western countries. Thus it was that the Ionian islands, and especially Corcyra, of which Thucydides[10] says that it was an excellent station for a coasting voyage to Italy and Sicily, were disqualified in the earliest times, and only at a later period served to guide the Greeks on their way to colonise the west. Italy, on the other hand, had a completely western aspect: its south-east provinces, Apulia and Iapygia, never influenced the history of the country; while the districts on which its future development was destined to depend—Campania, Latium, and Etruria—opened on the Tyrrhenian Sea. Thus the two countries were left to pursue their own courses independently of one another.

Geography of the Iliad and Odyssey.

The point which we have just noticed serves further to elucidate the interesting question of Homeric geography. As we have seen that at a remote period of their history the Greeks were but slightly acquainted with the western countries, we should expect to find that the localities of their earliest poems would be accurately described, only so far as they belong to continental Greece and to the neighbourhood of the Ægean. And this is precisely what we discover to be the case. The geo-

[10] Thuc. i. 36.

graphy of the Iliad is everywhere definite, and shows carefulness of description such as is not found in later Greek poets. The topography of the Plain of Troy is accurately drawn, allowance being made for poetical adaptation and the necessities of the story; and the same thing may be said of the neighbouring region. The chain of Ida, with Gargarus, its highest summit, and the most commanding point of all the surrounding country, which is consequently chosen as the fitting seat of Zeus;[11] the promontory of Lectum, in which it terminates towards the Ægean;[12] the islands of Tenedos, Lemnos, Imbros, and Samothrace, in their respective positions;[13] the Hellespont, and the opposite coast of Thrace,[14] are all faithfully given. Again, when places on the continent of Greece are mentioned, the local epithets, which are applied to them, are, with rare exceptions, singularly appropriate, as Eratosthenes[15] remarked in ancient times, and, as most modern travellers have observed. But when we come to the geography of the Odyssey, the same thing does not apply. We seem at once to have entered upon a region of fable; and this arises not merely from the character of the story—from our having passed from the *chanson de*

[11] Il. xiv. 352, xv. 152.   [12] xiv. 284.
[13] Compare together Il. xiv. 230, xiii. 33, xxiv. 78, xiii. 12, and xxiv. 753.
[14] ix. 72.   [15] Quoted by Strabo, i. 2, § 3.

gestes to the *roman d'aventures*—but also from ignorance of the localities themselves. It has, indeed, been maintained by M. Burnouf,[16] that the Odyssey was composed in western, as the Iliad was in eastern Greece, and that the local descriptions are as exact in the one as in the other. To prove this he relies principally on a supposed confusion between the Bosphorus and the Straits of Messina, from which he argues the author's ignorance of the former, and on the omission, or infrequent mention, in the similes of the Odyssey, of certain wild animals, such as the lion, the boar, and the wolf, which he regards as either peculiar to, or more commonly found in, Asia, and which are frequently introduced in the Iliad. But, independently of the fact that the boar and the wolf, at all events, were frequently found in parts of continental Greece, which, in default of other evidence, might be proved by the numerous names of places derived from them, the difference of subject of the two poems—the one being a tale of war, the other of peace—would be a sufficient explanation of the more frequent introduction in the former of them of such objects of comparison. Such arguments, indeed, are slippery ground; and with regard to the general question, it may reasonably be doubted whether any of the descriptions of places to the west of Greece are based on real knowledge. The claims of Corcyra to

---

[16] *Revue des deux Mondes,* vol. lxv. p. 736.

represent the Homeric Phæacia were long ago satisfactorily disposed of by Professor Welcker;[17] and, notwithstanding the trouble that has been expended in exploring the antiquities of Ithaca, it is extremely difficult to reconcile the topography of that island with what we find in the Odyssey. So far am I from believing that western Greece was the cradle of that poem, that it appears to me that almost the only really reliable piece of geography that it contains is the description of the course pursued by the Greek chieftains through the Ægean sea after leaving Troy.[18] Here the poet is treading on safe ground; he conducts them from Tenedos to Lesbos, and there represents them as debating which of two routes they should take across the sea to the shores of Greece: whether they should steer straight to Eubœa, through the open sea, leaving Psyra on their left; or whether they should keep between Chios and Cape Mimas on the peninsula of Erythræ, from whence they would be able to follow the line of the northern Cyclades as far as Geræstus, the southern Eubœan promontory. The former of these routes, according to the ideas of navigation of that time, could only be attempted in fair weather, and accordingly they did not venture upon it until they had received a favourable omen from Poseidon. All this is most accurately delineated, and shows an exact knowledge of the localities; but as soon as the poet passes Cape Malea, he enters

[17] *Kleine Schriften*, ii. 1 foll.   [18] Od. iii. 159–178.

on the realm of fiction, which the west long continued to be to the people of the east.[19]

The three basins of the Mediterranean.

The Mediterranean naturally divides into three great basins, which are partially shut off from one another by corresponding headlands of Europe and Africa. The easternmost of these, to which Greece properly belonged, is formed by the island of Crete together with the coast of the Cyrenaica, which here bends forward to meet it. Westward of this, the central basin is defined by a much more strongly marked limit, where the extreme point of the Carthaginian territory, now Cape Bon, approaches closely to Sicily. The third section includes the remaining portion as far as the Straits of Gibraltar. This triple division, it should be observed, is not an accidental one, but is based on the geological conformation of the Mediterranean basin; so much so, that, as Humboldt, who was the first to point out this fact, has remarked,[20] nature seems to aim at separating the western from the central section, and as late as the year 1831 a volcanic island was upheaved from the sea between the coast of Sicily and that of Africa. Now, as we have seen, it was only with the first of these, and only with a limited part of it, that the Greeks were acquainted in early times; and when they made their way into the second, their progress

---

[19] Mommsen says (i. 139), "In the Homeric poems the horizon scarcely extends beyond the eastern basin of the Mediterranean." [20] *Cosmos*, ii. 481 (Otté's Translation).

was for a long time a very gradual one. It is curious to trace how cautiously they feel their way along the coast of Sicily. All the earliest colonies—Naxos, Syracuse, Leontini, Catana, and Megara Hyblæa—were founded on the eastern side. Nearly half a century elapsed before they made their way round to the southern coast, and founded their first city, Gela; and it was considerably later that they explored the northern side of the island and established themselves at Himera. Even subsequently to this, notwithstanding the bold track which carried the Phocæans to Massilia, and their other adventurous voyages,[21] Greek knowledge of geography did not extend far west of Sicily. Hercules the traveller, you will observe, is a Phœnician god. It is he who is the tutelary deity of the city of Gades, and gives his name to the Pillars. Though the story of his bringing back the oxen from the west is undoubtedly a fragment of a solar myth, yet the accounts of the places where it was localised all come from Phœnician sources.

The great continent which formed the southern boundary of the Mediterranean was little known to the Greeks, and presented few attractions to them. Independently of their dislike of the open sea, which had to be crossed before Africa could be reached, they were discouraged by the want of rivers on that coast, at the mouths of which they might have established themselves.[22] Even the islanders in early times seem Africa.

[21] Herod. i. 163.   [22] E. Curtius, *History of Greece*, i. 457.

hardly to have turned their thoughts that way. When the people of Thera, according to the story given in Herodotus,[23] being ordered by the Delphic oracle to found a colony in Libya, endeavoured to obtain information about that country, they could find but one man, Corobius of Crete, who had ever been there, and he had been carried thither against his will by contrary winds. There certainly was no regular communication between Greece and Africa until later times, and even then the Hellenic colonies did not spread there as the prosperity of Cyrene would lead us to expect. With Carthage the Greeks were not brought directly into contact; it was in Sicily that the two peoples first met in arms, and the decisive battle of Himera permanently checked the advance of the Carthaginians in that quarter.

Ancient authorities on the geography.

Having thus taken a survey of the outer geography of Greece, let us proceed to notice briefly the two great authorities on whom we have to rely for an account of the ancient condition of the country—Strabo and Pausanias. While naming these, we must not, of course, forget that much valuable information is also to be obtained from other classical writers, and especially historians; but the notices which they furnish are given incidentally, and for anything like a systematic account we must look to professed geographers, and of these the two that I have named are far the most important. The first of them, Strabo, who

Strabo.

[23] iv. 151.

lived in the Augustan age, was a native of Amasia, a city of Pontus, on the banks of the Iris, where the famous tombs of the kings of that country still remain. His work, which is comprised in seventeen books, is a treatise on universal geography, and for such a task he was especially qualified by his comprehensive mind, vast learning, and extensive travels. So great was the estimation in which he was held in ancient times, that by the later Greeks he is regularly spoken of as *the* Geographer. He availed himself of all the materials that were at his command at that time, and drew largely from other writers, especially from Eratosthenes, whose works are now lost, but who must have been a man of even superior ability, and, notwithstanding that he preceded Strabo by more than two centuries, seems to have been better acquainted with mathematical geography. By the use of these, confirmed by his own careful observation and inquiry, he communicated to the men of his time a knowledge of the world which was not enlarged for several centuries.[24] Unfortunately, the 8th, 9th, and 10th books, which are devoted to Greece, are the least satisfactory part of his work. This arises from two causes. In the first place, he had himself seen but little of the country: had he penetrated but a short distance into the Peloponnese he would not have stated that no remains of Mycenæ were in existence,[25] whereas they have subsequently

---

[24] Niebuhr, *Lectures on Ethnography and Geography*, i. 21.
[25] viii. 6, § 10.

been described by Pausanias, and are still visible. As his object in writing was to make his book readable, he endeavours all through to compress his information within a moderate compass, and he may have been influenced by the idea that Greece had already been sufficiently described. Leake believes that he visited especially the coasts of Greece, because the distances he gives by sea are more accurate than those in the interior,[26] but this is probably to be accounted for by his having followed in the former the measurements of Eratosthenes. As it is, he falls into serious errors. We have already seen that he places Sunium almost as far south as Malea; he is also very far out in his conception of the position of the Isthmus, for he measures the breadth of the Peloponnese by drawing a line to that point from Cape Chelonatas in the west of Elis,[27] showing thereby that he regarded it as being to the extreme east of the country. Both these facts imply that he had an erroneous notion of the points of the compass in Greece. But a second, and certainly not less influential, cause of want of thoroughness in his description of this country, is the antiquarian point of view from which he regards it. As soon as he sets foot on Greek soil his method seems to change, and from delineating scientific and historical geography he turns to the discussion of passages of Homer. This, no doubt, was partly owing to the spirit of the age,

---

[26] Leake, *Athens and the Demi of Attica*, i. 32.
[27] viii. 2, § 1.

for the men of that time had thoroughly accustomed themselves to look upon Greece as interesting only in the past, and as possessing no present importance.[28] But at the same time he was completely enslaved by his veneration for Homer, so that he devotes a large part of the long introduction to his work to combating the views of Eratosthenes, who had ventured to depreciate the authority of the great poet as a teacher of general geography, and had limited the accuracy of his information to Hellenic lands. Hence, when he comes to Greece itself, Homer becomes his text-book, and the examination of his geographical statements is his principal occupation. Still, we must not ignore the amount of valuable information which he has handed down to us; and he has all the merit of a critical writer. His etymologies of the names of places, when he ventures upon them, are often worthy of respect; thus his derivation of the river-name Crathis from κεράννυμι or κίρνημι, "to mix"—ἀπὸ τοῦ κίρνασθαι τὴν ὀνομασίαν ἔχων, as he says[29]—is probably right. He equally shows his penetration and good sense here and there in his interpretation of myths; we shall have to refer subsequently to his explanation of the story of the contest of Hercules and the Achelous for the possession of Deianeira.[30]

In presenting to you the other great geographer of Greece, Pausanias, I introduce you to a very quaint *Pausanias.*

[28] E. Curtius, *Peloponnesos*, i. 120.
[29] viii. 7, § 4.　　　　[30] x. 2, § 19.

figure. He is the thorough archæologist. What Anthony-a-Wood was to Oxford, what Ambrosio Morales was to Spain, that Pausanias was to Greece. If I was required to describe him in few words, I would say, "Take Herodotus, and eliminate all his wit (using that term in its widest sense), and you will have Pausanias." He has all, and more than all, the δεισιδαιμονία of his great predecessor; in speaking of the mysteries he uses almost the same expressions of awe; he echoes his sentiments about the nemesis that attends on overweening prosperity, when contrasting the deserted condition of Megalopolis with the great hopes with which it was founded;[31] he regards the wickedness of the times as the reason why the men of his age never were changed into gods;[32] he retains all the old reverence for the oracles, saying that he cannot doubt the truth of the story of the Alpheius passing under the sea, because it had been confirmed by the god at Delphi.[33] His appetite for relics is astonishing. At Aulis he is shown some of the wood of the plane-tree mentioned by Homer in connection with the augury of Calchas;[34] in the temple of Minerva Alea at Tegea he carefully noted down the skin of the Caledonian boar, which he tells us was quite worn away by time, and had lost all its bristles;[35] at Delphi he sees a stone, which was reported to have been the one given to Cronos to

[31] viii. 33, § 1.   [32] viii. 2, § 5.   [33] v. 7, § 3.
[34] ix. 19, § 7.   [35] viii. 47, § 2.

swallow in the place of his son;[36] at Sparta he finds hanging from the roof of a temple the egg to which Leda was said to have given birth.[37] With regard to this last, it would be interesting to know whether it was broken or entire. He also possesses, though in a very inferior degree, Herodotus' quaint power of observation; and this leads him into numerous digressions, which, though but slightly connected with the subject on hand, often contain valuable information. Thus he describes the meteorological and other phenomena that have accompanied earthquakes in Greece;[38] he mentions the peculiar colours of springs in various parts of the world;[39] he discusses the question why oil should be required to preserve ivory statues in some places, and water in others, according to the climate.[40] He takes a peculiar interest in trees, noticing, among other points, the immense height of the cypresses at Psophis,[41] and the girth of the plane-trees near Pharæ, within the trunks of which banquets used to be held;[42] and in a digression he mentions the relative ages of the oldest trees existing in the Greek sanctuaries.[43] He is a thoroughly uncritical writer, and hence the etymologies which he introduces are of the most far-fetched and unreasonable description: he derives the name of the river Balyra in Messenia from βάλλειν λύραν, because Tha-

[36] x. 24, § 6. [37] iii. 16, § 1. [38] vii. 24, § 7.
[39] iv. 35, § 9. [40] v. 11, § 10. [41] viii. 24, § 7.
[42] vii. 22, § 1. [43] viii. 23, § 5.

myris was said to have cast away his lyre there,[44] and that of Lycorea, a place in the upper regions of Parnassus, from λύκων ὠρυγαί, because at the time of Deucalion's flood the inhabitants were conducted to this refuge by the howling of wolves.[45] In all this he is the representative of his age, which was an etymological one, and simply fanciful in its etymologies. In a spirit worthy of a scholiast, he piles one explanation on the top of another; you have them all before you, and he does not mind which you choose. A notable instance of this is his account of the name Ozolæ, as applied to the western branch of the Locrians.[46] It may come from ὄζος, "a branch," in which case it is connected with a story of a vine having miraculously sprung out of a log of wood to which a dog gave birth, and the shoots of this gave their name to the inhabitants. Or it may come from ὄζειν, "to stink," and if so, may be derived from a version of the story of the Centaur Nessus, which related that he escaped wounded from Hercules, and died in that country, and that as he was left unburied there arose a smell. Or it may have been from the stinking water of a river, or from the abundance of the asphodel plant, the flower of which has a strong odour. Or lastly, the inhabitants, being primitive herdsmen, clothed themselves in the untanned skins of animals, which caused them to be offensive to their neighbours. Similarly, though

[44] iv. 33, § 3.   [45] x. 6, § 2.   [46] x. 38, § 1.

many of the myths he relates are the most transparent allegories, he is quite incapable of seeing through them. As might be expected, he is completely destitute of humour.

But while we thus notice the shortcomings and oddities of Pausanias, we must not shut our eyes to his surpassing merits. Thanks to him, we possess a more complete knowledge of the topography, the art, and the mythology of Greece, than of those of any other nation of antiquity. He is not, in the proper sense of the term, a geographer, for the features of the country have little interest for him, and even mountain ranges are passed by almost unnoticed, unless some legend is attached to them. But in describing cities he is unrivalled. With extraordinary diligence he went through the whole country in a succession of tours, and after finding out the local guides or *cicerones* in each place, wrote down a full account of all that was to be seen, together with all the traditional stories. His book, which he calls an Itinerary (Ἑλλάδος περιήγησις), was a subsequent redaction of these journals. The period too at which he travelled was especially fitted for the work he had in hand, for at no time, probably, had the monuments of Greece been so numerous and in so good preservation as in the latter half of the second century A.D., when he lived. Here and there, indeed, he tells of towns deserted and temples in ruins, though these, in all likelihood, were not more numerous than the crumbling abbey churches in England at the present day; but, on the other hand, we must remember that the Emperor Hadrian, in the early part of that century, had been a great restorer of public buildings, and that Greece had been greatly indebted to his liberality. It was the moment when the work of centuries had been completed, and destruction had not yet set in. And the diligence of Pausanias is equalled by his accuracy. It is the work of modern explorers to compare the ruins that they find with his descriptions, and they may be confident of finding them correspond. With his book in your hand, you can go round the sites of the ancient cities, and reconstruct them as they stood. As it has been admirably expressed, in following him from point to point, "you feel that you are following an invisible guide—a ghost among ghosts."[47] And, notwithstanding his veneration for the objects he saw, and his love of art, he is never betrayed into sentimental enthusiasm or dilettante criticism. His strongest exclamation, when speaking of the most splendid statues of antiquity, is "they are worth seeing" ($\theta \acute{\varepsilon} \alpha \varsigma$ $\ddot{\alpha} \xi \iota \alpha$). He describes the pictures in the Pœcile at Athens and the Lesche at Delphi in the clearest, but at the same time the simplest language. This rare self-restraint gives all his statements the stamp of truth.

The latest antiquarian discovery that has been made in Greece forcibly illustrates the accuracy of

[47] Dean Stanley, in Sir T. Wyse's *Impressions of Greece* p. 316.

Pausanias. In describing the funeral monuments at Athens along the road from the city to the Academy, he mentions those of the warriors who fell before Corinth.[48] When commenting further on this, he leads us to understand that in the battle alluded to the Lacedæmonians defeated an army of Corinthians, Athenians, Argives, and Bœotians, and this seems to be the engagement mentioned by Xenophon in the Hellenics,[49] which occurred in the year B.C. 394. Now in the course of excavations in 1871 in the outer Ceramicus, which lay beyond the walls of the ancient city to the north-west, among the monuments of the Sacred Way leading to the Academy there was found one with the following inscription :—[50]

> " Dexilaus, son of Lysanias, of Thoricus,
> Was born under the archonship of Tisander,
> Died under Eubulides :
> One of the five knights at Corinth."

Without the notice in Pausanias we should have difficulty in discovering to what event this refers, but by his aid we may conclude, without much hesitation, that the five knights here referred to were persons

---

[48] i. 29, § 11.   [49] iv. 2, 9, foll.

[50] See Murray's *Handbook for Greece*, pp. 202-3. The original, which I take from a photograph, is as follows :—

ΔΕΞΙΛΕΩΣΛΥΣΑΝΙΟΘΟΡΙΚΙΟΣ
ΕΓΕΝΕΤΟΕΠΙΤΕΙΣΑΝΔΡΟΑΡΧΟΝΤΟΣ
ΑΠΕΘΑΝΕΕΠΕΥΒΟΛΙΔΟ
ΕΓΚΟΡΙΝΘΩΙΤΩΝΠΕΝΤΕΙΠΠΕΩΝ

who distinguished themselves by some special act of heroism on that occasion, for the archonship of Eubulides falls in the year 394.[51]

Modern explorers.

Shortly after Pausanias made his careful inventory of the Greek buildings, they must have begun to be forgotten and to fall into decay. Paganism was supplanted by Christianity, and two centuries later, in the reign of Theodosius, it became a forbidden creed. The curtain that then fell did not rise again until about a hundred years ago, when, after centuries upon centuries of misrule and barbarian inroad, explorers once more made their way into the interior of the country. I pass by Chandler, Dodwell, and Gell, to name one who made an epoch in the study of Greek geography, William Martin Leake. I cannot help speaking with something like enthusiasm of one so eminently fitted for his task, and whom Dr. Robinson, in the dedication of one of his volumes of *Researches in Palestine*, has called "the model traveller." We have to conceive of him as journeying with his watch and compass in his hand, making careful observations and accurate notes as he goes, with a keen eye for every feature of the country and every object in the

William Martin Leake.

---

[51] As the primary object of these lectures is historical geography, there is little need for me to speak of authors like Pomponius Mela, Marinus, and Ptolemy, however great their fame, since the object of their works was rather to determine the position of places, or to elaborate a scheme of mathematical geography. Of Stephanus of Byzantium I have spoken further on, in connection with the etymology of names

view. He brings with him a complete and well-digested knowledge of the whole range of classical authors, and a powerful memory which can reproduce any passage at pleasure; but, even with all this, it is difficult to understand how, being first in the field, he was able to notice so much, and to draw such certain conclusions. Let us take one or two instances of his remarkable geographical insight, under circumstances which must have given an extraordinary zest to this first plunge into an almost unknown land. The first shall be his discovery of the Styx. Before arriving at the spot he had no means of knowing what the appearance of that famous stream would be: the ancient authorities seemed to differ concerning it, some of them, apparently, not having seen it themselves: its position itself was not certain, all that he was able to discover being that it was a tributary of the Crathis, and flowed in a certain district in the north of Arcadia. What must have been his surprise and delight, on reaching the neighbourhood where he expected to find it, to see a waterfall 500 feet in height, completely justifying the Homeric description![52] And again, to take an instance of the application of the principle *ex pede Herculem*, let us see how from the fluting of a column he could reconstruct the temple of Jupiter at Olympia. When searching in the ruins of that place, he lighted on a single fragment of a Doric shaft of the friable limestone of which

[52] Leake, *Travels in the Morea*, iii. 160.

the neighbouring mountains are composed—the ἐπιχώριος πῶρος, of which Pausanias says the temple was built.[53] The only measurable dimension of this was the chord of the fluting, which he found to exceed a foot;[54] and accordingly, judging from the ordinary number of flutings in the Doric order, he concluded that the shaft was at least seven feet in diameter. This led him to believe that the temple to which it belonged was the great temple of Jupiter, and that it was a hexastyle, *i.e.* that it had six columns in the front; for the dimensions which Pausanias assigns to that temple are such, that it could not rightly have admitted of more than six columns of that size. Subsequent excavation has fully confirmed this conclusion.

Since Leake's time many able travellers have completed the work which he began; so that now little remains to be done except in the way of excavation. From this great results may be hoped: within a few years it has restored to us the famous Dionysiac theatre at Athens, and sooner or later it may yield great discoveries in other parts of the country.

[53] v. 10, § 3.   [54] *Travels in the Morea,* i. 27.

LECTURE II.

PRIMARY FEATURES OF THE COUNTRY—MOUNTAINS, COASTS, AND SEA.

The Mountains of Greece—Chains of Northern Greece : of Central Greece : of the Peloponnese—Their general Elevation—Distinguishing Characteristics—Results of their rocky Character—Descriptive Nomenclature of Greek Mountains—Other Sources of Mountain Names—The Sea, the determining Element—Maritime Character of the Greeks—Dangers of the Greek Seas—General Character of the Winds—The Harbours and Islands—Ideas suggested by the Islands—The Islands off the Coast—The Promontories of Greece—Their Influence on the History—Points of contact with Foreigners—Nomenclature of Greek Promontories.

THE most characteristic feature of Greece is its mountains; they ramify through the whole country, and form a part of every view. When the poet Gray spoke of Greece as a land

> "Where each old poetic mountain
> Inspiration breathed around,"

he laid his finger on what is most distinctive in Greek landscape. The names of the mountains occur continually in the Greek poets from Homer downwards; a great part of the mythology gathers round them, as the homes of the gods, and the most frequent scene of their intercourse with men; on them in great measure depends the character of the nation and of its several branches; and they constantly modify the

[margin: The mountains of Greece.]

course of historical events, and especially of military operations. It may be well, therefore, to begin by considering them; and after tracing the principal lines that they follow, to attempt to give some idea of their appearance.

<small>Chains of Northern Greece.</small>

The main chain of northern Greece, which chiefly determines the conformation of the country, is the well-defined backbone, which runs from north to south under the names of Scardus and Pindus. This remarkable mountain wall, which from every point of view presents a most imposing appearance, as it divides the continent into two equal halves, may not inaptly be compared to the *spina* of an ancient circus, with a *meta* or goal standing at either end. At its northern extremity, where it rises from the great central table-land of European Turkey, which in modern history has become famous as the field of Cossova, the scene of the great defeat of the Servians by the Turks, who then first established their power in Europe—it reaches at one spring the height of between 7000 and 8000 feet in a peak which was unnamed in antiquity, but is now called, no doubt from its shape, by the Slavonic name of Liubatrin, or the "Lovely Thorn." At the further end it reaches a similar elevation in Mount Typhrestus—or, as it is more commonly but less accurately called, Tymphrestus[1]—at the head waters of the Spercheius,

---

[1] See on this point Bursian, *Geographie von Griechenland*, i. p. 88, *note*.

which, from its pyramidal form and commanding situation, is one of the most conspicuous mountains of central Greece. The division between Scardus and Pindus is marked by the one break in the continuity of the chain, where the river now called Devol, rising on the eastern side, cuts through it to its very base on its way to the Adriatic. With this single exception, these mountains form a complete watershed between the two seas. At the centre of the Pindus stands Mount Lacmon, in every respect an important position, as being the point of divergence of the principal rivers and mountains of northern Greece. Here on the one side the Aous, the Arachthus, and the Achelous, on the other the Haliacmon and Peneius, take their rise; and at the same place the Cambunian range runs eastward towards Mount Olympus, and to the north-west, the chains of Tymphe and Ceraunia, which form the northern boundary of Epirus, make their way towards the Acro-Ceraunian promontory. The ground on the two sides of the great central barrier is wholly different in its formation. To the west, throughout Illyria, Epirus, and Acarnania, the whole of the country to the sea is occupied by a confused mass of rugged mountains, radiating in different directions, and dividing from one another a succession of irregular river-valleys; while on the opposite side the Scardus and Pindus are flanked by extensive plains, with rich alluvial soil, generally elevated themselves, though deeply sunk amid the rocky walls that surround them. The principal of these, after the plain of Thessaly, is that of Pelagonia, in Upper Macedonia, the original home of the Macedonian race. The mountains that bound these plains on the east, and are themselves offsets from Scardus, form a well-defined chain, and are continued in the Pierian mountains until they reach Olympus, standing as a huge warder to defend the approach to Greece, on the southern side of which they are still farther prolonged in Ossa and Pelion, which intervene between Thessaly and the sea. These mountains of the Giants form a continuous rampart, for, while the defile of Tempe, which separates Ossa from Olympus, is too narrow and winding to break the chain effectually, Ossa and Pelion, though there is a marked depression between them, yet, as Herodotus remarks,[2] mingle their roots with one another. Beyond them, again, the line of lofty heights once more rises in rugged Euboea; and even at its southern extremity it does not finally come to an end, as it is continued in the islands of Andros, Tenos, and others of the northern Cyclades.

Chains of Central Greece.

We must now return to Mount Typhrestus, which is the starting-point of a number of other chains. Directly to the east, and forming the southern boundary of Thessaly, is Othrys, the "Brow," a name it well deserves from the great elevation at which it overhangs the plain of Malis and the gulf of the same

[2] συμμίσγοντα τὰς ὑπωρέας ἀλλήλοισι. Herod. vii. 129.

name—for Ὄθρυς is a dialectic form of ὀφρύς ³—whereas on the other side its height appears less, because the Thessalian plain rises considerably towards its foot. To the south-west diverge the irregular Ætolian mountains, the best defined among which is Mount Corax, which forms a conspicuous object from the sides of Parnassus; while parallel to Othrys, forming the southern boundary of Malis, the no less lofty Œta runs in the direction of Thermopylæ. But those which may be regarded as the most lineal descendants of the main chain of Pindus are the mountains which, taking a south-easterly course, and trending towards the Corinthian gulf, are successively known by the famous names of Parnassus in Phocis, and Helicon in Bœotia, after which, as Cithæron and Parnes, they separate the last-named country from Attica, throwing off spurs southwards towards the Saronic gulf in Ægaleos and Hymettus which bound the plain of Athens. Again, from the end of Œta another and less well-marked branch skirts the Euboic gulf, passing through the territory of the Epicnemidian and Opuntian Locrians and the north of Bœotia, until it joins the end of Parnes, thus completing the enclosure of the Bœotian plains; after which, when it has thrown up the lofty pyramid of Pentelicus, overlooking the plain of Marathon, it sinks towards the sea at Sunium, to rise once more in the outlying islands. Finally, the important mountain of Geraneia, which blocks the approach to the isthmus, may be

---

[3] G. Curtius, *Grundzüge der Griechischen Etymologie*, p. 266.

regarded as an offshoot of Cithæron. Thus Greece is defended by a succession of outworks, and first the Cambunian mountains, afterwards Othrys and Œta, and finally Cithæron and Geraneia, have to be passed before the Peloponnese can be reached.

Mountains of the Peloponnese.

That country which has been called the Acropolis of Greece is itself a mass of mountains. We might almost apply to it the quaint Montenegrin legend, in which that people describe the origin of their land,— that when the Almighty was passing over the face of the earth to sow it with mountains, he chanced to let fall there the bag that contained the rocks, and the boulders rolling out covered the surface of the country. Only there is this difference—that in Montenegro the mountains lie at random and confused, while here, as everywhere in Greece, they have a distinct organisation. Between the mountains of Peloponnese and those of the rest of Greece there is no connection, for though Geraneia might seem to serve as a link to join them, yet in reality they are rather to be regarded as radiating from Arcadia, which is the highland district of the country. Those that rise nearest to the Isthmus in the Corinthian territory were called in ancient times the Oneian mountains, a name which Strabo wrongly applies to Geraneia;[4] from these the land slopes gradually upwards towards Cyllene in the north-east of Arcadia, which marks the commencement of the most important chain in the peninsula. Here

[4] ix. 1, § 8.

three mighty peaks, all over 7000 feet high—Cyllene in the east, Aroanius in the centre, and Erymanthus in the west—together with the mountains that join them, form a continuous line, which effectually separates Arcadia from Achaia. The other principal chains, which either bound or intersect Arcadia, take a direction at right angles to this. Towards the confines of Argolis, running directly south from Cyllene, and bounding on the east the plains of Mantineia and Tegea, rise successively Artemisium and Parthenium, and these are afterwards continued in the range of Parnon, which forms the eastern limit of the valley of Sparta, and ultimately runs off into the promontory of Malea. In the centre, following the same direction, is Mænalus, Pan's own mountain, to the south of which stretches the great barrier between Laconia and Messenia, and after Olympus and Parnassus the highest point in Greece—Taygetus, which, after reaching an elevation of somewhat less than 8000 feet above Sparta, sinks down towards the Tænarian promontory. The ranges of western Arcadia have a less distinctly marked character, but in the south they attain a considerable height in Lycæum, and are continued by Mounts Ithome and Eva to the extremity of Messenia. The only other mountains that remain to be noticed are those of Argolis, which separate from Mount Artemisium and bear towards the south-east, but are not equally well defined with the rest, though their outline is fine when seen from the Saronic Gulf.

Their general elevation.

Having thus seen how completely Hellas was a land of mountains, so that, in whatever part of the country a Greek lived, these prominent objects everywhere met his eye, we naturally proceed to inquire what their appearance was, what features of the view the inhabitants had always before them. And first, as to their elevation. We have seen, in tracing their ramifications through the country, that several attain a very considerable height; but in reality this is not confined to a few. The characteristic feature of Greek scenery is not the predominance of one or two lofty summits, but the conspicuous magnitude of many. Olympus, indeed, which rises sublime above the rest, not only in fame and the veneration it attracted, but also in elevation, being within a little of 10,000 feet high, and consequently nearly 2000 feet above any of the others, forms an exception to this rule; but then, from its outlying position in the north of Greece, it stood alone, and hardly came into comparison with the rest. On the other hand, if we classify roughly together the mountains with whose names we are best acquainted, we shall find seven between 7000 and 8000 feet—Parnassus, Taygetus, Typhrestus, the three great summits of northern Arcadia, and Mount Corax in Ætolia; three above 6000—Athos, Ossa, and Œta; seven above 5000—Pelion, Othrys, Mount Dirphe in Euboea, Artemisium and Mænalus in Arcadia, Parnon in Laconia, and Panachaicum near the straits at Rhium; between 4000 and 5000—Helicon, Cithæron, Parnes,

Geraneia, and Lycæum; and above or near 3000—Parthenium in Arcadia, Pentelicus and Hymettus in Attica, and Arachnæum in Argolis: to these must be added many peaks of lesser note, and, in particular, many of the Pindus chain. When standing on the summit of Parnassus, which commands the most extensive view in Greece, reaching from the north of Thessaly to Arcadia, and from the entrance of the Corinthian Gulf to the extremity of Attica, most of these summits are visible, and the effect produced is —not as in looking from Etna over Sicily, where everything is so dwarfed below you as to resemble an outspread map, nor yet as in some Alpine views, where the attention is absorbed by one overpowering object —but that the eye passes on from point to point, and rests equally on one after another of this federation of mountains. It will also have been noticed that in the elevations that have been given there is nothing which can be termed prodigious, nothing that can affect the mind with wonder independently of admiration. At the same time, for several months of the year, many of these mountains are deeply covered with snow; even as late as the month of May, Olympus, Parnassus, and Taygetus present all the appearance of snow mountains, though none of them are actually within the limit of perpetual snow. In the case of the first of these this is implied in the epithet "very snowy" (ἀγάννιφος), which Homer applies to it,[5] and

[5] Il. i. 420.

also in that of "radiant," or "dazzling" (αἰγλήεις);[6] and this latter feature explains its name, for Olympus, being derived from λάμπω,[7] signifies "the shining one," and we may thus account for the almost generic use of the word in Asia Minor and elsewhere, since the highest mountains in all parts of the world have received their names from their whiteness. The same poet distinguishes Taygetus by the epithet "exceeding lofty" (περιμήκετος),[8] which again corresponds to the meaning of the name, for we learn from Hesychius that ταῦς meant "great," so that Taygetus (Ταΰγετος) signifies "of gigantic growth."[9]

Distinguishing characteristics.
Besides the general elevation of the Greek mountains, there are other features which impart to them a peculiar character. The hard limestone of which they are composed is apt to break away, and thus produces those sharply-cut outlines, which stand out so clearly against the transparent sky of Greece. In most cases these are bare, but here and there, especially in the lower ranges, they emerge from enveloping forests. Archilochus' description of the island of Thasos, as "an ass's backbone, covered with wild wood,"[10] is as appropriate now as when he wrote, the

---

[6] Il. i. 532.

[7] G. Curtius, *Gr. Etymologie*, 240, 654. Cf. Pape, *Wörterbuch der Gr. Eigennamen*, s. v.

[8] Od. vi. 103. [9] E. Curtius, *Peloponnesos*, ii. 307.

[10] ἥδε δ' ὥστ' ὄνου ῥάχις
ἕστηκεν ὕλης ἀγρίης ἐπιστεφής.

Archil. Fragm. 18, in Bergk's *Poetæ Lyrici Græci*.

gaunt but picturesque line of its dorsal ridge standing prominently out from its wooded heights. From this comparison of a bare range of mountains to the skeleton of an animal, we can understand the name Oneium, or "the ass's back," which is given to the chain in the neighbourhood of Corinth; and the way in which these outlines are formed is aptly described in a remarkable passage of Plato's Critias,[11] by the similitude of a body wasting in sickness. It is this feature, with its numerous points, that is signified by another Homeric epithet of Olympus, "many-crested" (πολυδειράς);[12] and it can nowhere be better illustrated than on the northern side of that mountain as seen from the plains of Pieria. There its full proportions are visible from base to summit, rising in tremendous precipices, the "barrier crags of precipitous Olympus" of the Orphic poet of the Argonautica (Οὐλύμπου βαθυσκοπέλου πρηῶνας ἐρυμνούς),[13] until the whole is crowned by a long line of sharp, bare crests, such as have been described. These are all the more striking because of the contrast presented to them by the southern peaks of Olympus, which are seen from the side of Thessaly, and are blunt and rounded in their forms, being composed, not of limestone, but of some kind of igneous rock, and form but a poor contrast to the graceful conical summit of Ossa. The precipitous character of the cliffs in Greece is represented by the term "beetling" (ὀφρυόεις), which is common in Homer, and the idea of

[11] *Crit.* p. 111, B.   [12] Il. i. 499.   [13] 462.

which we have already seen in the name Othrys, "the Brow." But the epithet which perhaps more than any other will approve itself to the traveller is "many-folded" (πολύπτυχος): this, and the corresponding adjective πολύκνημος,[14] describe the buttresses which descend from the mountain sides, divided as they are again and again into minor ridges and valleys, cut out with exquisite sharpness, and often feathered with trees. The resemblance that the minute articulation of these presents to a spider's web, or perhaps to the insect itself, seems to have given the name Arachnæum, or "Spider-mountain," to the lofty peak which overlooks the plain of Argos, and on which Æschylus placed the last of the fire-beacons that conveyed Agamemnon's message to Clytemnestra. It appears also in Cyllene, the "mount of hollows," derived from κυλλός, a kindred form of κοῖλος, which reminds us of the graphic description of this aspect of nature in Virgil:—

Dum montibus umbræ
Lustrabunt convexa[15]—

"long as the shadows shall traverse the mountain hollows," a feature of scenery which is especially con-

[14] The words κνημός πολύκνημος are generally regarded as implying woodland, and this idea may have been associated with them, but it does not belong to their original meaning; the connection between them and κνήμη, "the leg," is probably the same as between *suffrago*, "the bend of the leg," and *anfractus*, in Latin. See Rost and Palm's *Lex.* s. v. κνημός.

[15] Æn. i. 607.

spicuous in these rifted mountains when the sun is low. Both this and the last-named peculiarity are expressed with regard to the Corinthian highlands by the proverbial description, Κόρινθος ὀφρυᾷ τε καὶ κοιλαίνεται[16]—" Corinth is beetle-browed and full of hollows." One other Homeric descriptive epithet remains to be noticed, that of "quivering with foliage" (εἰνοσίφυλλος), which, owing to the destruction of vegetation since classical times, has for the most part lost its significance; but in the case of Mount Pelion, to which Homer applies it, it is still suitable, for that mountain continues to be the best wooded in Greece. In the neighbourhood of the Ægean, it may be remarked, the largest amount of vegetation is to be found on the eastern slopes of the mountains, the reason being that the chains in Greece have a tendency towards the south-east, and consequently the eastern side has a somewhat northerly aspect, and is less liable to be scorched by the reflection of the burning sun from the rocks. This is especially noticeable on Athos, Olympus, Ossa, and Pelion.

We may notice in passing two indirect results of the rocky character of Greece. The first of these is the facilities it offered for purposes of building. In every part of the country the most admirable materials were at hand for constructing walls, and consequently from a very early period the inhabitants devoted themselves to the art of fortifying

Results of their rocky character.

[16] Strabo, viii. 6, § 23.

cities. This accounts for the magnificent specimens of ancient military architecture which remain in Greece, a notable instance of which is to be found in the ruins of Tiryns, which Homer himself calls "well walled" (τειχιόεσσα).[17] Hence from the first the art of defence was superior to that of attack, a circumstance of incalculable importance to civilisation, because the security which it caused introduced a settled order of things, and so encouraged peaceful arts. When we consider how clumsy were the instruments of siege warfare, even as late as the Peloponnesian war, and then look at the remains of the fortifications which are found at intervals of a few miles from one another all over the face of the country, we can fully understand the difficulties attendant on offensive strategy. It would be interesting to trace further, how the same cause tended to promote that city life which had so powerful an influence on Greek institutions. The second result which we may consider of the stony nature of the land is a very insignificant one, but serves to illustrate a frequently recurring Homeric incident. In the descriptions of the battles before Troy we find that when a hero has expended his missiles, and wants a stone to throw, he has only to stoop to the ground, and finds one ready to his hand. Now there is nothing unnatural in this either in the west of Asia Minor or in Greece, for in both these countries

[17] Il. ii. 559.

the soil is strewed with fragments of the same hard limestone rock (χερμάδια); and to these at the present day the traveller is frequently forced to have recourse as a defence against the ferocious shepherds' dogs which abound in the country. This is exactly what the swineherd Eumæus is described as doing in the Odyssey,[18] when the disguised Ulysses is attacked by those animals (σεῦεν κύνας ἄλλυδις ἄλλῃ πυκνῇσι λιθάδεσσι)—after that wily hero has had resort to the plan which is still practised in the mountain districts of Greece, of sitting down in the midst of them as a suppliant, after throwing away the staff he carried in his hand.

In examining the characteristics of Greek mountains, we observed that in some prominent instances these were described by the names that they bore. If we now proceed to investigate their nomenclature somewhat more carefully, we shall discover the same thing in a variety of other cases. The subject is naturally an intricate one, because the names of mountains are usually among the most primitive in a country, and consequently may be derived from words or roots only partially known to the classical literature, and may have suffered considerable modifications in the course of years. We should not therefore look for more than a moderate degree of certainty, and may well be content if the etymologies do not violate the ordinary laws of philology,

Descriptive nomenclature of Greek mountains.

[18] Od. xiv. 30-36.

and follow the analogies according to which such names are usually imposed.

The same feature of snowy brightness which we have seen to be expressed by the name Olympus (Ὄλυμπος), is found in that of another mountain derived from the same root λάμπω,—viz. Lampeia (Λάμπεια) in the north of Arcadia, which Statius, who in his Thebaid introduces frequent topographical descriptions, perhaps following Greek authorities, calls "white with snowy heights"—*candens jugis Lampia nivosis.*[19] The elevation of the summits is marked by a variety of names—Ceraunia (Κεραύνια), the "thunderhills," in Epirus, from their tendency to attract storms; Mænalus (Μαίναλος), "the wild," "the tempestuous,"[20] from the same cause; and Typhrestus (Τυφρηστός), either from τυφώς "whirlwind" or τῦφος "smoke,"[21] on account of the clouds that gather round it; Thaumasion (Θαυμάσιον) in the south-west of Arcadia, which even out-tops the neighbouring Mount Lycæum, from the wonder it arouses; and similarly Ptoum (Πτῶον) near the Copaic lake, derived from πτοέω "to terrify," and Phrikion (Φρίκιον) near Thermopylæ, from φρίσσω, "to shudder" (Schreckhorn), on account of the awe they inspire; and the same thing is expressed by Hypatos (Ὕπατος) "the highest," in Bœotia, which is so called in con-

---

[19] Theb. iv. 290. [20] Pape, *s.v.*
[21] G. Curtius, *Gr. Etymol.* 205.

trast to the low hills around it.²² Next, these points are considered as commanding extensive views: Ephyra ('Εφύρα), "the look-out place," the old name of Corinth, referring to the height of the Acrocorinthus, and derived from ἐφοράω, "to survey,"²³ is found in six other places in Greece; one of the highest summits of Taygetus is called Euoras (Εὐόρας), that is "belvedere," and it may well have been from this that Lynceus looked, when, according to the story, "he went to Taygetus, and trusting to his swift feet climbed to the summit, overlooking the whole country of Pelops the Tantalid."²⁴ But the most important mountain that was thus regarded was Ossa, "the watch-tower,"—derived from ὄσσομαι,²⁵—the title of which is amply justified by the position of its sharp peak, commanding, as it does, an extensive prospect over the plains of Thessaly on the one side and the wide Ægean on the other. The precipitous character of the rocks is described in Ithome ('Ιθώμη) which, like Ithaca, is derived from ἰθύς, "straight, steep,"²⁶ and in like manner in Acarnania we find a city in a steep position called Ithoria ('Ιθωρία); in Bœotia also there is a peak named

---

[22] Bursian, *Geographie von Griechenland*, i. 216.

[23] G. Curtius, 647. Cf. Signia in Latium.

[24] E. Curtius, *Peloponnesos*, ii. 204.

[25] G. Curtius, 407. E. Curtius, *Geographische Onomatologie*, 158.

[26] Ebel, quoted by E. Curtius, *Peloponnesos*, ii. 190.

Orthopagus (Ὀρθόπαγος) or "steep tor;" and in the neighbourhood of the pass of Phyle, between Cithæron and Parnes, a precipice bore the name of Harma (Ἅρμα) or "car," from the resemblance of the rounded face of rock to the ἄντυξ or rail of a chariot.[27] The sharply cut ridges appear in the Τομαῖον ὄρος or "knife-edge," in the neighbourhood of Pylos in Messenia; of which Stephanus of Byzantium says that it is like a graving tool (ἐοικὸς σμίλῃ); in Mount Scollis (Σκόλλις), between Elis and Achaia, the πέτρη Ὠλενίη of Homer, which is connected with σκολιός, "crooked, winding,"[28] thus representing the irregular paths along the hillsides; in Helicon (Ἑλικών), which probably is connected with ἑλίσσω, and so called from its "winding" outline; and in the Attic deme of Probalinthus (Προβάλινθος)—from πρὸ and βάλλω—the name of which describes its position on the projecting spurs of Mount Pentelicus. The deep intervening valleys are noticed in Lacmon (Λάκμων) "rifted," which is akin to λάκκος "a hollow," and λακίς, "a rent;"[29] in Mount Cnemis (Κνῆμις), the abode of the Epicnemidian Locrians, which corresponds to the epithet πολύκνημος already noticed; and in Mount Cotylæum (Κοτύλαιον) in Eubœa, from κοτύλη,[30] a word which expresses a variety of hollow objects. But the class of names, which perhaps more than any other are used to represent the many conspicuous summits of Greece, is that derived from roots signi-

[27] Bursian, i. 252, 333. [28] E. Curtius, *Peloponnesos*, ii. 105.
[29] G. Curtius, 147. [30] E. Curtius, i. 344.

fying "head" or "horn," such as *kar* of κάρα, *kor* of κορυφή, and *ker* of κέρας, of which last a lengthened form *karn* is found, corresponding to the Latin *cornu* and our "horn." In Greece, as in Switzerland, the comparison of a sharp peak to a horn was a familiar one. When Philip, son of Demetrius, was desiring to gain possession of Peloponnesus, he received the advice that he should " take the cow by the horns,"[31] which meant that he should seize the Acrocorinth and Mount Ithome, the natural fortresses of the north and south of the country. Accordingly we find the two marked summits at the end of the chain that divides the plain of Megara from that of Eleusis, called in ancient times Kerata (Κέρατα). Corinth itself, whose name the Athenians, in the true spirit of witty rivals, never failed to associate with the bug (κόρις),[32] is connected with κορυφή,[33] and thus continues to express a similar idea to that of her earlier name Ephyra. The form *karn* is seen most clearly in Halicarnassus[34] ('Αλι-καρν-ασσός), "Sea-horn-place," and is found also in Carneates (Καρνεάτης) in the territory of Sicyon, and in Acarnania, which signifies the " highlands."[35] The resemblance to a head is still further carried out in the names Corseia (Κόρσεια) in Bœotia and Thessaly, and Corsiæ (Κορσιαί) in Bœotia, which are derived from κόρση, the " temple." Finally, the important group of mountain

---

[31] Strab. viii. 4, § 8.
[32] Aristoph. *Nub.* 710 ; *Ran.* 439.   [33] G. Curtius, 132.
[34] Ibid. 136.   [35] Bursian, i. 107.

names which we find in Parnes, Parnon, and Parnassus, are thought by some to be derived from καρν—with the same change of κ into π which is seen in πότε for κότε and πῶς for κῶς: if this is considered inadmissible, they must be connected with πρών, πρανής and similar words, so that they will still express a corresponding notion of "projecting rocks." The name Pron is found attached to a mountain in Argolis. Other ideas by which mountains are represented are a breast, as in Titthium (Τίτθιον) above the Hieron of Æsculapius near Epidaurus, and probably also in Tithoræa (Τιθοραία)[36] one of the peaks of Parnassus; a knee, as in Gonnus (Γόννος) from γόνυ,[37] on an eminence near the exit of Tempe, and Gonussa (Γονοῦσσα) in Achaia, which latter we should be more disposed to derive from γόνος and similar words for the produce of the soil, were it not that Homer attaches to it the epithet "lofty" (αἰπεινὴν Γονόεσσαν);[38] a nail-head, as in Gomphi (Γόμφοι), in the south-west of Thessaly, with which we may compare Euryelus (Εὐρύηλος), or "broad nail," the excellent descriptive name for the highest point to which the ridge of Epipolæ rises above Syracuse; and a serrated jaw, as in Onugnathus (ὄνου γνάθος), or the ass's jawbone, the name of a promontory in Laconia. On the same principle Acontium ('Ακόντιον), or "spear-point," is

---

[36] The root τιθ is seen in τιθηνός, τιθασός, etc.
[37] Γόννοι· γόννα γὰρ οἱ Αἰολεῖς τὰ γόνατα.—Steph. B.
[38] Il. ii. 573.

applied to a mountain in Bœotia; and from fancied resemblances to animals we get Geraneia (Γεράνεια) "crane's bill," on account of a projecting point of that chain,[39] Corydallus (Κορυδαλλός), a part of Ægaleos, which bears the name of the tufted lark; and Corax (Κόραξ), the "raven," which was probably called from its appearance and not from the frequency of that bird, as in the latter case we should rather expect a derivative or composite form of the word. The sea-urchin also (ἐχῖνος), from its prickly shell, has given its name to the Echinades, the islands at the mouth of the Achelous, now partly joined to the continent by the deposit of that river, which present an extremely pointed outline;[40] from this some of their number were called Oxeiae (Ὀξεῖαι),[41] or "the sharp islands," like our name "the Needles."

To these mountain names we may add a number of others which cannot be so completely classified. From the colour of the rocks come Titanus (Τίτανος) in Thessaly, a word which means "lime" or "chalk," while Homer describes the place as the "white summits of Titanus" (Τιτάνοιό τε λευκὰ κάρηνα);[42] and Cnacalus (Κνάκαλος), a mountain near Orchomenus in Arcadia, which has been identified by the tint of its

<small>Other sources of mountain names.</small>

---

[39] Schol. Thuc. i. 105. ἀκρωτήριον νεῦον ἐπὶ τὴν μεσόγαιαν, from the beaked shape of which he derives it—ἀπὸ τοῦ σχήματος οὕτως ὀνομάζεται.
[40] Mure, *Tour in Greece*; i. 104, 105.   [41] Bursian, i, 119.
[42] Il. ii. 735.

cliffs,[43] for κνακός or κνηκός signifies "yellowish:" there is also a Mount Cnacadion in Laconia. From their material are derived Pelion, which can hardly be dissociated from πηλός, "clay," and may have been named from the deposits of its torrents by those dwelling at its foot, as at Iolcos and in other ancient cities; also Brilessus (Βριλησσός), if its etymology is βρῖ, an old form of βριθύ, "heavy," and λᾶς, "a stone,"[44] from the hardness of its marble masses. This, it should be remembered, is its original name, for that of Pentelicus, by which it is best known, was little used in antiquity, and was applied to it from its connection with the neighbouring deme of Pentele (Πεντελή) at its foot, which was probably named from some five-fold division. From their shape are called "the Altars" (Βωμοί), a number of hills in Ætolia;[45] Mount Dirphys in Eubœa, from a seat, to which its truncated summit, with a steep face of rock below, bears a resemblance—Δίρφυς being another form of δίφρος—as if it were the throne of some gigantic being, in the same way as Cader Idris, which somewhat resembles it in form, is the chair of the giant Idris, and Arthur's Seat at Edinburgh is the throne of that mythical hero; possibly also Cithæron (Κιθαιρών) from some fancied resemblance to a guitar (κιθάρα). Pindus is probably derived from πῖδαξ because it is rich in streams, just

[43] E. Curtius, *Peloponnesos*, i. 226.
[44] Pape, *s.v.*   [45] Bursian, i. 142.

as πολυπῖδαξ in Homer is an epithet of Ida;[46] Libethrium (Λειβήθριον), from λείβω, on account of its numerous fountains; Pangæus (Παγγαῖος), from the fruitfulness of its soil. Thornax, in Argolis and Laconia, is, like θρωσμός, a "springing of the ground," from θρώσκω, though Hesychius says θόρναξ signifies "footstool," and if this etymology be adopted, it should be compared with Dirphys. Erymanthus is regarded as the bulwark (ἔρυμα) of its land. Artemisium and Parthenium in mountainous Arcadia are both called after the huntress Artemis. Maciston (Μάκιστον), "the outstretched mountain," in Triphylia, describes the length of its ridge. Anchesmus ('Αγχεσμός), at Athens, derives its name from its neighbourhood (ἄγχι), to the city; Lycabettus (Λυκαβηττός), at the same place, when compared with the Homeric word for "a year," λυκάβας,[47] i.e. the "path of light," is shown to mean the mountain whence the solstices (τροπαὶ ἠελίοιο) were observed, for which purpose it was fitted by its height and conspicuous position;[48] while Mount Chaon in Argolis, from χάος, χαίνω, was called from the opening of the vast cavern at its foot, from which the stream of the

[46] The view, which has sometimes been maintained, that certain names in Greece are derived from Celtic roots, as Pindus from *Pen*, Axius from *Usk*, is probably erroneous, because there is no evidence of any Celtic race having ever settled in that country. On the ν of Πίνδος, see G. Curtius, *Gr. Etymol.* 51.

[47] Od. xix. 306.   [48] Welcker, *Griechische Götterlehre*, i. 477.

Erasinus issues forth.[49] A few received their names from the animals found there:—Lycæum (Λύκαιον), from the wolf; Coccygium (Κοκκύγιον), in Argolis, from the cuckoo; Chelydorea (τὰ Χελυδόρεα), near Cyllene in Arcadia, the scene of the invention of the lyre by Hermes, from the tortoise (χέλυς), which animal also appears in Cape Chelonatas (Χελωνάτας), in the west of Elis. Œta again (Οἴτη) is probably "sheep's tor," from ὄϊς, "a sheep;"[50] and Ægaleos (Αἰγάλεως) and Ægiplanctus (Αἰγίπλαγκτος) are called from the "goat" (αἴξ). Still fewer received their names from their vegetation, though we might have expected this to be a common source of nomenclature:—Elæon (Ἐλαιόν), on the confines of Messenia and Arcadia, from the olive; Minthe (Μίνθη), in Triphylia, from mint; and Narthakion (Ναρθάκιον), in Thessaly from the *ferula* (νάρθηξ). It is to be noticed that the special name for a wooded mountain, Ida (Ἴδη, "wood,") does not occur on the continent of Greece.

The sea the determining element.

The mountains, then, are the most prominent feature of Greek landscape; but, notwithstanding this, Strabo is right when he says that the determining element of Greek geography is the sea.[51] Speaking of his predecessor Ephorus, he represents him as having regarded this as pointing out the true direction to be followed in describing the country (ἡγεμονικόν τι τὴν θάλατταν κρίνων πρὸς τὰς τοπογραφίας), and then he adds

[49] Smith's *Dict. of Geog.* i. 201.　　[50] G. Curtius, 350.
[51] viii. 1, § 3.

approvingly, "we, too in like manner, ought to follow the nature of the ground, and take counsel of the sea" (οὕτω καὶ ἡμῖν προσήκει ἀκολουθοῦσι τῇ φύσει τῶν τόπων σύμβουλον ποιεῖσθαι τὴν θάλασσαν). Accordingly he divides Hellas into four peninsulas, or, as he calls them, chersoneses. The first of these is the Peloponnese, formed by the gulf of Corinth, running deep into the land from the Sicilian sea, and the Saronic gulf from the Ægean. The second comprises not much more than the mountain region of Geraneia, as its isthmus is the ground between Nisæa and Pagæ, the two ports of Megara; and, as a matter of fact, there is reason to believe that at one period the sea flowed both to the north and south of that mountain, as, according to the ancient legends of the Megarians, it was said to have done at the time of the flood of Deucalion, when Geraneia stood out from the water like a rocky island.[52] The third is marked by a line drawn from the Crissæan gulf to Thermopylæ, including Attica, Bœotia, and Phocis; while the fourth is determined by the deep indentation of the Ambracian and Maliac gulfs. Whatever we may think of this as a scientific division of the country, it certainly proceeds on a true principle; and this, it should be observed, regulates at once the physical and the political geography of Greece. For Hellas, in proportion as she stretches farther south, becomes more maritime, and at the same time more truly Hellenic. If we

[52] E. Curtius, *Peloponnesos*, i. 8.

start from the Hæmus as our base, we find in Thrace, Macedonia, and Illyria, extensive inland regions, the only part of which that bears a resemblance to Greece proper is Chalcidice, which in its political relations as well as its outward aspect belongs to the southern portion of the country. It is only where the continent contracts in width, at the parallel of Mount Olympus, that Hellas begins with Thessaly; and in a more limited sense it may be restricted to the district south of that region, where Mount Typhrestus, with its great lateral ranges, corresponds to the deep gulfs already noticed. From this point land and water begin mutually to influence one another, the mountains projecting into the sea, and the sea penetrating into the interior, so that the seaboard and the inland districts formed not two countries but one, being combined into an organic whole. This is what Cicero refers to when he says, "The remark I have made about Corinth I may perhaps with much truth apply to Greece generally; for the Peloponnese itself lies almost entirely in the sea, and there are none of the inhabitants, except the people of Phlius, whose territories do not touch the sea; and outside that again, the only tribes placed away from the sea are the Ænianes, Dorians, and Dolopes."[53] The Peloponnese is the culminating point of the maritime character of the country, and is so, at the same time,

---

[53] *De Republica*, ii. 4.

of its Hellenic life. Thus it is with justice that Karl Otfried Müller[54] compares Greece to a body, whose members are different in form, but between which a mutual connection and dependence necessarily exists. The northern districts are the nutritive organs, which from time to time introduced fresh and vigorous supplies: Attica and the islands may be considered as extremities, which served as the active instruments of the body of Greece, and by which it was kept in constant connection with others; while the Peloponnese seems formed for a state of life included in itself, occupied more with its own than external concerns, and whose interests and feelings were self-centred.

As might be expected from the inhabitants of such a country, the Greeks soon came to regard the sea as their natural element. The epithet "*dissociabilis*," which Horace applies to the ocean, represented a point of view the exact opposite of that of the Greeks. To them it was the highway of nations—the "watery paths," as Homer expresses it, (ὑγρὰ κέλευθα)—an idea, which was embodied in one of their most familiar names of the sea, πόντος, which is connected with πάτος and the Latin *pons*, and signifies "the bridge" or "means of passage."[55] They had watched its moods, and noticed the deeply-tinted and ever-shifting colours peculiar to the Ægean, as we see from the Homeric epithets applied to it—" dim " (ἠεροειδής), *Maritime character of the Greeks.*

[54] *Dorians*, i. 75.
[55] Max Müller, *Lectures on the Science of Language*, ii. 321.

from its misty, faint horizon, "twinkling" (μαρμάρεος and γλαυκός), "violet-hued" (ἰοειδής), "wine-coloured" (οἶνοψ), "purple" (πορφύρεος), "grey" (πολιός), "dark" (μέλας), and "black" (κελαινός).[56] We even find in these poems the description of a phenomenon which has been noticed in those seas in modern times—how in calm water a hollow swell, or, as Homer calls it, a "mute wave," will suddenly arise, the forerunner of a storm, though there may be no air stirring.[57] So the feelings of Nestor, when from his tent, where he is tending a wounded comrade, he hears the tumult of battle thickening round the Greek entrenchment, are described by the following comparison:—

ὡς δ' ὅτε πορφύρῃ πέλαγος μέγα κύματι κωφῷ,
ὀσσόμενον λιγέων ἀνέμων λαιψηρὰ κέλευθα,
αὔτως, οὐδ' ἄρα τε προκυλίνδεται οὐδ' ἑτέρωσε,
πρίν τινα κεκριμένον καταβήμεναι ἐκ Διὸς οὖρον.[58]

"So doth the darkly rolling sea presage,
  With hollow swell, the coming tempest's rage;
  While yet nor here nor there its waves are driven,
  Till Jove send down the threatened gale from Heaven."

Dangers of the Greek seas. Yet the sea which the Greeks had to navigate was not in all respects a safe sea. The dangers of rounding Malea were especially dreaded, and this circumstance give rise to the proverb, "Double Malea, and forget your home" (Μαλέας δὲ κάμψας ἐπιλάθου τῶν

[56] Ulrichs, *Reisen in Griechenland*, i. 12.
[57] Mure, *Tour in Greece*, i. 83.   [58] Il. xiv. 16.

οἴκαδε).[59] It was at this point that the currents of the Sicilian and Ægean seas met one another, and the effect of this, and of the adverse winds, was so great, that Strabo ascribes to it in great measure the prosperity of Corinth, because traders from the east preferred to land their goods there and carry them across the isthmus. Both Agamemnon and Ulysses are represented in the Odyssey as being driven out of their course by storms and currents off that promontory.[60] Indeed the very large number of inscriptions that there are in the Anthology on sailors who met their death by drowning[61] would seem to imply that generally the risk was very considerable. This is the natural result of the numerous high peaks and promontories that rise out of the Ægean, and form points of attraction to the storms, so that even at the present day the Greek sailors dread to round Mount Athos during the winter, and Xerxes was so far from being unreasonable in cutting through the isthmus of that peninsula after the experience of Mardonius, that it would even now be worth the while of an enterprising government to renew his work. Hence, as we have seen when speaking of the very gradual progress of geographical knowledge among the Greeks, with the half-decked vessels that were in use in Homer's time, they used to creep round the coasts, and were afraid to trust themselves to lengthened

[59] Strabo, viii. 6, § 20. [60] Od. iv. 514, ix. 80.
[61] *Anthol.* Ἐπιτύμβια; nos. 263 foll.

voyages, and even this timid navigation was confined to certain seasons of the year.

General character of the winds. It is true that these dangers were considerably lessened by the regularity with which certain winds blow in Greece, so that, notwithstanding their occasional violence, the experienced seaman can be prepared for them. Such were the Birdwinds (ὀρνιθίαι ἄνεμοι)—so called because they brought the birds of passage—which blow in the spring from the north, and the Etesian winds from the same quarter during the summer. So too, in the description of Phormio's engagement at the mouth of the Corinthian gulf, we are told by Thucydides[62] that that commander waited for the east wind, which used regularly to blow at daybreak; and at the present day the direction of the winds at the straits is so regularly east and west, that they are described by the sailors as "the gulf going out" and "the gulf going in."[63] This arises from the wind drawing up the Saronic gulf, and thence through the deep funnel formed by the lofty mountains on either side of the Corinthian gulf, so that in those parts it may be constantly east, when it is south in the open sea. But at the same time nowhere is navigation more dangerous than in this inland bay,[64] owing to the sudden gusts which descend through the ravines or from the mountain summits; and so elsewhere along the coasts the

---

[62] ii. 84. [63] Leake, *Morea*, iii. 207-8.
[64] Ulrichs, *Reise*, i. 4.

light and fickle winds, suddenly rising and as suddenly falling, render navigation uncertain. The difficulty is further increased in places by the confined nature of the seas. As you look along the narrow winding bays of the Euripus and the Euboic sea from the hill on which Aulis was built, you have no difficulty in understanding how Agamemnon's fleet should be detained by adverse breezes, as Æschylus says, "causing sore delay and famine, and detaining ships in harbour" (κακόσχολοι νήστιδες δύσορμοι).[65] It has even been suggested with some plausibility that this feature of the Saronic gulf was the source of the proverb, "*Non cuivis homini contingit adire Corinthum.*"[66] The original form of that saying, to which Horace has given a somewhat different meaning, was οὐ παντὸς ἀνδρὸς εἰς Κόρινθον ἔσθ' ὁ πλοῦς, which Strabo[67] explains to refer to the extravagant demands of the Hetæræ of that luxurious city, which ruined the traders who resorted there. But if, as is likely enough, the proverb originated in Athens, it is not improbable that the stress may have been laid on the last word, and that it may have been intended to express the difficulty of navigating the confined sea between the two cities, owing to the treacherous nature of the winds.[68]

But while the Greek mariner thus learnt a lesson of caution and hardihood from the uncertain seas with

The harbours and islands.

---

[65] Æsch. *Ag.* 194.   [66] Hor. *Ep.* i. 17, 36.
[67] viii. 6, § 20.   [68] Mure, *Tour in Greece*, ii. 133-4.

F

which he was familiar, he was at the same time favoured by the innumerable harbours, and the islands with which the coasts were fringed. The first of these, the harbours, which are formed by the windings and indentations of the coast, that make the seaboard of Greece of such extraordinary length in proportion to the area of the country, offered a fitting starting-point, and a welcome refuge in case of danger, while at the same time they facilitated the export and import trade of the country. The islands, on the other hand, as they followed one another in irregular chains, and were separated only by narrow spaces of sea, were an encouragement to enterprise, especially towards the east, in which direction, as has been before remarked, both they and the harbours pointed. Guided by these, the course of Greek emigration towards Asia Minor took two main lines, one by a central route through the Cyclades, the other farther to the south from the extremity of the Peloponnese, by Crete, Casos, Carpathos, and Rhodes. If we may judge from the silence of Homer, it was only the latter of these chains in which considerable Hellenic settlements were formed at an early period, as they alone are mentioned as having furnished contingents to Agamemnon:[69] those that composed the former, from the steepness of their rocks and the want of fertility in the soil, hardly presented sufficient attractions to compete with the rich continent that lay beyond. At the present day, the

[69] Il. ii. 645, foll. *See* Grote, *History of Greece*, ii. 313.

terraces into which their sides are laboriously shaped, and which from their sunny character are excellently adapted to the growth of vines, require to be artificially provided with earth brought from below; and the appearance of the islands themselves, as you sail among them, is that of a long, narrow, and lofty mountain chain, half submerged in the sea. These striking and romantic objects exercised a charm over the quick imagination of the Greeks, whether they saw their shifting forms pass in succession one before the other, or, looking at them from a distance, saw them, as Homer says— *Ideas suggested by the islands.*

ὡς ὅτε ῥινὸν ἐν ἠεροειδέϊ πόντῳ[70]—
"Spread like a shield upon the misty sea."

Hence they conceived of them as moving objects, and gave them the name of νῆσος, or "floating land," from νέω, "to swim;" and from a lengthened form of the same word, νήχω, one island in particular, Naxos, "the Swimmer,"[71] got its title. So, too, we find that both the Strophades off the west coast of Peloponnese, and the Æolian islands to the north of Sicily, bore the earlier name of Plotæ:[72] the name Strophades itself probably embodies the same conception of their shifting their position;[73] and from the analogy of that group we might even fancy that the term Cyclades meant, not merely

---

[70] *Od.* v. 281.   [71] G. Curtius, *Gr. Etymologie*, 286.
[72] *See* Pape, *s. v.* Στροφάδες and Πλωταί.
[73] Liddell and Scott's *Lex. s. v.* στροφάς.

those that lie round, but those that circle round, the sacred isle of Delos.⁷⁴ In the case of Delos this notion passed into a legend, and that island, which before had wandered on the surface of the sea, and had borne the name of Asteria from its likeness to a star—ἀστέρι ἴση—as Callimachus explains it⁷⁵—was reputed to have been fixed by chains to the bottom of the sea by the power of Zeus, that it might afford a secure resting-place for Leto when she was about to give birth to Apollo and Artemis; or, as some reported, it was the Far-darter himself who had made it fast, a version of the story which Virgil has adopted when he says—

> Sacra mari colitur medio gratissima tellus
> Nereidum matri et Neptuno Ægeo;
> Quam pius Arcitenens oras et litora circum
> Errantem, celsa Gyaro Myconoque revinxit,
> Immotamque coli dedit et contemnere ventos." ⁷⁶

> Encircled by a billowy ring
>   A land there lies, the loved resort
> Of Neptune, the Ægæan King,
>   And the grey Queen of Nereus' court :
> Long time the sport of every blast,
>   O'er ocean it was wont to toss,

---

⁷⁴ Bursian (ii. 178) would derive Prote also, the name of the island off Pylos, from πλωτή; but the change from λ to ρ is not admissible in classical Greek. It is better to regard it, with E. Curtius (*Peloponnesos*, ii. 183), as meaning "the first," *i.e.* the land first sighted by the sailor in approaching Messenia from the open sea.

⁷⁵ Callim. *Del.* 38. ⁷⁶ Æn. iii. 74.

> Till grateful Phœbus moored it fast
> To Gyaros and high Myconos,
> And bade it lie unmoved, and brave
> The violence of wind and wave.
> *Conington's Translation.*

From this again, by an easy transition, arose the idea that these wandering rocks clashed together, which has taken form in the story of the Planctæ as told in the Odyssey,[77] and this came to be especially associated with the two volcanic islands, which stand one on either side of the entrance of the Bosphorus from the Euxine, and were called Symplegades, because they were supposed to close on the ships that passed between them, thus symbolising the risk of shipwreck in that narrow passage.

The islands which lie off the coast have further to be regarded as serving in time of war as a base for offensive operations against the neighbouring country. Greek history affords frequent illustrations of the way in which they were turned to this purpose. What Ireland, as some think, might be to England in case of a war between that country and France, that the island of Cythera was to Sparta. During the Peloponnesian war, in B.C. 424, we hear of it as being occupied by the Athenians under Nicias,[78] in consequence of which the Lacedæmonians were seized with the greatest panic; and again, in the year 393, it was occupied by Conon after the battle of Cnidus.[79] This

The islands off the coast.

---

[77] xii. 61.   [78] Thuc. iv. 54, 55.   [79] Xen. *Hell.* iv. 8, § 7.

danger had been foreseen by the Lacedæmonian sage Chilon, who said that it would be more advantageous to his countrymen if sunk to the bottom of the sea;[80] and from the recollection of this remark, Demaratus, king of Sparta, advised Xerxes to despatch 300 of his vessels to that point, that they might detach the Spartans from the common cause of Greece by causing them anxiety at home. Similarly, from the position of Sphacteria on the Messenian coast, we can see what a vulnerable point that island would have been, had not the neighbouring headland of Pylos been even better fitted for hostile occupation; and when the Athenian fleet were preparing to engage the Spartans in that quarter, they were able to make the island of Prote, a little way from the coast, their head-quarters.[81] In like manner, Ægina, which Pericles was wont to call the eyesore of the Piræus, had been a cause of such serious apprehensions to the Athenians some time before the outbreak of the Peloponnesian war, that in the second year of that war, though the Æginetans were their tributaries, yet from fear lest they should side with their enemies, they carried out the harsh resolve of expelling the whole population.[82] And with regard to Eubœa, which commanded the other side of Attica, Demosthenes says that at one period the pirates that made it their head-quarters so infested the neighbouring sea as to prevent all navigation. [83]

[80] Herod. vii. 235.
[81] Thuc. iv. 13.   [82] Ibid. ii. 27.   [83] *De Cor.* p. 207.

It remains to speak of the promontories,[84] which exercised a great influence on the development of the country. We may divide these into various kinds. First, there are those which the Greeks distinguished by the name of ἀκτή, extensive tracts projecting into the sea, and usually distinguished from chersoneses by being joined to the continent, not by a narrow isthmus, but by a broad base, though in one remarkable instance, that of the peninsula of Mount Athos, which was called Acte, this does not apply; usually also flanked by rocky coasts, though here again there is an exception in Actium ("Ακτιον), the scene of Augustus' great victory, which is level. The most important of these tracts were Argolis, which was called the Argolic Acte, and Attica, the name of which, as Strabo[85] and other ancient writers inform us, was originally 'Ακτικη and 'Ακτή. Next there are tongues of low land, to which was applied the word for a ribbon, ταινία, for this, being derived from τείνω, "to stretch," was used for anything narrow and outstretched. Such were especially the headlands of the coast of Achaia, formed by the winter torrents descending from the Arcadian mountains, which, after pushing forward their deposit into the sea, were themselves

The promontories of Greece.

---

[84] On this point I may refer generally to E. Curtius' essay in the *Götting. Gel. Anz.*, Nachr, 1861, pp. 143 foll., *Beiträge zur geographischen Onomatologie der griechischen Sprache*, which is in fact devoted to the subject of Greek promontories and their names.   [85] Str. ix. 1, § 3.

turned aside by the action of the waves, which heap up sand in front of them, and so divert them into another channel. Lastly, there were the ἄκραι or ἀκρωτήρια, properly so called, the bluffs or headlands like Sunium, with which the coast abounded; though it is to be observed that the ancients did not usually restrict the name, as we do, to the extreme end, but included, as in the case of Tænarum, the neighbouring mountain chain that formed it, and particularly the highest point of it.

Their influence on the history. One of the earliest purposes which these promontories served, was to act as points which the seaman might make for on a voyage. In the infancy of navigation it was natural that a certain number of prominent positions should be chosen, with reference to which the ship's course might safely be regulated, and more especially those which formed a boundary between different spaces of sea. When these were once gained, they could follow the coast this way or that towards their destination. When the heroes in the Odyssey are crossing the Ægean, they make for Geræstus;[86] and, what is still more remarkable, when Agamemnon is on his homeward voyage, he directs his course towards Malea, on the way to Argos.[87] Hence, as we have already seen in the case of the last-named promontory, the limits of the navigation of a certain period were marked by the headlands; and

[86] iii. 177.
[87] Ibid. iv. 514. *See* E. Curtius, *Peleponnesos*, ii. 300.

when it became necessary to define the waters that belonged to particular states, a line was drawn with reference to these. Thus the Corcyreans regarded Actium as their maritime limit, for this is implied by their warning off the Corinthians at that point before the commencement of the Peloponnesian war;[88] and the Syracusans took the same view of the Iapygian headland, at which point Hermocrates says they ought to wait for the approach of the Athenians.[89] And further, when the knowledge of the sea increased, the promontories were of service to geography, as furnishing positions by which the distances and relative positions of places and districts might be determined, and as enabling persons to form an approximate conception of the shape of countries, and sometimes also to give them corresponding names, as in the case of Trinacria for Sicily.

But the most important influence which the promontories exercised on the Greeks was their bringing them into connection with foreign peoples. The name of Malea is considered by some authorities to be of Semitic origin, signifying a "a jawbone,"[90] and as we find the neighbouring promontory called Onugnathos or "the ass's jawbone," it has been suggested that the latter name was also given by the Phœnicians, and we should thus have an explanation of the plural form Μαλέαι, which is frequently found, and implies

Points of contact with foreigners.

---

[88] Thuc. i. 29.   [89] Ibid. vi. 34.
[90] Bochart, quoted by Curtius, *Peleponnesos*, ii. 330.

that there was more than one headland so called. In like manner Tænarum is thought to be derived from the Semitic "tinar" "a rock,"[91] though it may very well be derived, like ταινία, from τείνω, with reference to its outstretched projection. However this may be, those headlands and the bay they enclose, together with the neighbouring island of Cythera, were the great head-quarters of the purple-fishing, and it is usually in connection with that branch of industry that we meet with Phœnician settlements on the coasts of Greece. On the island of Cranaë, close to the Laconian shore by Gythium, they established one of their principal factories, and were thus brought into connection with the natives. Herodotus, at the commencement of his history, has left us a description of what used to occur at such places of meeting[92]— how the Orientals used to open a bazaar and expose their tempting wares for sale, by which means they secured to themselves a large profit, and found opportunities of carrying off the daughters of the land to sell in the slave-markets of the East. But those occasions not only introduced the inhabitants to new materials and fabrics, but also made them acquainted with a variety of inventions necessarily associated with commercial intercourse, and in particular with numbers, weights, and measures. In like manner these outlying points were of importance for the introduction of

[91] Bochart, quoted by Curtius, *Peleponnesos*, ii. 325.
[92] Herod. i. 1. *See* Curtius, *History of Greece*, i. 40.

foreign elements of religious worship, as, for instance, of that of Aphrodite, the goddess of Cythera, as she continued to be called, born from the sea-foam, who had a sanctuary at Cranaë, from whence her rites penetrated to Sparta. The mixture of races that arose from this has left a significant trace behind it in the name of the headland near Cranaë, Migonium (Μιγώνιον). And just as we have traced the presence of these strangers on the promontories nearest to the lower chain of islands that connect Greece with Asia, so by the line of the southern Cyclades we find them introduced into Argolis. There, at the extreme end of the Acte, at Hermione, which was famed for its purple, we again meet with their fisheries,[93] and from that point they started to establish themselves on the one side at Nauplia, on the other at Corinth. Thus there is especial and local significance in the words of Clytemnestra in the Agamemnon,[94] when she says "There is a sea, and who shall drain it dry? producing in abundance the juice of purple, ever fresh for dyeing garments, which may be exchanged for money."

> ἔστιν θάλασσα—τίς δέ νιν κατασβέσει;—
> τρέφουσα πολλῆς πορφύρας ἰσάργυρον
> κηκῖδα παγκαίνιστον, εἱμάτων βαφάς.

Thus too we find the explanation of the story of Sisyphus at Corinth, who is the father of Porphyrion, that is the purple trade, who founds the worship of Melicertes, that is the Tyrian Melcarth, and whose

[93] Curtius, *Peloponnesos*, ii. 579.   [94] Æsch. *Ag.* 958.

76 LECTURES ON THE [LECT. II.

name, being a reduplication of σοφός, and his corresponding character, represents the sharp practice of traders. This is confirmed by the appearance of the shell of the purple-mussel on the Corinthian coins, and by the prominence given to the worship of Aphrodite in that city.[95]

<small>Nomenclature of Greek promontories.</small>

In conclusion, let us endeavour to classify the names of promontories in Greece, as far as we can discover their etymologies.[96] A certain number are general terms, signifying "headland" or some similar idea: Acritas, the southernmost point of Messenia; Acte, in several parts of Greece; Actium, on the Ambracian gulf; Derrhis, in Sithonia, i.e. δειράς, a projecting ridge; Coryphasium, the other name of Pylos, from κορυφή; Rhium or "foreland" (ῥίον), at the entrance of the Corinthian gulf; and Chersonesus or Cherrhonesus, in the east of Euboea, in Argolis near Cenchreae, and in Ætolia; besides which it is found in many other peninsulas out of Greece Proper. From their position are called Amphiale or "sea-girt," in Attica; Pontinus or "sea-mountain," near Lerna; Amphipagus, the southernmost promontory of Corcyra, the "mountain fixed all round" (cf. ἀμφιπαγής); Platamodes, in western Messenia, from πλαταμών, a "ridge of rocks;" Pylos, from πύλη, as commanding the entrance to the country, just as Juvenal[97] calls

---

[95] Curtius, *Peleponnesos*, ii. 517, 590.

[96] These are for the most part derived from E. Curtius' essay, mentioned above. [97] iii. 4.

Cumæ *janua Baiarum*. From the dangers they caused to navigation—Colyergia, from κωλύειν ἔργον, a promontory at the south of Argolis, where two currents meet; similar to which is Zelasia, or "jealousy corner," a promontory of Magnesia, near Aphetæ, at the entrance of the Pagasæan gulf; Eryx in Sicily, the "restrainer;" Araxus, in the north-west of the Peloponnese, the "wave-breaker;" Rhœteium, in Troas, from the sound of the waves (ῥοῖζος), and Plemmyrium, in Sicily, from the flood-tide (πλημμυρίς); Scyllæum, the easternmost promontory of Argolis, from σκύλλειν, "to rend," and also Scylletium, the place in Bruttium which Virgil calls *navifragum Scylacœum*,[98] both which names are connected with that of the monster Scylla, who represented the dangers of navigation, and was supposed to have her abode on promontories;[99] Marpessa, also, from μάρπτειν, "to seize," the headland in Paros, of which Virgil speaks as *Marpesia cautes*.[100]

Others are called from their shape, as Speiræum, in the territory of Epidaurus, from its twisted or circular form (σπεῖρα): from their likeness to animals and to parts of the body, Leon in Eubœa, Chelonatas, "the tortoise-rock," in Elis; Ichthys, "the fish," in the same country; Cynosura, "the dog's tail," near Marathon and elsewhere; Onugnathus, in Laconia, "the ass's jawbone;" Bucephalon in the north, and Bucephala

[98] Æn. iii. 553. [99] Preller, *Griechische Mythologie*, i. 483.
[100] Æn. vi. 471.

in the south of Argolis, "the ox's head;" Buporthmos, near Hermione, "ox-ford"—in which word the latter part probably refers to the narrow channel between its extremity and the island of Aperopia, the former perhaps to the horns of the neighbouring bay; [101] and Mycale, which is derived from the same root as μυκτήρ, "nostril," and is used to designate a promontory in the same way as *næs*, *ness*, in northern countries :[102] from their resemblance to inanimate objects—Zoster, "the girdle," in Attica; and Drepanum and Zancle, "the sickle," in Achaia and Sicily. Other peculiarities have suggested other names. From their colour come Leucate in Leucadia and Leucimme in Corcyra, and also Pyrrha, in the northern part of the Pagasæan gulf. From caves and hollows in the rocks—Olmiæ, a projection of Geraneia in the Corinthian gulf, from ὅλμος,[103] "a trough or hollow;" Pharygium, or "jaws," in the south of Phocis; Thyrides, "the windows," as an extraordinary precipitous face of rock to the west of Tænarum, now Cape Grosso, was called in antiquity,

---

[101] E. Curtius, *Peloponnesos*, ii. 453, 454.

[102] G. Curtius, *Gr. Etymol.* 148. E. Curtius, *Onomatologie*, 155. It is true that μυκτήρ and similar words are derived from a root signifying "to blow the nose;" but it is likely enough that from this a substantive was derived, signifying the nose itself, and so a projection.

[103] The aspirate of this word is not necessarily an objection to this etymology, for if, as G. Curtius (p. 322) thinks, ὅλμος is derived from ἴλλω, the aspirate would only represent a lost digamma.

from its caverns, which are the resort of innumerable doves;[104] Canastræum, the southernmost point of the peninsula of Pallene, from κάναστρον, "a basket," in the same way as κώρυκος, "a wallet," as being a hollow receptacle, is used as a name for caverns; Lacinium, in Bruttium, from λάκκος, a "hollow or rent;" and Caieta in Italy, the Greek form of which, Καιάτα, is connected with καιάδας, the pit at Sparta, and refers to the vast caverns (σπήλαια ὑπερμεγέθη) which Strabo[105] mentions as existing there. From the vegetation and animals—Ampelos, at the extremity of Sithonia; Crithote, from κριθή, "barley," in Acarnania; Platanistus, the northern promontory of Cythera; Opus, a headland in the south of Phocis, perhaps from ὀπός, "silphium;" Struthus, in the south of Argolis, from the sparrow; and Circæum, in Italy, from the hawk. Some, too, were called from places of worship erected upon them—as Artemisium in Euboea, Poseidium in Epirus, in Phthiotis, and in the peninsula of Pallene, Nymphæum at the extremity of Athos, Æneium in Chalcidice, projecting into the Thermaic gulf, and Æantium in Magnesia.

[104] E. Curtius, *Peloponnesos*, ii. 281.   [105] v. 3, § 6.

LECTURE III.

SECONDARY FEATURES OF THE COUNTRY: RIVERS, SPRINGS, LAKES, CAVERNS, GORGES.

The Rivers of Greece—Perennial Streams and Torrents—Features of the Larger Rivers—Homeric Descriptions of the Torrents—Character of the Water—Etymologies of Greek River-names—Legends suggested by Rivers—Sacredness of Fountains—Their Appearance in Antiquity—Warm Springs—Legends connected with Fountains—Lakes with no Outlet—Drainage of the Plains—Subterranean Passages or Catavothras—Famous Caverns—Waterfall of the Styx—Gorges—The Acheron—Vale of Tempe.

The rivers of Greece. IN describing the geography of an extensive inland country, it would be necessary to give the rivers equal prominence with the mountains, since, while the latter represent the barriers that defend a territory, and separate one tribe from another, the rivers are means of transit and arteries of communication. But in a narrow country like Greece the courses of the streams are not of sufficient length to allow of their attaining any considerable volume, so that none of them are navigable except for boats, and very few even for these. In Thrace and Macedonia, where there is an extensive tract to be drained, we find rivers of greater size—the Hebrus, the Nestus, the Strymon, and the Axius—which last river in particular

Homer celebrates for its fertilising water, as "the fairest stream that flows in all the earth"—

'Αξιοῦ, οὗ κάλλιστον ὕδωρ ἐπικίδναται αἶαν[1]

but even these, though barges are floated down them at the present day, could not be made permanently serviceable without a large outlay of money and labour, owing to the violence of their current. It was rather from the value of their water that the Greek rivers came to be so highly estimated. In that thirsty land, where light-soiled plains filled up the spaces between the stony hills, everything was valued which could refresh the surface and encourage the fertility of the soil. Hence they were called ποταμοί, or waters for drinking. It would not be true to say that water was scarce in Greece, because it was eminently a land of fountains; but the need of it was sufficiently great to cause the inhabitants to prize all that they could obtain. To this fact we must refer for the explanation of the sacred character attached to innumerable sources, and the legends attached to every river and every fountain.

It may be well at starting to distinguish the Greek rivers into two kinds, the perennial streams and the torrents. A river like the Spercheius, which rises at the base of the lofty Typhrestus, and is supplied by tributaries from Othrys and Œta, which flank it on either hand throughout its course, though its volume is diminished during the hot season, never fails

Perennial streams and torrents.

[1] Il. ii. 850.

throughout the year; but with the rivers of Attica this is not the case. The Cephisus, indeed, which is fed by copious sources on the side of Mount Parnes, has a constant supply of water, and Strabo is probably in error, when he speaks of it as having been completely dry in the summer in ancient times;[2] but it does not reach the sea, being drawn off into numerous channels for the irrigation of the neighbouring olive groves and gardens; and this would seem to have been the case also in antiquity from Sophocles' description—"the sleepless fountains of Cephisus, which stray forth from their channels" (ἄϋπνοι κρῆναι Κηφισοῦ νομάδες ῥεέθρων),[3] and accounts for the renowned fertility of the neighbourhood of Colonus and of the Academus. The Ilissus, however, is a mere brook, and notwithstanding its beautiful source in Mount Hymettus, which Ovid has so gracefully described,[4] stands in pools a great part of the year, and during the summer is completely dry. Still more was this the case in the plain of Argos, which Homer has characterised as "very thirsty" (πολυδίψιον), and which still shows the dryness of its soil by its numerous windmills. There the brooks which descend the steep mountain-sides are at once sucked in and disappear from sight, and the stony channels remain dry except after violent rains.

Features of the larger rivers.

The rivers on the west side of the Pindus chain,

[2] ix. 1, § 24. [3] O. C. 685, foll.
[4] *Ars. Am.* iii. 687.

like the mountains and the entire conformation of that district, are different from what we find elsewhere in Greece. The Aous in Illyria, flowing north-westwards towards Apollonia, beyond the Acroceraunian promontory, and the Arachthus and Achelous, which take a southerly direction—the one through Epirus to the Ambracian gulf, the other through Acarnania to the southern sea—are all violent streams, which force their way through narrow valleys between the irregular mountain ranges. The other perennial rivers, with few exceptions, bear a strong likeness to one another in the features of their course. Rising in the upland country, they flow through one or more inland plains, and after being confined for some distance in a narrow gorge, pass through a maritime plain into the sea.[5] Thus the Peneius, rising in the inmost recesses of the Pindus, traverses the whole length of the Thessalian plain, then forces its way by the gorge of Tempe between the precipices of Olympus and Ossa, and at length reaches the Thermaic gulf, after intersecting the alluvial soil which skirts the base of those two mountains. The Alpheius, taking its rise in the south of Arcadia, and winding towards the north-west through that country, after passing through the upland plain of Megalopolis, descends by the mountain passes to Olympia, below which place the plain opens out to the sea. The Eurotas, which starts from the same

[5] Forchhammer, in the *Geographical Society's Journal*, xii. 29.

point—the ancients regarded the two rivers as having actually a common origin[6]—traverses for some time an upland valley, until it flows through a gorge into the plain of Sparta, and at its southern end enters another ravine, so narrow as hardly to admit of its passing (διεξιὼν αὐλῶνά τινα μακρόν, as Strabo says),[7] and traverses the maritime plain of Helos, the name of which is justified by the marshes on the sea-coast. The Pamisus also, the river of Messenia, passes successively through the Stenyclerian and Messenian plains, which are separated from one another by the counter-forts of Taygetus approaching Mount Ithome.

Homeric descriptions of the torrents.

The numerous torrents (χείμαρροι) are the natural result of the configuration of the country, for the steep limestone mountains have but little of a spongy surface to act as a reservoir for the rain, and consequently the channels are only filled after violent storms, or during the winter season, except so far as they are supplied by perennial springs. The water of these, however, is soon absorbed in the upper part of their course, and the white bed is exposed to the scorching rays of the sun, though often beautifully diversified during the summer by a flush of pink colour from the oleander bushes which fringe the banks. It is especially at the time of the autumn rains that the greatest floods take place, and the sudden swelling and violent rush of the stream has

---

[6] Strabo, viii. 3, § 12. Pausan. viii. 44, § 4; 54, § 1.
[7] Strabo, *l. c.*

furnished Homer with some of his finest similes. Such is the passage in the fourth book of the Iliad, where he thus describes the shock of battle :—

> ὡς ὅτε χείμαρροι ποταμοί, κατ' ὄρεσφι ῥέοντες,
> ἐς μισγάγκειαν συμβάλλετον ὄβριμον ὕδωρ
> κρουνῶν ἐκ μεγάλων, κοίλης ἔντοσθε χαράδρης·
> τῶν δέ τε τηλόσε δοῦπον ἐν οὔρεσιν ἔκλυε ποιμήν.[8]

> As when, descending from the mountain's brow,
> Two wintry torrents from their copious source
> Pour downward to the narrow pass, where meet
> Their mingled waters in some deep ravine,
> Their weight of flood ; on the far mountain's side
> The shepherd hears the roar.
> Lord Derby's Translation.

And again, in a similar passage in the sixteenth book, the poet specifies the time of year :—

> ὡς ὑπὸ λαίλαπι πᾶσα κελαινὴ βέβριθε χθὼν
> ἤματ' ὀπωρινῷ, ὅτε λαβρότατον χέει ὕδωρ
> Ζεύς, ὅτε δή ῥ' ἄνδρεσσι κοτεσσάμενος χαλεπήνῃ,
> οἳ βίῃ εἰν ἀγορῇ σκολιὰς κρίνωσι θέμιστας,
> ἐκ δὲ δίκην ἐλάσωσι, θεῶν ὄπιν οὐκ ἀλέγοντες·
> τῶν δέ τε πάντες μὲν ποταμοὶ πλήθουσι ῥέοντες,
> πολλὰς δὲ κλιτῦς τότ' ἀποτμήγουσι χαράδραι,
> ἐς δ' ἅλα πορφυρέην μεγάλα στενάχουσι ῥέουσαι
> ἐξ ὀρέων ἐπὶ κάρ· μινύθει δέ τε ἔργ' ἀνθρώπων.[9]

> As in the autumnal season, when the earth
> With weight of rain is saturate ; when Jove
> Pours down his fiercest storms in wrath to men,
> Who in their courts unrighteous judgments pass,
> And justice yield to lawless violence,

---

[8] iv. 452, foll.   [9] xvi. 384, foll.

> The wrath of Heav'n despising ; ev'ry stream
> Is brimming o'er ; the hills in gullies deep
> Are by the torrents seam'd, which, rushing down
> From the high mountains to the dark blue sea,
> With groans and tumult urge their headlong course,
> Wasting the works of man.
> *Lord Derby's Translation.*

In the latter of these two passages, where the torrents are described as furrowing the mountain sides, we have the derivation of the word χαράδρα, "a stream," from χαράσσω, "to scratch or furrow," whereas in the former it is used of the bed which is thus carved out. Accordingly, Charadrus is found as the name of several such rivers in different parts of Greece. It is hard to doubt that floods such as these suggested the magnificent description of the combat between Achilles and the Scamander, in the 21st book of the Iliad, when the river-god rises up in defence of his favoured city, forces the hero from his stream, and pursues him with a mighty wave over the plain, calling to his brother Simois to hasten to his aid.[10] This is exactly what happens in the upper part of the Trojan plain, when the Mendere, as the Scamander is now called, after continued rainfall bursts out from the narrow defile behind the site of ancient Troy.[11]

Character of the water. A word should be added on the water of these rivers. Travellers are frequently disappointed, on visiting Tempe, to find the Peneius a white and

---

[10] Il. xxi. 233.
[11] See my *Researches in the Highlands of Turkey*, i. 38.

turbid river, which it is in the spring, though later in the summer it has a pale green colour which is pleasing to the eye. It is, however, never clear; and this circumstance gave rise to the poetical fable which Homer relates, that its tributary, the Titaresius, being a branch of the dread stream of Styx, would not mix with it, but flowed on its surface like oil;[12] for the Titaresius is a pellucid river, and like the Rhone and the Arve at Geneva, the waters of the two can be seen flowing separately for some distance below their confluence. Strangely enough, Strabo just inverts Homer's statement, and makes the Peneius the clear river, being misled apparently by the epithet "silver-eddying" ($\dot{\alpha}\rho\gamma\nu\rho\sigma\delta\dot{\iota}\nu\eta$), which is applied to it.[13] The same want of clearness is found in most of the larger Greek streams, as the Spercheius, the Bœotian Cephisus, and, though in a less degree, the Alpheius; the Eurotas, however, at Sparta, is a beautifully pure river, and thus seems to have an especial right to its name, "the fair-flowing." The water of most of the smaller streams is clear; the epithet "black" ($\mu\acute{\epsilon}\lambda\alpha\nu$ $\ddot{\upsilon}\delta\omega\rho$), which Homer applies to them, refers not to their colour, but to the deep, dark look which water, and especially pools of water, assume, when looked at from above. Hence Mavro-nero, or "blackwater," is a common name for rivers among the modern Greeks; and we find Melas as a proper name of

---

[12] Il. ii. 751, foll.
[13] ix. 5, § 20. Leake, *Northern Greece*, iii. 896.

several streams in ancient Greece. Other names which are derived from the colour of the water, are— Cnacion (Κναχιών) in Laconia, from the same word, κναχός, "yellowish," which we have seen giving its name to Mount Cnacalus; and Glaucia (Γλαυκία) in Bœotia, from γλαυκός, signifying either its pale-grey hue or glancing surface; and especially Phœnix (Φοῖνιξ), the name of a small stream, mentioned by Herodotus,[14] near the entrance of the pass of Thermopylæ, which is easily identified by the deep-red sediment that it leaves in its channel, being strongly impregnated with iron.

Etymologies of Greek river-names. A further examination of the etymologies of Greek river-names yields us results not less interesting than what we have seen in the case of mountains, and we shall find that the groups into which they fall correspond in many ways to the different kinds of rivers already noticed.[15] To take first the torrents, and those that are violent in their course: the name Arachthus (Ἄραχθος)—from ἀράσσω to "smite or dash"—occurs both in Epirus and Ætolia; Thyamis—from θύω, "to rush"—in Epirus;[16] Thoas, an old name of the

---

[14] vii. 200.

[15] Since this was written, I have seen Mr. Ferguson's interesting book *The River-Names of Europe*, and I find that he has been led (pp. 19, 20) to much the same classification for the continent generally, which I have found applicable to Greece.

[16] Leake (*Northern Greece*, iv. 97) thinks this name came from θύα (which he takes to mean "juniper,") and says that tree is common along its course; but it is not certain what the Greek tree θύα was.

Achelous, and Teutheas,[17] a river of western Achaia, from θέω, "to run;" Acidon (Ἀκίδων) in Triphylia, like Acis in Sicily, from its arrowy course (ἄκων, javelin); Cycloboros, at Marathon, from its eating away its banks in all directions—κύκλος and βιβρώσκω; Crathis in Achaia, as well as in Magna Græcia, from κεράννυμι, describing the mixing of the torrent streams, or the seething of the water; Buphagus (Βουφάγος), "devourer of oxen," in the territory of Megalopolis, a name which recalls the modern Greek name for a violent stream, Γαϊδαροπνίκτης, or "donkey-drowner;"[18] and Peiros in Achaia, which like Peirene, the fountain at Corinth that makes its way through the rocks from the Acropolis to the lower city, signifies "the piercer" —from πείρω. From the noise of their streams are derived the Kelados and Keladon in Arcadia; the Boagrios, from βοή and ἄγριος, in Locris, which also bore the name of Manes (Μάνης) or "the Lunatic;" the Bruchon (Βρύχων), from βρύχω, "to roar," and Crausindon—perhaps for Κραυγίνδων[19]—from κράζω, both on the side of Mount Pelion; Bomucas, an old name of the Eurotas, the "bellower," from βοῦς and μυκάομαι; and a group of names, Neda and Nedon in Messenia, and Nestus in Thrace, from a root *nad*, which does not appear elsewhere in Greek, but is used for a river in Sanscrit, and signifies "to roar."[20] The same feature

---

[17] E. Curtius, *Peloponnesos*, i. 450.   [18] Ibid. i. 405.
[19] Pape, *Wörterbuch*, s. v.
[20] G. Curtius, *Gr. Etymol.* 219.

of a sudden and violent stream is expressed by the comparison with various animals, distinguished either by their force or by the ferocity of their attack. Thus in Achaia we find a torrent called the "Ram" (Κριός); in the north of Arcadia the "Goat" (Τράγος); in Pieria, rushing from the steep ravines of Mount Olympus, the "Boar" (Σῦς), an animal with which we are familiar in Homeric battle-pieces as a metaphor for a sudden charge; and this name appears again in Achaia for one of the streams from the Arcadian mountains. The older name of the Evenus in Ætolia was Lycormas, "rushing like a wolf"—from λύκος, ὁρμάω; and the name Lycus itself appears in the Greek colonies. Lastly, the bull supplies the name of the Taurius (Ταύριος) near Trœzen, and the Bocaros, "bull's head," in Salamis.

Distinguished from these are the names of those rivers that pursue a gentler course, and flow partly through the plains. The name Asopus, which is best known in connection with the Bœotian stream, but which frequently recurs in other parts of Greece, is derived from ἄσις, the Homeric word for "mud" or "slime," and all the rivers to which it is applied are found to have clayey or muddy banks. The Cephisus, again, whether in Phocis or in Attica, is a quiet stream, and both its name and its laggard nature suggest a possible connection with κηφήν, the drone, and κωφός, "dumb." Similarly the Peneius may come from πήνη, "a thread,"[21] as describing the long extended line which it is seen to make through the plain of Thessaly; and the same thing will apply to the other river of the same name in the rich lands of Hollow Elis. The fertilising power of these streams is further expressed in a group of names—Alpheius, "the enricher," from ἀλφάνω, "to produce or yield"— which is illustrated by the epithet ἀλφεσίβοιος, "producing oxen," which Æschylus[22] applies to the Nile; and from the analogy of this it would seem that Pamisus signifies "the giver of property," from πάομαι, and πᾶμα, "a possession." Similarly in Arcadia the Aroanius is called from the tilled land (ἄροτος) which borders its stream; the Lusius (Λούσιος) in an upland plain in the south-west of that country, from the waters which it poured over a fertile district; and Arethusa, the name of eight fountains in different places, which is connected with ἄρδω,[23] and signifies "the waterer." Again, Probatia (Προβατία), or "sheep-stream," is the name of a tributary of the Cephisus in Bœotia. The winding courses of the streams furnish another source of nomenclature. This is expressed by Ilissus—derived from εἴλω, "to twist or wind"—and by Helixus ("Ελιξος), a stream in the island of Ceos, and Helisson ('Ελισσών), the river which divides in two parts the city of Megalopolis: the last of these is simply the participle of the verb ἑλίσσω, with a change of accent. Again, a tributary of the Achelous, with

[21] G. Curtius, 248.   [22] *Supp.* 855.   [23] Steph. Byz. *s. v.*

numerous windings, is called Campylus (Καμπύλος) or "the crooked." The snake was a natural object of comparison for this, and so we find a river Ophis in the territory of Mantineia: the name Ladon also signifies a snake, and was used to designate the serpent that guarded the gardens of the Hesperides. Pausanias mentions a legend concerning the Styx, that she was a daughter of Ocean, and married Peiras, by whom she had a daughter called Echidna.[24] Pausanias adds, "whoever this Peiras may be." When we see that the Styx joins the Crathis, which afterwards *pierces* through the Arcadian mountains, and *winds* through the rich lands of Achaia to the sea, we may be able to explain both who was Peiras ("the piercer") and who was Echidna ("the snake").

To these we may add some more general names from the fulness, or force, or beauty of the water:—Apidanus, "the water-giver," from the roots of the Latin *aqua* and δίδωμι,[25] for ἀπ is a natural corruption of ἀκ, and is found also in Μεσσάπιοι, the inhabitants of the heel of Italy, between the Adriatic and the Bay of Tarentum, and probably also in γῆ 'Απία (where the first vowel is long), which describes the Peloponnese from its maritime situation as the "waterland." The same form appears in the Indian languages, as Punjab, or the "five waters." Hence Anapus, which is found in Acarnania, as well as in Sicily, where it is more famous, would seem to be from ἀνά or ἄνω, together with this root, and to signify "upland stream." The

---

[24] viii. 18, § 2. [25] G. Curtius, 412.

Pleistus (Πλεῖστος) in the neighbourhood of Delphi is the "full stream," as also is Pimpleia; the Eurotas and Callirrhoe are the "fair-flowing;" and the Erasinus, as the beautiful stream of clear water is called between Argos and Lerna, the "lovely," from ἐράω—though if, as we are told, it bore also the name of Ἀρσῖνος,[26] it may be derived from ἄρδω, "to water, irrigate." Ismenus also means "lovely," if, as is probable, it is connected with ἵμερος, "desire;"[27] and Castalia probably is called from the purity of its water (καθαρός),[28] and also its power of purifying from guilt. The name Spercheius, again—from σπέρχω—describes the force of the stream; Strymon (Στρύμων) probably comes from σρυ, the original form of the root of ῥέω, "to flow,"[29] and consequently corresponds to our word "stream;" and in Doris we find a river Pindus, which, like the mountain of the same name, is derived from πῖδαξ, "a fountain." Nor must we altogether ignore the name Eridanus, which belongs to a confluent of the Ilissus in Attica, from which fact we may conclude that Herodotus,[30] when speaking of the semi-fabulous river of that name in the north of Europe, is right in saying that its appellation, at all events in this form,[31] is Greek; and that he is

[26] Pape, s. v. Ἐρασῖνος.
[27] G. Curtius, 359.   [28] Ibid. 128.
[29] Ibid. 316. Cf. Ferguson, *River-Names of Europe*, 58.
[30] iii. 115.
[31] It may originally be derived from Rhodaune; *see* Rawlinson's Herod. *in loc.*

not far wrong in adding, that it was invented by some poet—perhaps it would have been more true to say, by a poetic people—for it seems to have a mythological significance, as the "stream of morning" or "of light,"—$\mathit{ἠρι\text{-}δανός}$.

<small>Legends suggested by rivers.</small>

Having seen by how many images the courses of the rivers represented themselves to the minds of the Greeks, we cannot be surprised if we find them give birth to numerous legends. In more than one instance we have noticed that the violence of a torrent is symbolised by a boar. Now, at Psophis in the north-west of Arcadia—the ruins of which are to be seen in a romantic glen, shaded with plane-trees, at the meeting of three clear mountain streams, which have given to the place its modern name of Tripotamo—there was a story that a boar used to issue from Mount Erymanthus and ravage the city. But when at the head of a neighbouring valley we see the snowy peaks of that mountain, from which a river of the same name flows under the walls of the town, we have little difficulty in understanding the meaning of the Erymanthian boar. It is this which Hercules, the author of all great works by which man gets the upper hand of nature, has to subdue; that is to say, its ravages have to be checked by dams and dykes. The animal is not killed, but mastered and made serviceable.[32] Again, the names Taurios and Bocaros, which imply the com-

---

[32] Preller, *Griechische Mythologie*, ii. 194. E. Curtius, *Pel.* i. 388, 400.

parison to a bull or bull's head, and those derived from serpents, as Ophis and Ladon, will help us to the explanation of other familiar stories. When Deianeira in the *Trachiniæ* is describing the suitors who contended for her hand, she thus speaks of the Achelous:—

> μνηστὴρ γὰρ ἦν μοι ποταμὸς, Ἀχελῷον λέγω,
> ὅς μ' ἐν τρισὶν μορφαῖσιν ἐξῄτει πατρὸς,
> φοιτῶν ἐναργὴς ταῦρος, ἄλλοτ' αἰόλος
> δράκων ἑλικτὸς, ἄλλοτ' ἀνδρείῳ κύτει
> βούπρῳρος· ἐκ δὲ δασκίου γενειάδος
> κρουνοὶ διερραίνοντο κρηναίου ποτοῦ.[33]

The river Achelous came to woo,
In triple form my father suing for me;
First as a bull appearing visibly,
Then as a dragon wound his speckled length,
And then with human trunk and head of ox,
And from his shaggy beard there flowed the streams
Of his clear fountains.   *Plumptre's Translation.*

Here the allegory is transparent enough, and Strabo comments on it in the following manner:—" Some interpreters, conjecturing the truth from these things, say that the Achelous, like other rivers, was compared to a bull on account of its noises and the bends in its channel, which are called horns, and to a serpent from its length and its windings, and was said to have an ox's head (βούπρωρος) for the same reason as it is called 'bull-faced' (ταυρωπός); and that Hercules, who was usually beneficent, and, besides, was going to marry

[33] Soph. *Trach.*, 9 foll.

Œneus' daughter, forcibly confined the irregular current of the river by dams and dykes, and so drained a great part of the district bordering on the Achelous, as a favour to Œneus; and that this is the horn of Amalthea."[34]   Here, then, we have the explanation of the mythical contest of Hercules and the Achelous, and at the same time of the numerous comparisons of a river to a bull, which suggested to Horace the epithet *"tauriformis"* for the Aufidus. The combination of the figures in Sophocles' third image, where the bull's head is placed on the man's shoulders (ἀνδρείῳ κύτει βούπρῳρος), explains also the corresponding union of parts in the minotaur, *i.e.* the limbs of a bull with a man's face, which, as well as the former, and the more modified type, in which budding horns are added to the human head and figure,[35] are frequently found on coins, especially those of the Sicilian Greeks, and symbolise the rivers, which were rarer, and consequently more prized, in Sicily even than on the Greek continent. The same explanation should be given of the adventure of Hercules with the centaur Nessus, whose name is etymologically connected with the river-names Neda and Nestus. The scene of this is the Evenus, one of the fiercest and most treacherous torrents in Greece; the centaur, the ravisher, represents the violent impetuosity and destructive power of

---

[34] Strabo, x. 2, § 19.

[35] *See* Ruskin (*Stones of Venice*, i. 405), who classifies these figures together as the Androtauric type.

the stream; and Deianeira seems to mean the devastation it causes, and which Hercules strove to restrain.[36]

Another peculiarity of the Greek rivers, which gave birth to numerous fables, is their tendency to disappear underground during a portion of their course. This seems to have been the origin of the idea of the Alpheius passing through the sea; and we may notice that the earlier name of that stream was Nyctimus (Νύκτιμος), *i.e.* the river of night, and so of darkness, whereas it was afterwards regarded as the "enricher" (Ἀλφειός). Pausanias makes the following remarks with regard to it:—" The Alpheius appears beyond all other rivers to show the following peculiarity—I mean that it is wont often to disappear beneath the earth and reappear again. Thus, when it has made its way onward from Phylace and the place called the Confluence, it descends into the plain of Tegea; and after rising again in Asea, and joining its waters with the Eurotas, it again disappears a second time into the earth; then it reappears at the place called by the Arcadians the Fountains, and passing in its course the territory of Pisa and Olympia, falls into the sea above Cyllene, the port of the Eleans. Nay, even the Adriatic is not destined to check its course, for it carries its waters through that sea, wide and tempestuous though it be, and at Ortygia, in front of Syracuse, proves that it is

---

[36] Mure, *Tour in Greece*, i. 170.

Alpheius, and that it joins its stream with Arethusa."[37] The proof of his identity are the leaves and flowers that he is believed to throw up in the fountain, these being, as Moschus expresses it in his graceful poem on the subject, his bridal gifts—ἕδνα φέρων καλὰ φύλλα καὶ ἄνθεα καὶ κόνιν ἱράν;[38] and this belief has left its traces behind it, for a similar connection was believed not long ago to exist between Arethusa and the Jordan, since, in autumn, the fountain was said to throw up leaves of such trees as were known only to flourish on the banks of that river;[39] and in the islands of the Strophades, off the west coast of the Morea, there is a well where leaves and flowers, and even roots and shrubs, are reported by the inhabitants to be deposited by the Alpheius.[40] Pausanias, in another part of his work, justifies his belief in the legend by mentioning the perfectly natural phenomenon of the water of rivers being seen to pass through lakes without mingling with them, and he mentions as an instance of this the Jordan passing through the Sea of Tiberias.[41] The same writer mentions a similar peculiarity belonging to a river in Macedonia, under Mount Olympus, near the city of Dium, together with an accompanying story. "The river Helicon also flows there, and when

---

[37] Paus. viii. 54, § 2. See also the remarks of Grote, *History of Greece*, ii. 292, 293, *note*. [38] vii. 3.
[39] Marifiotti, quoted in Wilkinson's *Magna Græcia*, p. 15.
[40] Waddington, *On the Greek Church*, p. 105.
[41] v. 7, § 4.

it has run for the distance of seventy-five stadia, it afterwards disappears underground; and after an interval of about twenty-two stadia its water rises again, and taking the name of Baphyra instead of Helicon, descends to the sea as a navigable stream. Now the people of Dium say that at first this river flowed above ground throughout its whole course, but that when the women who slew Orpheus desired to wash off the blood in its water, it descended into the earth lest it should furnish them with its water as a means of purification from the murder."[42]

One more story may be added, also relating to Orpheus and to a neighbouring part of Pieria, to illustrate the way in which the violence of the torrents was regarded as an instrument of divine vengeance. "I have heard," he says, "another tale at Larissa, how that there was a city on Olympus called Libethra, on the side of the mountain facing Macedonia, and that not far from the town was the sepulchre of Orpheus. Now there came to the people of Libethra an oracle from Dionysus from Thrace, saying that when the sun saw the bones of Orpheus, their city was destined to be destroyed by a boar. Well, they, for their part, paid little heed to the oracle, for they did not think that that animal or any other was sufficiently great and powerful to overthrow their city, and that the courage of the boar was greater than its strength. But when it was the will of God, it happened to them as

[42] ix. 30, § 8.

follows. A certain shepherd, just about midday, rested himself against the tomb of Orpheus and fell asleep, and whilst he was sleeping, it came to pass that he sang some of the poems of Orpheus with a sweet and loud voice. At this, all who were keeping cattle or ploughing in the immediate neighbourhood left their work, and assembled to listen to the shepherd singing in his sleep. And it happened, as they were hustling one another, and contending for the nearest place to the shepherd, they overturned the gravestone, and the urn fell away from it and was broken, and then the sun saw what remained of the bones of Orpheus. And immediately after, during the following night, the god poured down violent rain from heaven, and the river Sys, which is one of the torrents on the sides of Olympus, cast down the city walls of the Libethrians, and overthrew the sanctuaries of the gods and the habitations of men, and drowned both the human beings and likewise all the animals that were in the city.[43]

Sacredness of fountains. Greece may truly be called a land of springs and fountains of water. They meet you in every glen, and gush out even from the tops of the mountains: Peirene flows from the summit of the Acrocorinth; Aganippe rises high up among the peaks of Helicon; and a similar perennial stream is found on the ridge of Mount Ithome. Hence arose, in a land where the rivers were accustomed soon to fail, the esteem in which they were held, and the sacred character

---

[43] ix. 30, § 9.

attached to them, so that the names of Callirrhoë, Hippocrene, Castalia, and Dirce, cannot be mentioned, without calling up the most familiar and most poetical associations. Of water, as of virtue, it may be said—

—— incolumem odimus,
Sublatam ex oculis quærimus invidi—

and therefore in a country like our own, where there is a more than sufficient supply, it is difficult to understand why the Greek poets lavish such praises upon it: but in Pindar's native land it is easy to explain why he said that water was the best of things (ἄριστον μὲν ὕδωρ). These were the children of Poseidon, as distinguished from the water that came from Zeus. The διϊπετὴς ποταμός, as the streams were called that were fed by the rain from heaven, was liable to dry up as soon as the clouds dispersed; but the fountains never ceased, and so they were regarded as parts of the great unchanging body of water, the offspring of the divine Ocean. Hence Poseidon held sway on the dry land as well as on the sea; he is *uterque Neptunus*, as Catullus [44] expresses it; and so in Aristophanes we find the following conversation:—

XP. νὴ τὸν Ποσειδῶ.
ΒΛ. τὸν θαλάττιον λέγεις;
XP. εἰ δ' ἔστιν ἕτερός τις Ποσειδῶν, τὸν ἕτερον.[45]

---

[44] xxxi. 3.
[45] Ar. *Plut.* 396. See Welcker, *Gr. Götterlehre*, ii. 682. The same idea is expressed by Æschylus (*Sept.* 307)—ὕδωρ τε Διρκαῖον, εὐτραφέστατον πωμάτων, ὅσων ἵησι Ποσειδᾶν ὁ γαιάοχος Τηθύος τε παῖδες.

"Ay, by Poseidon."—"Do you mean the sea-god?" "Yes, and by any other there may be."

Without them it would have been impossible for the country to have been as thickly strewn with cities as we see it to have been from the ruins which remain; and so in some districts, as for instance in the upland regions of Mount Pelion, notwithstanding the presence of abundant vegetation, the want of them prevented, as it continues to do at the present day, the formation of settlements. Hence, though we frequently find the remains of cisterns which served to help out the supply of water, the springs were in Greece, as they were still more notably in Palestine, a determining element in the choice of a position. This principle especially influenced the Greeks in founding their colonies, and thus we find the site of Cyrene on the African coast determined in preference to others by the copious fountain, which was subsequently dedicated to Apollo.

Their appearance in antiquity. We must not suppose that these sources were always very romantic spots in antiquity. Like many other features of the country, they now present to us rather the aspect which they presented to the early settlers than the features they wore when the land was crowded with cities and temples. The necessities of use must frequently have interfered with their appearance. Callirrhoë, which pours its waters from a projecting rock into the bed of the Ilissus, must have lost much of its beauty when it became Enneacrounos, or "the Nine Sources," especially if the channels for the water, which were bored through the rock, were fitted with pipes, as is sufficiently probable. Aganippe at the present day resembles the ordinary fountains of the country in presenting the appearance of a narrow erection of stone with a small iron spout, over which there is an ancient inscription; and it is Colonel Leake's opinion that several of the famous classical fountains were of this character. At the present day their neighbourhood, which we are accustomed to associate with nymphs, is everywhere the resort of washerwomen; and this may well have been the case of old, since Homer tells us concerning the fountains in front of the city of Troy, that the wives and fair daughters of the Trojans used to wash their garments there, "in peaceful times, ere came the sons of Greece"—

τὸ πρὶν ἐπ᾿ εἰρήνης, πρὶν ἐλθεῖν υἷας ᾿Αχαιῶν.[46]

There is one instance, happily, to which this disenchanting view does not apply: this is the fountain of Castalia, which must have presented nearly the same appearance in ancient that it does in modern times. It is a stone basin, of about 36 feet in length, with steps to descend into it, hewn in the natural rock. On the face of the rock behind are three niches, the middle and largest of which is thought to have been intended for a statue of Apollo, the other two for

[46] Il. xxii. 153-6.

figures of Pan and of the nymph Castalia. A thin stream of water issues from under these into the basin, and at the back there is a channel which served to carry off the superfluous water, when the basin was quite full; this office, however, it has no longer to perform, for an exit has been cut through the steps of the basin in front. I grieve to add that what I have described is no longer to be seen, for in 1870, during an earthquake, a fragment of rock which was detached from the cliff above crushed the basin, and its fragments have even concealed the water itself from view.[47]

Warm springs. The warm springs also were a prominent feature of the country. These were sacred to Hercules, so that the ἄδικος λόγος in the Nubes, when wishing to justify the use of warm baths, is able to appeal to the example of that manly hero—" Who ever heard of baths of Hercules being cold ? "

ποῦ ψυχρὰ δῆτα πώποτ' εἶδες Ἡράκλεια λουτρά ;[48]

The most famous were those of Thermopylæ, at which place the waters are still used for their beneficial influence. These issue from the foot of the mountain at several points, though there are two principal sources, and the water, though very clear, has a greyish-green colour from the sediment at the bottom, of which you may take up handfuls, if you put your hand in. It is called by Pausanias γλαυκότατον ὕδωρ.[49]

[47] Murray's *Handbook of Greece*, 247.
[48] Aristoph. *Nub.* 1051.   [49] iv. 35, § 6.

The water is hot, salt, and sulphureous to the taste, and in some places, where the stream is not strong, the green sediment floats in lumps on the surface. By this the banks are encrusted with a white crust, and for a long way below the ground is covered with an extensive tract of white deposit, which when stamped with the foot gives forth a hollow sound. This has done much towards changing the appearance of the famous pass. Still more considerable are the sources at the Baths of Hercules at Ædepsus in the north of Eubœa, which were used, we are told, by the dictator Sulla,[50] and have now been converted into an extensive bathing establishment. These, which are strongly sulphureous, rise a short distance inland at several points, and at last pour themselves steaming over the rocks, which they have yellowed with their deposit, into the Euboic sea. On the isthmus of Corinth near Cenchreæ were the lukewarm springs called the Baths of Helen, and at the peninsula of Methana in Argolis, near Epidaurus, were others, of the formation of which Pausanias has left us an account. "The inhabitants relate," he says, "that it was when Antigonus, son of Demetrius, was king of Macedon that the water first appeared; but it was not in the first instance water that appeared, but a mass of fire burst out of the earth, and after this ceased to burn the water rushed forth, which

[50] Plutarch, *Sulla*, 26, § 3. ed. Bekker. *Sympos.* iv. 4, § 1, ed. Duebner.

even down to my time continues to flow, hot and excessively salt." [51] Other warm springs which are mentioned by ancient authors have now either ceased to flow or have lost their temperature, as, for instance, those that Pausanias [52] mentions in the valley of the Alpheius, in the neighbourhood of which there were jets of flame; and on the other hand, there are warm springs now existing, which from their conspicuous position we should expect to have been mentioned, if they had been so in antiquity. These changes are quite natural in a country liable to be shaken by earthquakes.

Legends connected with fountains.

As might be expected, these fountains gave birth to innumerable legends, so that no feature of the country was equally prolific in that respect. Nowhere is the admirable paradox more thoroughly applicable, that a legend, to be permanent, ought to be "writ on water." Milton shows his usual fine appreciation of classical antiquity, when, in describing the downfall of paganism in Greece, he says—

> "From haunted spring and dale,
> Edged with poplar pale,
> The parting genius is with sighing sent."

Nothing is more striking in reading Pausanias, than the number of fountains that he enumerates, each with its appropriate myth; and this it is which attracts the old archæologist, who otherwise neglects the features of the country. In one place was a

---

[51] ii. 34, § 1.   [52] viii. 29, § 1.

source called Dionysias, because Dionysus called it forth by striking the earth with his thyrsus;[53] in another the water which issued from the ground with a foul odour was said to have derived this from the poison of the Hydra, a centaur who was wounded by the arrows of Hercules, having washed his wound there.[54] Here was the spring by which Actæon rested from the chase, and in which he saw Artemis bathing;[55] there was a fountain sacred to Ares, over which the god appointed a snake as guardian.[56] We may also notice the mythological connection between the horse and fountains; thus Peirene and Hippocrene, which rose on lofty summits, and were therefore regarded as an especial gift of God, were believed to have arisen from the footprint of Pegasus, whose name also implies that he symbolises a source of water ($\pi\eta\gamma\acute{\eta}$).

The lakes of Greece are a very peculiar feature of the country. This arises from the conformation of many of the valleys or upland basins, which are so hemmed in by mountains that no aperture is left for the escape of the water, and this is consequently forced to make a passage for itself underground. This is the case with every piece of water in Greece, with the single exception of the Lacus Lychnitis, now the Lake of Ochrida, at the head-waters of the Black Drin, which is the largest of them all, but was little known

Lakes with no outlet.

[53] iv. 36, § 7.   [54] v. 5, § 10.
[55] ix. 2, § 3.   [56] ix. 10, § 5.

in ancient times, until the Romans constructed the great Egnatian Way from the Adriatic to the Ægean, which skirted its shores. The Lacus Pambotis, now the lake of Joannina, in Epirus; the Lacus Ascuris, which lies more than 3000 feet above the sea in the highlands of Mount Olympus; that of Bœbe in the south-east of Thessaly; the Copaic lake in Bœotia; those of Stymphalus and Pheneus in Arcadia; and others of less size and note in various parts of the country, all present this peculiarity. The level of these lakes frequently rises and falls, and at times they disappear altogether, an occurrence which has happened most remarkably in the case of the lake of Pheneus. That beautiful basin, which, as you look down upon it from the surrounding fir-clad heights, resembles in many respects our own Derwentwater, is now a glassy expanse of water, but in the early part of this century Leake[57] described it as a green plain, marshy in parts, which was its character also in Pausanias' time;[58] and Mr. Clark, who visited it about fifteen years ago, was so unprepared for its present appearance, that he humorously compares his feelings to those of Pizarro, "when he stared at the Pacific, silent upon a peak of Darien."[59] These changes have naturally aroused superstitious feelings in modern as well as in ancient times: thus there was an old prophecy amongst the modern Greeks, that Greece

[57] *Travels in the Morea*, iii. 141, foll.
[58] Pausan. viii. 14, § 1.   [59] Clark's *Peloponnesus*, 312.

would never be free until the lake was replenished; and so it came to pass that shortly before the Allied Powers declared the freedom of Greece, the waters reappeared.[60]

Even where a lake was not formed, the draining of a district by the disappearance of the waters underground was not an uncommon phenomenon in Greece. This was what took place in the plain of Mantineia, at the southern end of which, we are told by Thucydides,[61] when Agis wished to provoke his enemies to an engagement, he forced the water back over that plain. This, which the historian adds was a frequent cause of war between Tegea and Mantineia, took place in the following manner.—Between the plains in which those two cities lie, and which in reality form one great expanse, was the mouth of the subterraneous passage by which the surface water escaped; and consequently, if this was stopped, or the approaches to it dammed, the neighbouring lands were immediately flooded. For the same reason, in consequence of the absence of cultivation resulting from the stagnant waters, the upper part of the plain of Mantineia, which has insufficient natural drainage, was called Argon Pedion, or the uncultivated plain. The water from this was believed by the ancients to pass under Mount Artemisium, and to appear in the sea on the Argolic coast near Thyrea. That remarkable fountain, which, though it does not in reality

Drainage of the plains.

[60] Linton, *Scenery of Greece*, 83.   [61] v. 65.

descend from the Argon Pedion, is probably the issue of a stream from the plain of Tegea, bore in antiquity the name of Deine, and may still be seen about 1000 feet from the shore, rising in the midst of the salt water with a column of such volume as to force itself above the sea-level, and throw off concentric eddies all round.[62] It may illustrate the twofold function of Poseidon, as the god of fresh water as well as of the sea, to mention what Pausanias tells us with regard to this spring,[63] that the Argives used there to sacrifice horses to him, by letting them down into the water with bits in their mouths. And even the stagnant waters of the plains were not without their influence on Greek development. It was in the swampy lands bordering the Copaic lake that the reeds grew from which the flutes were made that caused the Thebans to be so famous for their music, and which gave rise to the poetic art in that country, of which Hesiod and Pindar were the great representatives. For what the marbles of Pentelicus were to Athenian sculpture, as its material or suggestive cause, that the reeds of the Copais were to the poetry of Bœotia.

Subterranean passages or catavothras. When Virgil, in relating the story of Aristæus, represents him as finding his mother Cyrene at the head-waters of the Peneius—

> Pastor Aristæus, fugiens Peneia Tempe,—
> Tristis ad extremi sacrum caput adstitit amnis—[64]

---

[62] E. Curtius, *Peloponnesos*, ii. 373. [63] viii. 7, § 2.
[64] Virg. *Georg.* iv. 317, 319.

and as there seeing the great rivers flowing underground—

> Omnia sub magna labentia flumina terra ;[65]

he is, whether consciously or not, an excellent exponent of Greek geography. For, in the first place, the spot which he has chosen, on the side of Mount Lacmon, is, as we have noticed, the starting-point of five of the largest rivers in Greece; and besides this, the idea of subterraneous courses was everywhere familiar to the Greeks. We have seen this in the case of some rivers, like the Alpheius, which occasionally disappear, but it was far more common in the outlet of lakes. Aristotle gives the following account of the phenomenon :—"That there are such chasms and openings in the ground is clear from the rivers that are engulfed. Now this happens in many parts of the earth, as, for instance, in Peloponnesus, where there are several instances in the neighbourhood of Arcadia. The reason is that, whereas that is a mountain district, it has no channels leading from the cavities of the ground to the sea. For when a district is filled and has no vent, it finds for itself a passage vertically, by the force of the water that presses from above."[66] The numerous words used in Greek to describe it, show how familiar it must have been to the ancients. Thus the subterranean passage itself was called βάραθρον (in Arcadia ζέρεθρον),

---

[65] Ibid. 366.   [66] Ar. *Meteorol.* I. cap. xiii. § 27.

βόθρος, πόρος, ῥεῖθρον ὑπόνομον, ἔναυλος, ἔκρυσις. The entrance was termed χάσμα, the exit ἔκρηξις, ἐκβολή, ἀναβολή, ἀναχοή.[67] The modern name is Catabothron, a corruption of καταβάραθρον, and in some places χωνεύτρα or the "digester."[68] It is not often possible to see the exit of the water from a lake, because it is usually covered. In some cases the mouths are small, so as almost to present the appearance of water filtering through shingle; but in others, as for instance in the lake of Stymphalus, an escarpment of rock runs down sheer into the water, and at the foot of this there is an arched cavern through which the lake is discharged. The waters of this lake, according to Herodotus,[69] after passing under Mount Chaon, reappear as the Erasinus in Argolis. A similar opening at the exit of the lake of Pheneus is described by Catullus, who compares it to the absorbing character of Laodamia's love :—

———— tanto te absorbens vertice amoris
Æstus in abruptum detulerat barathrum ;
Quale ferunt Graii Pheneum prope Cyllenæum
Siccare emulsa pingue palude solum ;
Quod quondam cæcis montis fodisse medullis
Audit falsiparens Amphitryoniades.[70]

———— so wert thou hurried there,
Upon the whirling torrent of thy love,

---

[67] Ulrichs, *Reisen in Griechenland*, i. 223.
[68] Leake, *Northern Greece*, i. 410.   [69] vi. 76.
[70] lxviii. 109.

> Into a steep-down gulf, as dark and deep
>   As that which erst, in Grecian story famed,
> Near Pheneus' city by Cyllene's steep,
>   From oozy marsh the fertile soil reclaimed.[71]

Strabo[72] makes the following remarks on the outlets of these two Arcadian lakes:—"I have already mentioned the extraordinary phenomenon relating to the Alpheius and Eurotas, as also that the Erasinus now makes its exit into the Argive territory from the Stymphalian lake, whereas formerly there was no discharge, because the subterranean channels (βέρεθρα), which the Arcadians call ζέρεθρα, were blind and did not allow a passage to the water, so that the city of the Stymphalians, though now it is as much as five stadia from the lake, was then situated upon its banks." (The text gives πεντήκοντα here, but it should certainly be πέντε, which just corresponds to the actual distance).[73] "The reverse," he continues, "was the case with the Ladon, because its stream was once checked by its sources being blocked up; for the subterranean channels near Pheneus, through which the passage was, were broken up by an earthquake, and stopped the stream even to the deep-seated veins of its source." There is good reason to believe that Strabo, and others in antiquity, were right in tracing a connection between the Ladon and this lake, as the distance

---

[71] In the last line but one I have ventured to alter Mr. Theodore Martin's translation, who renders it—"Where rolls Peneus by Cyllene's steep."

[72] viii. 8, § 4.   [73] See Leake, *Morea,* iii. 145.

between them is not great, and they correspond in position. The safest test in such a case would be the overflow of the one corresponding to the subsidence of the other, but this does not appear to have been observed. The most remarkable, however, of all the catavothras were those of the Copaic lake, for there nature was assisted by the hand of man. The natural emissaries which carry its waters into the Euboic sea are in the main three, while a fourth drains some portion into a smaller lake called Hylice. The course of the former of these is about four miles, after which the water again emerges, and forms a river before flowing into the sea. But these natural outlets, which the water had made for itself in the course of ages, were found insufficient for the drainage of the plain, and at some very early period, of which we have no record, probably when the Minyæ held sway at Orchomenus, two gigantic tunnels were excavated to carry off the standing water of the lake. The smaller of these communicates with the lake Hylice, but the larger, which runs towards the sea, is cut through the rock for the distance of nearly four miles, with fifteen vertical shafts let down to it at intervals from above: some of these reach to a depth of more than 100 feet.[74] At the time when these were in working

---

[74] See the notice and plan in Smith's *Dictionary of Geography* (vol. i. p. 411), which are derived from Forchhammer's *Hellenica;* also an excellent account in Murray's *Handbook for Greece* (p. 241).

order, the Copaic lake could not have existed, and the whole of the rich plain now covered by it was under cultivation—a circumstance which would readily explain the early prosperity of the neighbouring Orchomenus. But they appear soon to have become ruined, though they were partially cleared by Crates at the command of Alexander.[75]

In a country where the mountains are thus honey-combed at their base, we cannot be surprised at finding numerous caverns above ground. The most remarkable of these, both in size and fame, was the Corycian cave, which is situated at the side of a small plain some distance above Delphi, among the summits of Parnassus. The opening by which it is entered is somewhat more than six feet in height, and when you are within, you descend for some distance, and ascend again to reach the farther end. It is 330 feet long, and nearly 200 wide, and 40 high; and at both ends fine stalactites hang suspended from the roof, while at the inner end there are stalagmites rising from the ground to meet them. Through a narrow entrance at its extremity there is a passage into another and smaller cave. It is easy to understand how, in the dim light within, the stalactites and other glimmering objects would assume to the imaginative Greeks the forms of Pan and the Nymphs, the divinities to whom

Famous caverns.

---

[75] Strabo, ix. 2, § 18. The lake appears to have existed in some form in the Homeric period, for Homer says—λίμνῃ κεκλιμένος Κηφισίδι (*Il.* v. 709).

it was sacred, and who were the companions of Dionysus in his revels on Parnassus; as Sophocles says—"Thee above the rock with double crest, the flashing smoke beheld, where the Corycian nymphs proceed in Bacchic revels"—

> σὲ δ' ὑπὲρ διλόφου πέτρας
> στέροψ ὄπωπε λιγνύς, ἔνθα Κωρύκιαι νύμφαι
> στείχουσι Βακχίδες—[76]

or, as Æschylus has described it—"I venerate too the nymphs, where lies the Corycian rock, hollow, tenanted by birds, the resort of deities:"—

> σέβω δὲ νύμφας, ἔνθα Κωρυκὶς πέτρα
> κοίλη, φίλορνις, δαιμόνων ἀναστροφή.[77]

To this spot also it was that, as Herodotus relates,[78] the Delphians fled for refuge at the time of the Persian attack on the oracle, when they bestowed their movables within the Corycian cave. In this circumstance we find the one point of correspondence between the history and use of caves in Greece and Palestine, both of them countries of limestone caverns; for whereas in the latter they either served as refuges for the brigand, the outlaw, and the persecuted, or else formed the natural place of sepulture,[79] in the former they were regarded as the homes of the deities, and were constantly associated with the mythology. In the side of the Acropolis at Athens may still be seen the shallow cavern which Pausanias[80] describes as the one

[76] *Ant.* 1126. [77] *Eum.* 22. [78] viii. 36.
[79] Stanley, *Sinai and Palestine*, p. 150. [80] i. 28, § 4.

dedicated by the Athenians to Pan after the battle of Marathon, before which engagement that deity met the courier Pheidippides on Mount Parthenium returning from Sparta, and charged him to remonstrate with the Athenians for neglecting one so kindly disposed towards them:[81] and under the Areopagus, at its north-eastern angle, where the shadow falls gloomily, is the deep cave of the Eumenides, with its pool of dark water, the scene of the disappearance of Œdipus. Very remarkable also was the one mentioned by Pausanias, where Melampus, the ancient seer, cured the mad daughters of Prœtus by means of secret sacrifices and expiations.[82] This was situated on the side of Mount Aroanius in Arcadia, and may well be the huge hollow in the rock, at the foot of a precipice 300 feet in height, in front of which now stands the extraordinary monastery of Megaspelion; *i.e.* μέγα σπήλαιον, or "the great cave." Lastly, we must not omit to name what was the most frequented of all, on account of the oracle it contained, the cave of Trophonius, in the deep ravine of the Hercyna behind Lebadeia.

It is not a little surprising that in a land of mountains, such as Greece, we should find hardly any waterfalls. In fact, if we except the fine cascade of the Thyamis in the north of Epirus, which is not noticed by any ancient author, the only fall worth

<small>Waterfall of the Styx.</small>

---

[81] Herod. vi. 105.
[82] viii. 18, § 7. See Hettner, *Athens and the Peloponnese*, p. 188.

mentioning is that of the Styx in Arcadia. The appearance of that stream and its surroundings are fully equal to its ancient fame, and justify the infernal character that has been attached to it. Beneath one of the highest summits of the snowy Aroanius, near a place where two ranges of rocks meet and form a chasm, there is a perpendicular cliff of great height, the face of which is deeply tinged with an iron hue. From the top of this there drops a thin stream of water, which in one or two places is slightly broken by the rock against the side of which it falls, and about half-way down it is joined by another still narrower stream which descends parallel to it from above. Its full height is calculated at 500 feet. During a great part of the year its waters are lost in the snow which lies at its foot, so that both its source and its exit are concealed, and at all times its position is so inaccessible that it has not yet been reached by any traveller. Thus from early times it was regarded by the Greeks with the deepest awe, and served to localise for them their primæval traditions about a river of Hades. This they conceived of as a great stream falling down in a sheer cataract to the underworld, and there running with a mighty stream to infinite distance;[83] and with their usual fondness for the real they represented it to themselves by what they found here. Accordingly, Homer speaks of it as the " down-dropping water of Styx" (τὸ κατειβόμενον

---

[83] Clark's *Peloponnesus*, 306.

Στυγὸς ὕδωρ),[84] and the "precipitous streams of the water of Styx" (Στυγὸς ὕδατος αἰπὰ ῥέεθρα) ;[85] and Hesiod, with still greater definiteness, describes it as the "cold water which is poured down from a lofty inaccessible cliff" (ὕδωρ ψυχρὸν ὅ τ' ἐκ πέτρης καταλείβεται ἠλιβάτοιο ὑψηλῆς),[86] and the "primæval imperishable water of Styx, which it pours down through a precipitous spot" (Στυγὸς ἄφθιτον ὕδωρ ὠγύγιον, τὸ δ' ἵησι καταστυφέλου διὰ χώρου).[87] Then it was regarded as the highest object of adjuration to the gods ;[88] and in later times we hear from Herodotus[89] that it had a similar idea attached to it, so that Cleomenes, when he was desirous of making a solemn league with the Arcadians, led their chief men to Nonacris, and administered to them an oath on the waters of the Styx. Pausanias describes it as dropping over a precipice the like of which in height he had never seen,[90] and relates the local legends about it, concerning its poisonous character, which caused death to man and beast, and how its water would break almost any vessel into which it was poured—fragments of which stories have been perpetuated among the inhabitants of the valley down to the beginning of this century.[91] It has even been suggested[92] that when the dread goddess Styx is spoken

---

[84] Il. xv. 37.
[85] viii. 369.   [86] *Theog.* 785.   [87] Ibid. 805.
[88] Il. xv. 38.   [89] vi. 74.   [90] viii. 17, § 6 ; 18, § 4.
[91] Leake, *Travels in the Morea,* iii. 166, 167.
[92] Preller, *Griechische Mythologie,* i. 28.

of in the Theogony as inhabiting a palace overshadowed with rocks and raised on silver pillars to heaven—

κλυτὰ δώματα ναίει
μακρῇσιν πέτρῃσι κατηρεφέ᾽· ἀμφὶ δὲ πάντῃ
κίοσιν ἀργυρέοισι πρὸς οὐρανὸν ἐστήρικται—[93]

by the silver pillars are meant the dripping streams; and that when, in the Odyssey, Homer speaks of the "rock in Hades, and the junction of two resounding rivers"—

πέτρη τε ξύνεσίς τε δύω ποταμῶν ἐριδούπων—[94]

he refers to the double waterfall;[95] but, for my own part, I greatly doubt whether the ancient poets used to carry description so far.

Gorges—the Acheron. It remains to speak of the gorges in Greece, which form one of the most imposing features of the landscape. We have just described one of the infernal rivers; let us now turn to another, the Acheron. The scene of this is Thesprotia, and consequently it is not far distant from Dodona, the home of the earliest religious associations of the inhabitants of the country. Pausanias expresses his opinion that Homer derived the idea of his "Inferno" from this spot, and adopted the names of the rivers in this part of Thesprotia;[96] and we learn from Herodotus that the Greeks of his time used to seek responses there at the ancient

---

[93] Hesiod, *Theog.* 777. [94] Od. x. 515.
[95] Hayman's *Odyssey*, p. lv. Appendix D.
[96] Paus. i. 17, § 5.

oracle of the dead.[97] Certainly lofty rocks, as well as rivers and a marsh, entered into the Greek conception of those regions, and Aristophanes speaks of the " cliff of Acheron dripping with blood " (Ἀχερόντιός τε σκόπελος αἱματοσταγής).[98] The scene, though a perfect contrast to the Styx, is an equally fine embodiment of the idea it represents. It is the deepest and darkest ravine in Greece, and between its precipitous rocks, for the distance of from two to three miles, the white waters of the stream roar along through chasms and clefts which they have worn away in the course of ages, leaving no room even for the path, which has to be carried along the sides of the cliffs far above, in some places as much as 500 feet above the water. But, notwithstanding these awe-inspiring features, it is at the same time a most romantic spot, for the sides of this passage are, for the most part, richly clothed with foliage, trees and shrubs clinging to every available point, whilst among so much luxuriance the light-grey rocks peep out in the most enchanting manner. Sometimes nothing intervenes between you and the stream but a few trees which have fastened their roots in the fissures of the rocks, and the dull roar of the surging waters may be heard, softened by the distance, while, above, the mountain summits tower at a great elevation on either side. At the mouth of the gorge, where it suddenly comes to an end, was the marsh, the Palus Acherusia, in the neighbourhood of which was the oracle.

[97] Herod. v. 92.   [98] Ar. *Ran.* 471.

Vale of Tempe. From this place, which embodied to the Greeks so many dread conceptions, let us turn to another, which they were accustomed to associate with rural delights, the Vale of Tempe. This also was a chasm, cloven in the rocks, as the fable tells us, by the trident of Poseidon, between Olympus and Ossa; but, though it possesses every element of the sublime, yet its features are soft and beautiful, from the broad winding river, the luxuriant vegetation, and the glades that at intervals open out at the foot of the cliffs, which distinguish it from ordinary passes and enable us to recognise in it the Tempe of the poets. Its length is about four miles and a half, and throughout it is flanked by lofty rocks of grey limestone finely tinted with red; these are highest towards the middle of the pass, where the precipices in the direction of Olympus descend steeply, so as completely to bar the passage on that side; but those which descend from Ossa are the loftiest, rising in many places not less than 1500 feet from the valley. The plane-trees which shade the banks of the Peneius along its tranquil reaches are especially conspicuous for their growth, and from among them, here and there, copious streams of clear water gush out through beds of spreading fern. Strange to say, out of all the descriptions of this famous valley that have come down to us from ancient authors, whether poets or prose writers, whether Greek or Latin, there is not one that can be spoken of as fairly accurate.

LECTURE IV.

PHYSICAL CONDITIONS OF THE COUNTRY—SOIL AND MINERALS—EARTHQUAKES AND VOLCANIC ACTION—CLIMATE AND WINDS—VEGETATION.

Nature of the Soil—The chief Products—Minerals—Marbles—Earthquakes in Antiquity: in Modern Times—Greece near a Volcanic Centre—Eruptions in Historic Times—Climate of Greece—Contrasts in Different Districts—The Winds in Homer—Their Subsequent Nomenclature—Character of the Several Winds—"Temple of the Winds" at Athens—Distribution of the Vegetation—The Forests—Important Trees in Antiquity—Lesser Growths and Shrubs—Flowers.

THE soil of Greece is for the most part light and thin, and requires very careful agriculture to develop its produce. This feature, which Thucydides has noticed in the case of Attica (τὸ λεπτόγεων),[1] belongs not only to the mountain sides, but also to the maritime plains, and had considerable influence on the development of those districts, because their inhabitants were led at an early period to take to the sea. To this rule there is one remarkable exception, the plain of Messenia, the soil of which was the most fertile in Greece, and thus became the primary source of all the misfortunes of that ill-fated country. The inland plains, on the other hand, being deeply sunk in

Nature of the soil.

[1] Thuc. i. 2.

mountain basins, which, as we saw in the last lecture, are subject to frequent inundations, and in other ways well provided in respect of their water supply, afforded the richest land; especially those of Thessaly and Bœotia. This accounts for the fame of the Theban and Thessalian cavalry, for it was only in the plains that the horse could be reared; and for the same reason that animal was usually an accompaniment of oligarchy, because it was associated with fertile soil and consequent wealth. Aristotle remarks in the *Politics*[2] on this aristocratic character of the horse, and he instances its use among the Chalcidians and Eretrians in Eubœa. It is in the former of those two states that we find a class of nobles called Hippobotæ, and their existence is sufficiently accounted for by the extensive Lelantian plain between Chalcis and Eretria, which was afterwards occupied by Athenian cleruchs. Otherwise the Greeks possessed few horses, and imported those that they required, especially from Sicily. The plains of Greece are also important to the history as having been the principal battlefields of the country: in them were fought the great engagements of Marathon and Platæa, and at a later period those of Leuctra, Mantineia, and Chæronea.

The chief products.
The principal products of the country were corn, wine, and oil. But notwithstanding the careful cultivation, the first, at all events, of those articles of

[2] vi. (iv.) 3, 3.

consumption failed to suffice for the wants of the population. When Herodotus tells us that Xerxes, when he was at Abydos, saw ships laden with corn from the Pontus sailing through the Hellespont,[3] on their way to Ægina and the Peloponnesus, the need of such importation is proved for that early period; and later on great quantities were introduced into the ports of Greece both from the Black Sea and from Sicily. In other respects also the consumption of the country was largely supplemented from abroad; and what Pericles says in his funeral oration, that every article came to them from every land, and that they had as full fruition of the products of their neighbours as of their own,[4] might be applied, though with less force, to the Greeks at large. In Elis a considerable amount of flax was grown; and in Pausanias' time we find the extremely rare product, cotton,[5] in that district. That this is what he means by βύσσος seems tolerably clear, as he distinguishes it from both flax and hemp;[6] but it was not found elsewhere in Greece, and had probably been introduced by the Phœnicians. The mountain sides afforded extensive pasturage for cattle, and it is well to remember that, notwithstanding the city life which we associate so constantly with Hellenic institutions, a large part of the population were

---

[3] Herod. vii. 147.   [4] Thuc. ii. 38.
[5] Pausan. v. 5, § 2.
[6] vi. 26, § 4. *See* E. Curtius, *Peloponnesos*, i. 438; ii. 10.

engaged in pastoral occupations. And, lastly, their flowery slopes produced the honey of which we hear so much in ancient times. To this Aristotle assigns a separate place as a distinct branch of economic science,[7] in the same way as Virgil regards it as an important part of rural industry. Before the introduction of sugar, when honey was the only substitute for that article, the keeping of bees was an employment of first-rate consequence.

Minerals. When we come to look below the surface of the soil, we find Greece only moderately provided with mineral wealth.[8] For gold she had to look beyond her boundaries—to Thrace, to Asia Minor, and to the distant east. The use of gold was certainly known in early times, for we find the mention of it in the Homeric poems, but it was a rarity, and even Sophocles speaks of Indian gold as an unfamiliar article.[9] Though the earliest coins from Asia Minor are of that metal, there were none struck at Athens before the Macedonian period; indeed there is good reason to believe that the first gold coinage in Greece proper was of the time of Alexander the Great. But the islands of Siphnos[10] and Thasos[11] both possessed gold mines, and those of Scapte Hyle on the Thracian coast opposite the last-named island were of considerable

---

[7] *Pol.* i. 11, § 2.

[8] Kruse's *Hellas*, i. 327, foll. *Dictionary of Antiquities:* articles *Aurum, Argentum, Æs.*

[9] *Ant.* 1038. [10] Herod. iii. 57. [11] vi. 46.

value.¹² Copper, however, was tolerably abundant on the continent, as we should conclude from the constant use of it and of bronze in the heroic age for armour and other purposes. The Achæans in Homer are regularly spoken of as being cased in bronze (χαλκοχίτωνες), and their spears were tipped with it (δοῦρε δύω κεκορυθμένα χαλκῷ) ;¹³ the god of war is called χάλκεος Ἄρης, and the oracle which declared to Psammitichus the coming of Greek mercenaries to Egypt spoke of them as "men of bronze."¹⁴ So abundant was it, that a coppersmith was regarded as a name equivalent to a worker in metal, and so we find χαλκεὺς σιδήρου.¹⁵ A large supply of this seems to have come from Cyprus, in which island the town of Temesa is mentioned in the Odyssey¹⁶ as a mart for copper; but the most considerable mines were those of Eubœa, from which the town of Chalcis took its name; and the recurrence of the name in Ætolia, Triphylia, and elsewhere in Greece, would lead us to suppose that there were many other such mining stations. Iron was also worked at Chalcis, in Bœotia, in the island of Seriphus, and especially in the southern part of Mount Taygetus. For purposes of exchange, however, the most important metal was silver, so that it is striking, in comparing the coinage of Greece with that of the Sicilian colonies, to see how much larger the proportion of silver pieces is in the former. Thus it

¹² Ibid. and Thuc. iv. 105.   ¹³ Il. iii. 18.
¹⁴ Herod. ii. 152.   ¹⁵ Od. ix. 391.   ¹⁶ i. 184.

was that the word for a silver piece (ἀργύριον) became the Greek equivalent for money. The richest veins of this were found at Laureium in Attica, and the proceeds of these mines were among the largest sources of revenue to the Athenians, so that Aristophanes makes his chorus of birds promise his audience, that if they give him the preference, owls from Laureium— *i.e.* silver pieces with the usual emblem of Athens— should never fail them.[17] Similarly, Æschylus, in the Persæ, when the chorus are describing the resources of Athens, makes them speak of its possessing a fountain of silver—

ἀργύρου πηγή τις αὐτοῖς ἐστι, θησαυρὸς χθονός.[18]

So minute were the subdivisions of the silver coinage, that a person is comically described as putting fish-scales into his mouth by mistake for coins.[19] At the most flourishing period of that city, many thousand hands were employed in those mines;[20] and though Strabo tells us that in his day they hardly yielded anything, yet he adds that a considerable amount of silver was found in the scoriæ, in consequence of the unskilfulness of the smelting processes of the ancients.[21] At the present day a large amount of lead is being obtained in the same way, and the value of what was exported in 1869 was £177,000 sterling.[22] The

[17] Ar. *Av.* 1106. [18] Æsch. *Pers.* 235.
[19] Ar. *Vesp.* 790.
[20] Boeck, *Economy of Athens*, p. 658. [21] ix. 1, § 23.
[22] Murray's *Handbook of Greece*, p. 216.

name Λαυρεῖον—from λαῦρα a "lane"—signified the streets of shafts in the hill-side; and these, though ruined, may still be seen.

The Greek mountains also possessed a rich treasure in the veins of marble concealed within them. In many parts of the country the common rocks are composed of a fine-grained limestone nearly resembling marble, and this was serviceable not only for building fortifications, but also for finer work, such as was required in theatres and temples; and the use of it accounts for the sharpness of the outlines in many of the remains now standing. But besides this there were numerous places where the finest marble of different colours could be found.[23] Most famous amongst these was Pentelicus, which afforded a material of unrivalled purity and whiteness for building the Athenian temples, and along whose sides, as seen from Athens, white lines, marking the projecting veins, form a conspicuous object. Only second to this was the white marble of Paros, which was extensively used for sculpture and architecture. From Attica also came the blue marble of Hymettus, slabs of which—the *trabes Hymettiae* of Horace[24]—used to be transported to Rome for the construction of palaces. Among the others the most famous were the green and white marble of Carystus in Euboea, the modern Cipollino, and the green porphyry of Laconia.

<small>Marbles.</small>

Throughout its history Greece has been a country <small>Earthquakes in antiquity.</small>

[23] Kruse's *Hellas*, i. 337. [24] *Od.* ii. 18, 3.

much exposed to shocks of earthquake. Of Laconia in particular, Strabo tells us that it was liable to be shaken (εὔσειστος ἡ Λακωνική),[25] and from the accounts of that author and others Euboea seems to have been a centre of similar movements; but these do not appear to have extended far, and this is corroborated by Aristotle's remark[26] that the earthquakes are local, and often confined to a narrow area. Both before the Persian and Peloponnesian wars the island of Delos seems to have been shaken, though the repetition of the occurrence must have been forgotten by the Greeks, as Herodotus[27] and Thucydides[28] speak of those occasions respectively as having been unique in its history: and from the fact that this sacred spot was regarded as exempt from such visitations—as the oracle says, "Delos' self will I shake, which never yet has been shaken"—we may gather that in the surrounding islands the phenomenon was not uncommon. Especially famous was the great earthquake at Sparta in B.C. 464, which gave occasion to the revolt of the Helots, and the outbreak of the third Messenian war.[29] Of this we are told that it laid the city in ruins, and rolled down huge masses of rock from the highest peaks of Taygetus.[30] Again, in B.C. 426, the Peloponnesians gave up their annual invasion of Attica on account of the violence of the earthquakes;[31] and in

---

[25] viii. 5, § 7.   [26] *Meteorol.* ii. 8, § 44, ed. Ideler.
[27] Herod. vi. 98.   [28] Thuc. ii. 8.   [29] Ibid. i. 101.
[30] Plutarch, *Cim.* 16.   [31] Thuc. iii. 89.

this instance we are able to trace the main direction of their movement, for Thucydides tells us that the island of Atalanta on the coast of the Opuntian Locrians was inundated, and also the town of Orobiæ on the opposite coast of Eubœa, from whence the shock pursued a north-easterly course to the island of Peparethus. The same district, together with the whole neighbourhood of the Maliac gulf, was the scene of the earthquakes mentioned by Strabo,[32] when he tells us that part of the promontory of Cenæum and the Lichades islands were sunk in the sea, and the warm springs at Ædepsus and Thermopylæ ceased flowing for three days, after which those of Ædepsus burst out again in fresh sources; also that the city of Heracleia in Trachis, and those of Oreos and Lamia, with many others, were more or less shaken down; that the Spercheius changed its course, and that a triple wave arose at the entrance of the Euboic sea, which rushed in three different directions. From the same writer we learn that a fountain at Chalcis on the Euripus was once dried up by a similar cause, and a mud volcano formed in the Lelantian plain, after which the island ceased to be shaken.

But the most famous of all the disasters caused by earthquakes in antiquity was the destruction of the cities of Helice and Bura, near Ægium, on the coast of Achaia. This happened in the year B.C. 373, two years before the battle of Leuctra. The earthquake

[32] i. 3, § 20.

occurred in the night, and the former of those two towns, which had been the place of meeting for the league of the Achæan cities, suddenly sank in the earth, and was covered by the sea. Pausanias, in describing it, says—"The sea came up over a great part of the country, and encompassed Helice all round: even the grove of Poseidon was so covered by the wave that only the tops of the trees were visible. And as the god suddenly caused an earthquake, and the sea rose at the same moment, the wave dragged down Helice with all its inhabitants."[33] At the same time the town of Bura was also destroyed. The occurrence was attributed to the wrath of Poseidon, whom the citizens of Helice had offended; and in such a case, where sea and land combined to work the mischief, it was natural that it should be referred to his agency; but in other instances also the Greeks believed that earthquakes were caused by the waters having penetrated into hollows beneath the ground,[34] and the same deity whom they regarded as the "holder of earth" (γαιήοχος), because, as they looked from the sea, they saw the dry land rise from its surface, they also spoke of as the "shaker of earth" (ἐννοσίγαιος) because such movements were attributed to him.

Earthquakes in modern times.

Of the frequency of earthquakes in Greece during the Middle Ages we have melancholy evidence in the ruined state of the temples and other great public buildings in that country. No doubt the hand of man

---

[33] vii. 24, § 12. [34] Welcker, *Griechische Götterlehre*, i. 627.

caused much destruction throughout that period, for to half-civilised persons, who possess no instruments for quarrying, a squared stone is always a tempting object; but in many cases it required a more powerful agency to dismember the massive work of such skilful architects. In modern times they have been equally violent. In 1817 the neighbourhood of Helice was again the scene of a similar disaster. On that occasion the earthquake was preceded by a sudden explosion, which was compared to that of a battery of cannon. The shock which immediately succeeded was said to have lasted a minute and a half, during which the sea rose at the mouth of the river Selinus, and extended so far as to inundate all the level immediately below Vostitza (the ancient Ægium). After its retreat not a trace was left of some warehouses which had stood on the shore, and the sand which had covered the beach was all carried away. In Vostitza 65 persons lost their lives, two-thirds of the buildings were entirely ruined, and five villages in the plain were destroyed.[35] In 1853 another terrible earthquake laid the greater part of Thebes in ruins, and at Athens at the same time, for six or seven weeks, two or three earthquakes were the daily average, and one night as many as fifteen shocks were counted.[36] Subsequently, in 1858, almost every house in Corinth was destroyed, and even the massive monolithic columns of the temple

[35] Leake, *Morea*, iii. 402.
[36] Sir T. Wyse, *Impressions of Greece*, 64.

of Athena, which are the oldest in Greece, and have held their position since the seventh or eighth century before Christ, were seriously injured. Another again visited Vostitza in 1861.

<small>Greece near a volcanic centre.</small>

The frequent occurrence of these phenomena will appear less extraordinary when we learn that Greece lies close to a centre of volcanic agency. The exact locality of this is the island of Santorin, the ancient Thera, which we have seen within a few years in a state of eruption. Indeed, it is maintained by a great geological authority, Leopold von Buch,[37] that if a permanent crater were formed at that point it would be of the utmost service to Greece, because it would form a vent for the internal heat, and so relieve that country from the continual movements that arise from this cause. As it is, the traces of volcanic agency in the neighbourhood of the Ægean are very considerable. The earlier outbreaks, which are found in the north of that district, belong to the mythopœic age, and may be traced in connection with the fire-gods Hephæstus and Heracles. Lemnos, anciently called Æthaleia, or the "fire island," on which Hephæstus fell when cast by Zeus from heaven, and of which Sophocles speaks in the Philoctetes as if the fame of its fires still remained—

τῷ Λημνίῳ τῷδ' ἀνακαλουμένῳ πυρί—[38]

and

ὦ Λημνία χθὼν καὶ τὸ παγκρατὲς σέλας
Ἡφαιστότευκτον—[39]

---

[37] *See* E. Curtius, *Peloponnesos*, i. 58.
[38] Soph. *Phil.* 800.   [39] Ibid. 986.

on which, too, one of the mountains, Moschylus, was said to have emitted flames within historic times—still bears strong marks of the effects of volcanic action.[40] From hence, following the line of earthquake-movement, which we have seen to pass by the island of Peparethus, we arrive at the tract, also volcanic, which was so intimately associated with the life and death of Hercules, the Cenæan promontory and the opposite coast of Trachis. Here the traces remain in the hot springs already mentioned. Again, at Mount Laphystium in Bœotia—the place where, according to the natives, Hercules dragged Cerberus into the upper world[41]—there are a crater and warm springs.[42]

But it was at a later period that the greatest eruptions took place. The most celebrated was that which produced the mountain of Methana, on the coast of Argolis, opposite Ægina, about the year B.C. 282. Of this we have descriptions from Strabo and Ovid. Strabo says, "Near the city of Methone, in the bay of Hermione, a mountain seven stadia in height was thrown up after a fiery eruption had taken place, which by day could not be approached by reason of the heat and sulphureous smell, but at night was fragrant, and emitted light and heat to a distance, so that the sea boiled for five stadia from the shore, and was disturbed over an area of twenty stadia, and was

Eruptions in historic times.

---

[40] *Dict. Geog.*, art. "Lemnos." [41] Paus. ix. 34, § 5.
[42] Fiedler, *Reise durch alle Theile des Königreiches Griechenland*, i. 104.

choked with fragments of rock as great as towers.[43] The passage from Ovid, which Humboldt[44] speaks of as accurate in its scientific theory, is as follows—

> Est prope Pitthæam tumulus Trœzena, sine ullis
> Arduus arboribus, quondam planissima campi
> Area, nunc tumulus : nam, res horrenda relatu,
> Vis fera ventorum, cæcis inclusa cavernis,
> Exspirare aliqua cupiens, luctataque frustra
> Liberiore frui cælo, cum carcere rima
> Nulla foret toto, nec pervia flatibus esset,
> Extentam tumefecit humum : ceu spiritus oris
> Tendere vesicam solet, aut derepta bicorni
> Terga capro. Tumor ille loci permansit, et alti
> Collis habet speciem, longoque induruit ævo.[45]

> Near Trœzen stands a hill, exposed in air
> To winter winds, of leafy shadows bare :
> This once was level ground ; but (strange to tell)
> Th' included vapours, that in caverns dwell,
> Lab'ring with colic pangs, and close confined,
> In vain sought issue for the rumbling wind :
> Yet still they heaved for vent, and, heaving still,
> Enlarged the concave, and shot up the hill ;
> As breath extends a bladder, or the skins
> Of goats are blown t' inclose the hoarded winds :
> The mountain yet retains a mountain's face,
> And gathered rubbish heals the hollow space.
> *Translation by Dryden and others.*

Had this mountain existed in the time of Demosthenes it would have prevented him from enjoying a

---

[43] Strabo, i. 3, § 18.   [44] *Cosmos*, i. 239.
[45] Ovid, *Met.* xv. 296-306.

view of Athens from the island of Calaureia, for it directly intervenes between those two points.[46]

About 50 years later occurred another great display of volcanic activity at the island of Thera. That extraordinary place, which, together with the sister island of Therasia, encloses an almost circular harbour, is in reality a crater in the midst of the sea, and dates from a great antiquity; but on the occasion referred to we learn from Strabo[47] that flames rose from the water half-way between the two main islands for four days, so that the whole sea boiled and blazed, and that by these an island was ejected little by little, being lifted as it were by mechanical force, and composed of firestones, extending over an area of 12 stadia in circumference. This phenomenon has been repeated on several subsequent occasions, and we have most curious documents in modern Greek, both in verse and prose, relating to the eruption of 1650, and in Italian, describing that of 1707.[48] The last outburst has occurred within a few years from the present date. The lava of which the island of Thera is formed has decomposed in the course of ages, and, like that of Vesuvius, forms an excellent soil for the cultivation of the grape, so that the Santorin wine, which is produced there, is one of the finest wines in the Ægean. It is not a little remarkable that a spot so striking and so peculiar in its

---

[46] Stanley, on "Greek Topography," in *Classical Museum*, i. 78.
[47] i. 3, § 16. [48] Ross, *Inselreise*, i. 291, foll.

appearance should not have given birth to any legends.

Climate of Greece.

The climate of Greece is praised by Herodotus[49] as the best tempered in the whole world. When enumerating the excellent products of the extremities of the earth—the size of the animals in India, the abundance of gold, and the wild trees that bear wool instead of fruit; and, again, the frankincense and other spices of Arabia—he considers them to be counterbalanced by the Greek climate. Similarly, in the Platonic Epinomis[50] we are told that every Greek is bound to remember that the position of his fatherland is among the best of all, its excellence consisting in winter and summer being equally tempered. And even at the present day, though the destruction of forests and the decrease of the supply of water has heightened the extremes of heat and cold, and though the absence of proper cultivation, and especially of drainage, has caused the prevalence of malaria, yet for a great part of the year the climate of Greece is delightful. During the autumn, winter, and spring, Athens can be recommended as a residence, and Corfu is enjoyable in every season. The lofty mountains provide an inexhaustible supply of fresh breezes to temper the heat of summer, and the brightness of the southern sun moderates the cold of winter, while the extremes of both are qualified by the nearness of the sea. At the same time, as might be

[49] iii. 106. [50] p. 987, D.

LECT. IV.]   GEOGRAPHY OF GREECE.   139

expected in such a country, the varieties of climate are very great. While in the inland parts of Epirus you find upland pastures and bleak hill-sides, together with the cold and the thunderstorms which caused Dodona to be called "stormy" (δυσχείμερος), and the neighbouring mountains the Ceraunia, under the western slopes of Mount Taygetus the date ripens, citrons and oranges flourish abundantly, and the cactus and aloe are common plants. In the same way the varied elevation of the ground supplies a corresponding variety of temperature. At the end of June snow is still lying in the hollows beneath the peaks of Parnassus, when the heat at Delphi is almost insupportable ; and in August you may leave a burning sun in the plains of Macedonia, to be met by a snowstorm among the summits of Olympus.

It is in certain districts that these contrasts are most striking. Thus, in the Peloponnese, you may find deep snow in Arcadia, when Laconia is enjoying all the brightness of spring, and it is already summer in the plains of Messenia. The produce of the soil in those countries shows a corresponding difference ; for while the plain of Mantineia is rich in corn and wine, the mulberry tree, which decks with its bright green the valley of Sparta, is rare there, and the olive is not seen ;[52] and on the other hand the vegetation of the Messenian gulf is semi-tropical. The comparison of the temperature in Laconia and Arcadia is

Contrasts in different districts.

[52] E. Curtius, *Peloponnesos*, i. 233.

pointed by a story told by Pausanias,[53] that on one occasion the Spartans invaded the territory of Tegea, and were so benumbed by the cold which they found there owing to the snow, that the Tegeans, who had provided themselves with fire, and consequently did not suffer, were able to gain the mastery of them. The contrast between Bœotia and Attica in this respect was even greater. Hesiod describes the climate of his native Ascra as bad in winter, oppressive in summer, and never good—

Ἄσκρῃ, χεῖμα κακῇ, θέρει ἀργαλέῃ, οὐδέ ποτ' ἐσθλῇ—[54]

and this account is generally confirmed in modern times. I have never experienced such heat in any country as in the plains of Bœotia in the month of July, and several other travellers have spoken of the excessive cold they have met with there during the winter.[55] On the other hand, Attica has always been famous for its mildness. Though Herodotus gave the preference to the sky of Ionia on the Asiatic coast,[56] yet both Plato and the Attic comedians always speak with enthusiasm of their native climate,[57] and the fineness of the Athenian intellect was referred to the clearness of the Attic atmosphere. The air of Athens was said to be the purest of all; it is this which Euripides celebrates, when he speaks

---

[53] viii. 53, § 10.   [54] *Works and Days*, 640.
[55] See Kruse's *Hellas*, ii. 499; Wordsworth's *Athens and Attica*, 244.   [56] i. 142.
[57] See Welcker, *Gr. Götterlehre*, i. 38.

of the inhabitants as "ever walking gracefully through the most luminous æther"—

ἀεὶ διὰ λαμπροτάτου
βαίνοντες ἁβρῶς αἰθέρος—[58]

and another author says of Athens that a mist seems to be lifted from the eyes as you approach it, and the light appears to assume an unwonted brightness.[59] Those who approach this district from Bœotia almost always experience a change of temperature as soon as they descend from Cithæron or Parnes; and in the summer the heat is lessened by the sea-breeze, which in modern times is called ὁ ἐμβάτης, or that which sets towards shore.[60] Accordingly Xenophon is justified in saying "one would not err in thinking that this city is placed near the centre of Greece, nay of the civilised world, because the farther removed persons are from it, the severer is the cold or heat they meet with."[61]

The inland valley-plains, which are completely surrounded by mountains and only drained by subterranean outlets, such as those which we have already noticed in Bœotia and Arcadia, deserve a somewhat fuller notice, because of the peculiar character of their climatic influences. Being thus hemmed in on all sides, they admitted no regular current of air, and consequently the vapour that arose from the lakes, or where these were not formed,

[58] *Med.* 829.   [59] Aristides, *Panath.* p. 97, ed. Jebb.
[60] Bursian, *Geographie von Griechenland*, i. 8.   [61] *Vectigal*, i. 6.

from the undrained ground, found no vent and hung over the valley. Hence Aristotle[62] remarks that in Arcadia the still days were colder than the windy days; and he rightly assigns the cause, when he says, that when the wind could penetrate, it came warm from the sea, whereas at other times the exhalations made the air cold. This moist heavy atmosphere was the cause of the dull phlegmatic Bœotian temperament. *Athenis tenue cœlum, crassum Thebis*— Cicero remarks,[63] and hence arose the contrast between the inhabitants of the former and those *crasso sub aëre nati*. Similarly Polybius maintains that the Arcadians introduced music and other means of cultivation by law, in order to counteract the roughness of character and habits, which arose from the prevalence of cold and the dulness of the sky.[64]

The winds in Homer.

We have already spoken of the prevalence of certain winds in Greece, and of the direction taken by certain currents of air, in connection with the navigation; but it is important that a more definite account should be given of the character of the several winds, both with reference to the climate, and on account of their influence on the history. On several occasions their agency comes powerfully forward; most notably at the time of Xerxes' invasion, when the people of Delphi, being alarmed for themselves and for Greece, consulted the oracle, and the

---

[62] *Problem.* 26, 58, p. 947, Bekk.   [63] *De Fato*, 4.
[64] Polyb. iv. 21.

answer given them was, that they should pray to the winds, for they would be powerful allies to Greece.[65] After which, we are told, the Delphians erected an altar to the winds at Thyia, where there is an enclosure consecrated to Thyia, daughter of Cephisus, from whom that district derives its name; and in after times sacrifices continued to be offered to the winds. We must, however, distinguish at starting between the Greek names for the winds in earlier and in later times. Homer is acquainted only with four winds—Boreas, Eurus, Notus, and Zephyrus— which represent the four chief points of the compass. In the Iliad we meet with them in pairs; thus two of them are introduced in the description of the excitement in the assembly in the second book—

κινήθη δ' ἀγορὴ, φὴ κύματα μακρὰ θαλάσσης
πόντου 'Ικαρίοιο, τὰ μέν τ' Εὖρός τε Νότος τε
ὤρορ', ἐπαΐξας πατρὸς Διὸς ἐκ νεφελάων—[66]

and the two others in the ninth book—

ὡς δ' ἄνεμοι δύο πόντον ὀρίνετον ἰχθυόεντα,
Βορέης καὶ Ζέφυρος, τώ τε Θρήκηθεν ἄητον—[67]

while in the Odyssey all four are mentioned together—

σύν τ' Εὖρός τε Νότος τ' ἔπεσε, Ζέφυρός τε δυσαής,
καὶ Βορέης αἰθρηγενέτης, μέγα κῦμα κυλίνδων.[68]

In Hesiod also these are found, only the name of the east wind is not Eurus but Argestes—

'Αργέστην, Ζέφυρον, Βορέην τ' αἰψηροκέλευθον
καὶ Νότον—[69]

---

[65] Herod. vii. 178.   [66] Il. ii. 144.   [67] ix. 5.
[68] Od. v. 295.   [69] *Theog.* 379.

unless indeed we are to regard ἀργέστης, or "the clear wind," as an epithet of Zephyrus in this passage, in the same way as it is used in Homer of the south wind—ἀργέσταο Νότοιο[70]—for at a later period this became the title of the north-west wind.[71] These are not, like the wild storms, the brood of Typhœus,[72] but were borne by Eos to Astræus,[73] that is, by the morn to the starry sky—reference being made to what is usual in Greece, the rising of the wind at daybreak after a calm night. They are again the mythological parents of horses—as, for instance, those of Achilles, Xanthus and Balius—

> τοὺς ἔτεκε Ζεφύρῳ ἀνέμῳ Ἅρπυια Ποδάργη—[74]

and those born from the mares of Erichthonius—

> τάων καὶ Βορέης ἠράσσατο βοσκομενάων,
> ἵππῳ δ' εἰσάμενος παρελέξατο κυανοχαίτῃ—[75]

either to symbolise the swiftness of those animals, or perhaps the fertilising power of the wind, according to the idea expressed in Virgil—

> Ore omnes versæ in Zephyrum stant rupibus altis,
> Exceptantque levis auras, et sæpe sine ullis
> Conjugiis vento gravidæ, mirabile dictu,
> Saxa per et scopulos et depressas convalles
> Diffugiunt.[76]

---

[70] Il. xi. 306.
[71] The same doubt hangs over the passage *Theog.* 870, because of the two readings Ζεφύροιο and Ζεφύρου τε.
[72] *Theog.* 869.   [73] Ibid. 378.   [74] Il. xvi. 150.
[75] Ibid. xx. 223.   [76] *Georg.* iii. 273.

> They, turning all their faces to the west,
> Stand on a rocky eminence, to catch
> The light inspiring breeze, and oft without
> Embraces conjugal, impregn'd by wind
> (Miraculous to tell), o'er mount and cliff
> And lowlands of the valley scud away.
> Kennedy's Translation.

It is to be observed, with regard to this early division of the winds, that it necessarily involves some confusion, because, owing to the absence of sufficient distinction, winds exercising different influences have to be classed together. Thus it is that Zephyrus is at one time a soft gale, at another a violent wind (δυσαής), and is described as falling heavily upon the crops (λάβρος ἐπαιγίζων);[77] the reason being that the latter descriptions refer to the north-west wind, which always had that character. We should also notice that this wind as well as Boreas is represented as blowing from Thrace; and in that country was situated the cave that formed his dwelling, from which he is summoned by Iris to answer the prayers of Achilles that the pyre of Patroclus may be consumed.[78] This seems to imply not only that a north-west wind was intended, but also that the poem was composed in Asia Minor.

At a later time a more accurate subdivision of the winds was introduced, and the number increased to eight, the cardinal points being retained, and those intermediate between them being marked, in default of

Their subsequent nomenclature.

[77] Il. ii. 148.   [78] Ibid. xxiii. 200 and 230.

a more scientific system of mathematical geography, by the rising and setting of the sun in summer and winter; thus its rising in summer marked the north-east, in winter the south-east, and similarly its setting the other two points. The old names of the winds were retained for three of those that blew from the cardinal points—viz. Boreas, Notus, and Zephyrus; but Eurus became the south-east, while its place as the east wind was taken by Apeliotes. Of the other winds, the north-east was called Kaikias, the south-west Libs, and the north-west Argestes. This account, which is given by Strabo [79] on the authority of Aristotle and others, is corroborated by a monument still existing at Athens, which also supplies us with valuable information respecting the character of the various winds. This is the Horologium of Antonius Cyrrhestes, or, as it is commonly called, the Temple of the Winds, an octagonal water-clock, on the outside of which, underneath the cornice, are eight bas-reliefs, representing figures of the winds. The names are inscribed over them, and correspond to those just given, except in the case of the north-west wind, which is not called Argestes, but Sciron. Each of them has wings, and floats through the air in a nearly horizontal position, and bears, except in the case of Eurus, some emblem to describe its nature or the effect which it produces.[80]

[79] i. 2, § 21.

[80] These figures are admirably delineated in the plates to vol. i. chap. 3, of Stuart's *Antiquities of Athens*, where also the text is to be consulted. See also Kruse's *Hellas*, i. 322, foll.

It may be well for us to go through these *seriatim*, beginning with Boreas, as being the most important and most famous of all.

Boreas is represented as a bearded man of stern aspect, thickly clad, and wearing strong buskins; he blows into a conch shell which he holds in his hand as a sign of his tempestuous character. Of all the winds he is the most violent and the most frequent in Attica, so that he is to that part of Greece what the mistral is to the south of France. The Athenians, like Homer, placed his home in Thrace, so that they called the districts north of that country the lands beyond the north wind, or Hyperborean. The prevalence of this wind in Attica is shown by the close connection between him and that country in mythology, especially in the story of Thyia or Orithyia ('Ωρείθυια), whom he carries off to his northern home and makes his wife.[81] She is the daughter of the Cephisus, and signifies the fertilising mists which rise from the river during the night, and are borne about by currents of air—whence θυῖα, equivalent to θύελλα; but at dawn the north wind, which always rises in the Ægean at that time, descends and sweeps her away. The explanation of this myth is given unconsciously, but with great accuracy, by Hesiod, when he is describing this kind of weather in the Works and Days. There he advises Perses to provide himself with a thick

Character of the several winds.

---

[81] Welcker, *Gr. Götterlehre*, iii. 67. Preller, *Gr. Mythologie*, ii. 149.

cloak, and a cap to cover well his head and ears; "for," he adds, "the morning is cold when Boreas comes down, and in the morning the wheat-producing mist is spread over the earth from starry heaven upon the tilled lands of the wealthy; which having drawn its moisture from ever-flowing rivers, and then being borne aloft over the earth by a gust of wind (θυέλλη), sometimes turns to rain towards evening, and sometimes to a gale, when Thracian Boreas drives the dense clouds."[82] One of the daughters whom Orithyia bears to Boreas is Chione or the Snow-maiden, symbolising his frosts and snowstorms, of which Homer speaks in the Odyssey—

—— νὺξ δ' ἄρ' ἐπῆλθε κακή, Βορέαο πεσόντος, πηγυλίς.[83]

The connection of Boreas with Attica continued also in historic times. Before the great destruction of the Persian fleet on the rocks of Sepias, it is related that they received an oracle to the effect that they should call their son-in-law to their assistance. They therefore invoked Boreas, because of his marriage with Orithyia. "Whether indeed," Herodotus adds, "the north wind in consequence of this fell upon the barbarians as they rode at anchor, I cannot undertake to say; however, the Athenians say that Boreas, having assisted them before, then also produced this effect; and on their return they erected a temple to Boreas near the river Ilissus."[84] We hear of the same wor-

[82] *Works and Days*, 547, *seq.*   [83] Od. xiv. 475.
[84] Herod. vii. 189.

ship at Megalopolis in Arcadia, at a later time, when that wind was believed to have saved the city from Agis, king of Sparta. After describing how the inhabitants had been defeated in battle by the Lacedæmonians, and how afterwards threatening engines had been brought against the city, Pausanias[85] continues, "So Boreas was destined to be a benefit not only to the Greeks at large, in dashing a great part of the Persian fleet on the Sepian cliffs, but this wind also saved the people of Megalopolis from capture, for by the violence and continuance of his blasts he broke down Agis' siege-works and utterly ruined them." He then describes how Agis desisted from the attack, and subsequently yearly rites were instituted in honour of the wind-god.[86]

On either side of Boreas, on the Horologium, stand bas-reliefs of the two north winds, Sciron and Kaikias. The first of these, which is an excessively cold wind in winter, and in summer brings thunderstorms, and is in other ways injurious both to the vegetation and the inhabitants, is represented as holding in his hand a chafing dish to dispel the cold which he causes. This is the δυσαὴς Ζέφυρος of Homer, and the Strymonias of Herodotus,[87] which caused Xerxes, on his return from Greece, to be nearly shipwrecked. Kaikias is also an inclement wind, and is seen to carry a shield, the lower part of which is full of hailstones.

"Temple of the Winds" at Athens.

---

[85] viii. 27, § 14.   [86] viii. 36, § 6.
[87] Herod. viii. 118.

This is the Euroclydon, the violence of which we hear of in connection with St. Paul's voyage.[88]

To turn now to the south winds—Notus is the most rainy wind of all; he is represented with an inverted urn, the whole contents of which he is pouring out upon the earth. He is also regarded by the poets as a violent wind, for Hesiod warns his farmer, if he carries his produce across the sea, not to defer his return till the rising of its dread blasts—

> Νότοιό τε δεινὰς ἀήτας,
> ὅστ' ὤρινε θάλασσαν ὁμαρτήσας Διὸς ὄμβρῳ
> πολλῷ ὀπωρινῷ, χαλεπὸν δέ τε πόντον ἔθηκε.[89]

The south-west wind, Libs, is also a rainy wind, but is in every way milder than Notus, and hence his garments are light, and he and Zephyrus, alone amongst the winds, have their feet bare. But he is especially regarded as favourable to navigation, because he wafted vessels from Corinth to Athens and across the Saronic gulf; hence his emblem is the *aplustre* of a ship, which he holds in his hand.

In strong contrast with these two is the south-east wind, Eurus, who appears as an old man of scowling aspect, with his head half enveloped in his robes. His name signifies the "burning wind"—from αὔω, εὔω, "to burn or singe"—and he is described in the Odyssey as melting the snow which Zephyrus lets fall—

> ἥν τ' Εὖρος κατέτηξεν, ἐπὴν Ζέφυρος καταχεύῃ.[90]

---

[88] Acts xxvii. 14. [89] *Works and Days*, 675. [90] Od. xix. 206.

This is the Scirocco, the most parching and enervating of all the Mediterranean winds.

Lastly, we have to speak of the two winds which are intermediate between these groups, and are both distinguished by their milder character. Zephyrus is the true Zephyr of the poets, the harbinger of spring. His bas-relief represents him as a graceful youth, almost unclothed, with the fold of his robe filled with flowers. He is in mythology the beloved of Chloris (Χλῶρις), the young fresh vegetation; in Homer it is he who breathes refreshingly over the Elysian fields, and gives their fruitfulness to the gardens of Alcinous.[91] But the most instructive of all the figures is that of Apeliotes, the east wind, the characteristics of which are the opposite of all that we associate with it. He also has a gentle and beautiful face, and is regarded as the giver of good things, for his lap contains ears of corn, honeycomb, and a profusion of fruits. In Greece the east wind brings pleasant rains and favours vegetation, so that the Turks used to call it "a divine wind, wafting to them the blessings of God from Mecca."[92] The knowledge of this helps us to understand more easily Thucydides' meaning, when, in describing the escape from Platæa, he speaks of the ice on the moat as being thin and mixed with water, such as one might expect with an east rather than a north wind (οἷος ἀπηλιώτου ἢ βορέου).[93]

[91] Od. iv. 567, and vii. 119.
[92] Stuart's *Antiquities of Athens*, i. 22.   [93] Thuc. iii. 23.

Distribution of the vegetation.

It remains to speak of the vegetation of Greece, a large subject, which can only be treated very superficially, but without it an account of Greek geography would be incomplete. Curtius the historian, who is an excellent judge in consequence of his intimate knowledge of the country, remarks that "there is not on the entire known surface of the globe any other region in which the different zones of climate and flora meet one another in so rapid a succession."[94] The natural result of this is the greatest possible variety of trees and plants within a limited area, and an extraordinary fulness of natural beauty, whether dispersed over the mountain sides, or clustered together in the valleys and round the watercourses. We have already compared Greece and Italy in respect of the conformation of their surface; perhaps we may learn something also with regard to the distribution of vegetation in the former country, by comparing it with that of the neighbouring peninsula.

Niebuhr divides Italy into three distinct areas, according to the trees that flourish there.[95] First, there are the plains of Lombardy in the extreme north, occupying the entire space between the Alps and the Apennines, and between the sources of the Po and the Adriatic: in this region the olive is not found, or only shows a stunted growth. Southward of this, as far as the parallel of Terracina, is the pro-

[94] *History of Greece*, i. 3.
[95] *Lectures on Ethnography and Geography*, ii. 13-15.

per home of that tree; but in this second area the true plants of the south, such as the cactus and aloe, are only seen here and there, and are kept up with great labour and difficulty. It is the remaining portion of Italy, which, as being the country occupied by Greek settlements, is called by Niebuhr Greek Italy, that this semi-tropical vegetation is found, growing naturally and almost wild; and the palm is found at Naples, and increases in frequency as we proceed farther south. Now in Greece the Alpine region, corresponding to the mountains and valleys of Switzerland, is that which lies north of the Ægean and the parallel of Mount Olympus, comprising the Scardus district, upper Macedonia, and Thrace. You may pass through this from the Adriatic to the Ægean without seeing a single cypress tree, and it is only when you have descended the Axius for some distance from the highlands of the interior that the plane-tree begins to appear. In the plains of Thessaly, which correspond to those of Lombardy, and in all but the sea-coast of Epirus, the olive is wanting, and appears first in Phthiotis, and in the peninsula of Magnesia, where it is cultivated with great success. But Attica, as we know from the enthusiastic praises of Sophocles,[96] is the land in which it flourishes best; yet that favoured air will not allow the orange, much less the palm, to grow without especial care, whereas on the southern coasts of the Morea and in the islands, these trees are

[96] *Œd. Col.* 700.

much more abundant. In Greece, however, the great variety of elevation causes the products of different districts to be much less regular than in Italy; and the mean temperature of the whole country is lower. It is in ascending the lofty mountains that abut on the sea, that the zones of vegetation can be traced in the most impressive manner. Thus the shore of Mount Athos is fringed with myrtles, and its dells are filled with luxuriant plane-trees; as you mount its steep slopes, you are embowered in an undergrowth of arbutus, ilex, and branching heather, frequently festooned with creepers, or interspersed in the clearings with vineyards and groups of dark cypresses; but above the height of 1500 feet the region of chestnuts and other forest trees is entered, and the ridge of the peninsula is found to be thickly clothed with beeches. Still higher, on the great peak itself, the beech forests are again surmounted by pines, and from these the bare summit emerges, on the sides of which are found the violet and the pansy, and on its crest tiny saxifrages and other alpine plants.

The forests. We have ample evidence that Greece was, in parts at all events, a well-wooded country in ancient times. The trees, shrubs, and plants were so fruitful a source of nomenclature, that, even if other information were wanting, we might almost reconstruct the flora of the country from the names of places, as I hope to show on a future occasion. But the subject is often alluded to by ancient authors. Parnassus is called by Homer "a mountain clothed with wood" (ὄρος κατασειμένον ὕλῃ Παρνησοῦ),[97] and Euripides addresses it as "wooded rock of the Pythian god" (ὦ Πυθίου δενδρῶτι πέτρα);[98] and here and there the remains of noble pine-forests may be seen on its sides at the present day. Of Helicon Pausanias tells us that it was especially fertile and rich in trees (ἐν τοῖς μάλιστα εὔγεως καὶ δένδρων ἀνάπλεως),[99] and the woods of Cithæron form a graceful background to the silvan scenes in the Bacchæ of Euripides. From Parnes, again, came the wood which caused the deme of Acharnæ to be famed for its charcoal—the ἄνθρακες Παρνήσιοι of the Acharnians of Aristophanes.[100] The districts which were most famous for their oak-forests were Arcadia and Bœotia. In the oracle about Arcadia in Herodotus, the inhabitants are described as "acorn-eating men" (βαλανηφάγοι ἄνδρες),[101] and one part of the country was called Drymodes for the same reason. Pausanias in this part of his peregrination is continually mentioning them, and regards them as the cover for the wild animals that abounded there:[102] in one place he distinguishes several kinds, one of which is the cork-tree.[103] Nor was this dense woodland confined to the hill-sides; in the plain of Mantineia he describes the road from that city to Tegea as passing through an extensive forest named Pelagos, or the sea,[104] apparently from

[97] Od. xix. 431.　　[98] Herc. Fur. 790.　　[99] ix. 28, § 1.
[100] Acharn. 348.　　[101] Herod. i. 66.　　[102] viii. 23, § 9.
[103] viii. 12, § 1.　　[104] viii. 11, § 1.

its waving foliage; and again he speaks of these trees as numerous in the level ground between Tegea and the foot of Mount Parthenium.[105] He also notices those of Bœotia;[106] and in that country and Phocis we meet with the names Drymos, Drymia, Dryoscephalæ, etc. The beech does not appear to have been familiar to the Greeks; at all events its name, ὀξύα, does not occur in their writings in the same way as the other forest trees: it was found on Pelion,[107] but not in the same abundance as at present, for now it has driven out almost every other growth on the upper parts of that mountain. It is also plentiful in modern times on Pindus and Athos. The value of these forests for the timber they yielded was soon discovered: Aristotle speaks of it in the *Politics* as an important article of export,[108] and he also mentions ὑλωροί or commissioners of woods and forests,[109] who were appointed after a time in various states to see to the proper administration of them.

There is no need for us to enter at greater length into the different kinds of forest trees;[110] let us confine our attention to those trees, whether wild or cultivated, which had some special importance in ancient times.

[105] viii. 54, § 5.   [106] ix. 3, § 4.

[107] *Descriptio Montis Pelii*, in the *Geographi Græci Minores*, ed. Müller, vol. i. p. 106.

[108] iv. (vii.) 5, § 4.   [109] vii. (vi.) 8, § 6.

[110] For further information on this subject see Fiedler, *Reise*, i. 513, foll.

The pine of the Isthmus must always have been famous from its connection with the Isthmian games. On that occasion it composed the crown that was placed on the head of the victor, and this it is which St. Paul refers to when he says, writing to the neighbouring Corinthians, "Know ye not"—ye of all men may be expected to know—"that they which run in a race run all, but one receiveth the prize?"[111] The feathery light-green foliage of this tree must have been formerly, as it still is, one of the most graceful features in Greek scenery. It is also a useful tree, for from it, as from the other pines, the resin is obtained which is mixed with the wine to preserve it: in passing through a forest you will often notice a slit in the bark, down which the resin exudes into a cup hollowed out in the trunk below. We have evidence that resin was put to the same use in ancient times, and this custom was believed to account for the presence of the pine-cone on the top of the thyrsus of Bacchus.[112] But the most imposing of all the trees in Greece is the plane, which grows to an immense size, and in some districts is very abundant, especially in Euboea and in the valley of the Neda in Messenia. Pausanias speaks of the extraordinary growth of some that he had seen,[113] and regards them as among the

Important trees in antiquity.

---

[111] 1 Cor. ix. 24.
[112] Pliny, xiv. 19, xxiii. 1. Plutarch, *Symp.* v. 3, 1; quoted by Mure, *Tour in Greece*, ii. 203.
[113] vii. 22, § 1.

oldest trees in Greece:[114] the plane was certainly introduced in Homer's time, for it is mentioned once, though only once, in the Homeric poems.[115] Still, it was not an indigenous tree in Greece, and seems to have been introduced from Asia Minor. Its name, the *Oriental* plane, might lead us to look to the Phœnicians as its importers, but this was not the case, for it was not a Semitic tree.[116] That the date-palm, on the other hand, had this origin, is clear from its Greek name, φοίνιξ. The first specimen introduced was that of Delos, the πρωτόγονος φοῖνιξ of Euripides;[117] this is first mentioned in the Odyssey,[118] when Ulysses, in expressing his admiration of Nausicaa's beauty, tells her that he can only compare her to the palm at Delos, which caused him, though a much-travelled man, to stand still in amazement. In the Hymn to the Delian Apollo[119] it is celebrated as having been clasped by Leto, when about to give birth to Apollo and Artemis; and in later times it became more and more famous in Greece. Pausanias also mentions palms as growing at Aulis, but he adds that the climate was not sufficiently favourable to allow of their ripening:[120] there are a few at the neighbouring town of Chalcis at the present day. The pomegranate, too, bushes of which may occasionally be seen growing wild in

---

[114] viii. 23, § 5.
[115] Il. ii. 307. See Hehn, *Kulturpflanzen und Hausthiere*, p. 201.
[116] Ibid. p. 202. [117] *Hec.* 457.
[118] Od. vi. 162. [119] 117. [120] ix. 19, § 8.

Greece, came from the Phœnicians, and Aphrodite herself was said to have planted the tree in Cyprus.[121] But we find it already in the gardens of Alcinous, and it formed one of the ornaments on the chest of Cypselus, which was laid up at Olympia.[122] From its numerous seeds it was the emblem of fruitfulness, and consequently was much used in marriage ceremonies; so too, when Persephone was persuaded to taste of it in Hades, she at once became the lawful wife of her ravisher,[123] and the fruit was thenceforward sacred to her. The fig also came from abroad, and found its favourite home in Attica; so great was its repute, that Demeter was said to have bestowed it as a gift on the Eleusinian Phytalus, *i.e.* "the gardener," in that country. We have perhaps evidence of the same thing in the origin of the name συκοφάντης, which is said to have been first applied to those who gave information against persons exporting figs from Attica: if this is true, it would imply that a great value was set upon them. The chestnut, which now forms so beautiful an element in the vegetation of certain districts, was introduced, at a comparatively late period of classical times, from the interior or north of Asia Minor.[124]

Among the most characteristic of the lesser growths and shrubs we may mention the arbutus and bay, which are found on the hill-sides and in the gorges; the myrtle

Lesser growths and shrubs.

---

[121] Hehn, *Kulturpflanzen*, 156.
[123] Hymn to Demeter, 372.
[122] Paus. v. 19, § 6.
[124] Hehn, 284.

by the sea-shore, and the feathery tamarisk on the maritime plains; the juniper, the Greek κέδρος; the cytisus and judas tree, which with their bright yellow and lilac blossoms colour the slopes in spring; and the oleander in the river-beds during the summer. But one tree calls for more careful notice, both on account of its history, and of mistakes which exist with regard to it. This is the cypress, which forms a conspicuous object wherever it appears in the landscape, and is enumerated by Curtius[125] among the primæval growths of Greece. There is no tree, however, more closely associated with the Phœnicians, or which was more certainly introduced by them. Its original home was in the highlands of Afghanistan, and from thence it migrated first to Persia, where its spiry shape was taken as a symbol of fire-worship, and accorded it a sacred character, and afterwards to Syria and the coasts of the Mediterranean. There it appears as the gopher wood of which we hear in connection with the building of the ark, and this name, when transferred to Greek, forms κυπαρ, the stem of the Greek κυπάρισσος. It had arrived in Greece before Homeric times, for in the Homeric catalogue we find two names of places, Cyparissus and Cyparisseis,[126] derived from it, and in the Odyssey it is mentioned as growing in Calypso's garden.[127] From the hardness and fragrance of its wood we find it frequently used as a material for

[125] *History of Greece*, i. 41.
[126] Il. ii. 519, 593. Hehn, 195.   [127] Od. v. 64.

statues of the gods, and at the time of the plague at Athens the public coffins for the dead were made of it.[128] At a considerably later period it was introduced into Italy, where it was at first called the cypress of Tarentum, because it came by that city. Even at the present day it is doubtful whether this tree grows wild in the Greek peninsula: Colonel Leake believes that it does not,[129] and I myself have only seen it in the neighbourhood of dwellings and of sacred buildings, whether Greek or Mahometan.

Lastly, the flowers of Greece must not be entirely passed over, both on account of their mythological significance and their intrinsic beauty. The most plausible derivation that has been suggested for the name ’Αθῆναι is from ἀθ-, the root of ἄνθος, "a flower;"[130] and Lobeck proposed to translate it by *Florentia*. The favourite epithet of the place, we may remember, was "violet-crowned" (ἰοστέφανοι). It is a curious coincidence that the peasants' modern name for Athens is Anthena. Ulrichs was once walking in the neighbourhood of that city, and wishing to obtain evidence on this point, he inquired of a labourer how they called the place: his answer was, "They call it Anthena ("the flowery"), but it has no flowers."[131] This answer also illustrates the sad change that has passed over the country between ancient and modern times; yet when

Flowers.

---

[128] Thuc. ii. 34.   [129] *Northern Greece*, iii. 397.
[130] G. Curtius, *Gr. Etymologie*, p. 226.
[131] *Reisen in Greichenland*, i. 13.

we see the banks in spring scarlet with anemones, or the uplands covered with the pink blossoms of the gum cistus, from which the traveller treads out the aromatic odours, as he walks in quest of some romantic ruin, we seem to realise what Pindar meant by "the prime of purple-blossomed spring" (φοινικανθέμου ἦρος ἀκμά).[132] The anemones—white, violet, and red—symbolised, according to some, the blood of Adonis, according to others, the tears shed by Aphrodite for him ;[133] perhaps it was the pale-coloured flowers that symbolised the tears. Among the other plants with the names of which we are most familiar, may be mentioned the narcissus, cyclamen, gladiolus, and a great variety of orchids in the lower lands; the asphodel also, though that is a most disenchanting plant of the lily tribe, ragged and branching, with small white flowers; and the violet, daphne, and crocus, on the higher mountains. But in the case of many of these great caution is required in identifying them with those famous in classical times. When Sophocles, for instance, speaks of the "crocus with its golden sheen" (χρυσαυγὴς κρόκος),[134] we would fain regard this as the same with the splendid flower that displays its golden blossoms close to the snow on Parnassus and the mountains of Arcadia. But, in reality, there can be little doubt that it was the cultivated crocus, from which the saffron was obtained, and which was intro-

[132] *Pyth.* iv. 114.   [133] Preller, *Griechische Mythologie*, i. 273.
[134] *Œd. Col.* 685.

duced into Greece from the East, where it was prized as a dye for robes and slippers—the κροκόβαπτον ποδὸς εὔμαριν of the Persæ[135]—the sign of royalty and majesty. Again, of the ὑάκινθος of the ancients, with its marks, which some interpreted as αἰαῖ, some as the name Ajax, from whose blood it was thought to have sprung—*flores inscripti nomina regum*—though it is sometimes regarded as the iris or gladiolus, sometimes as the larkspur, yet almost all that we know is that it was not our hyacinth.[136] But the importance of many of these flowers to mythology causes the study of them to be of considerable value. Just as among trees the olive was sacred to Athena, the bay to Apollo, and the silver poplar to Hercules, so the narcissus, which derived its name from its narcotic scent, the emblem of death, was consecrated to the goddess of the nether world, Persephone, and her mother Demeter, μεγάλαιν θεαῖν ἀρχαῖον στεφάνωμα; the lily was borne by Aphrodite Urania in her hand; the violet and the rose were sacred to Dionysus, and other blossoms to other deities.

[135] Æschyli *Pers.* 660.
[136] See Liddell and Scott's *Lex. s.v.* ὑάκινθος. Pausanias (i. 35, § 4) distinguishes the flower of Ajax from the ὑάκινθος. Dierbach (*Flora Mythologica*, pp. 137, 142) identifies the former with the larkspur, the latter with the gladiolus. Fiedler (*Reise*, i. 839) regards the gladiolus as representing both.

LECTURE V.

APPEARANCE OF THE COUNTRY—EFFECT OF THE CONFORMATION OF GREECE ON THE CHARACTER AND POLITICS OF THE GREEKS.

Appearance of Greece—Classical Character of the Landscape—Symmetry of the Component Parts—Presence of the Sea—Did the Greeks appreciate Scenery?—Indirect Influence of the Aspect of the Country—The Mountains and the Sea—Their combined Influence—Greek Scenery and the Hellenic Mind—Influence of Soil and Climate—Effect on the Language—Greek Geography and Politics—Individuality of the States—Opposition between Neighbours—Balance of Power—Varied Forms of Civic Life.

Appearance of Greece. IN some of the preceding lectures we have touched upon a few of the individual features of the landscape in Greece, but before proceeding further it may be well to give some idea of the appearance of that country generally. I do not hesitate to say that the scenery of Greece is equal in beauty, if not superior, to that of any country in Europe. Though inferior to Switzerland in wildness, and to Italy in luxuriance, it unites those two qualities in a way which cannot be found in either of those regions, and in variety it far surpasses both. And, besides this, it possesses very peculiar features of its own. As soon as you see it, you feel that it is unlike anything you have seen before. Nor is this merely a first impression, for it recurs whenever you approach the Ægean from another country. Thus, in descending from Upper Macedonia to the sea on the shores of Chalcidice or in the neighbourhood of Olympus, you leave behind you broad masses of mountains, extensive sweeps of country, and uniformity of colour, to find yourself, as if by magic, in the midst of scenery delicate, bright, and varied, with an atmosphere, an outline, and a vegetation completely its own. It is true that in some parts, where trees and other softening features are wanting, its severity is apt at first to repel; but as Mure has well remarked, when speaking on this subject, the full perception of scenery of this class is in itself an acquired taste—as in fact are all our finer tastes in their more advanced stages.[1] The same education which the mind has to go through in order thoroughly to appreciate a Greek statue or temple, will fit it to understand and feel the beauty of Attic mountains.

Thus the first peculiarity to be noticed in Greek landscape, is what may best be described as its classical character. Unlike the jagged forms of other broken ranges, its mountains are never weird or wild, but are at once bold and delicate, and clearly cut, so as to deserve the epithet "aristocratic" which has been applied to them. This arises from the marble or hard limestone of which they are composed, and has been noticed in other places where the same kind

Classical character of the landscape.

[1] *Tour in Greece*, ii. 40.

of rock is found, as at Carrara, and in the ranges of Pamphylia, of which Sir Charles Fellowes says that they are "poetically beautiful."[2] The fine lines in the "Giaour," in which Byron has compared the aspect of modern Greece to the face of a corpse, so forcibly illustrate this point, that I cannot do better than introduce them here:—

> "He who hath bent him o'er the dead
> Ere the first day of death is fled,
> The first dark day of nothingness,
> The last of danger and distress,
> (Before Decay's effacing fingers
> Have swept the lines where beauty lingers,)
> And mark'd the mild angelic air,
> The rapture of repose that's there,
> The fixed yet tender traits that streak
> The languor of the placid cheek,
> And—but for that sad shrouded eye,
>   That fires not, wins not, weeps not, now,
>   And but for that chill changeless brow,
> Where cold obstruction's apathy
> Appals the gazing mourner's heart,
> As if to him it could impart
> The doom he dreads, yet dwells upon;
> Yes, but for these and these alone,
> Some moments, ay, one treacherous hour,
> He still might doubt the tyrant's power;
> So fair, so calm, so softly seal'd,
> The first, last look by death reveal'd!
> Such is the aspect of this shore;
> 'Tis Greece, but living Greece no more!

---

[2] *Asia Minor*, p. 189.

> So coldly sweet, so deadly fair,
> We start, for soul is wanting there."

This passage, which is intended by Byron to represent the political and social condition of Greece in his time, gives such an accurate description of its physical aspect, that it is hard to think that this could have been absent from his mind. The comparison to the features of the dead brings vividly before us all the delicacy, all the sharpness, all the severity, and at the same time all the tenderness of outline, which characterise it. The same thing has been excellently described in prose by Hettner in the following passage:—

"There can hardly be more beautiful mountains than those of Greece. They have not the peaked, zigzag outlines of ours. Their characteristic feature is the prevalence of the horizontal line; they seem to repose, therefore, even in ascending. They rest securely on a broad and massive base. The lines rise at first quite softly and gradually; suddenly they shoot up more boldly and aspiringly, but fall again into gentle levels, which introduce softness and repose. But the fresh vigour of the ascending lines is not yet exhausted; on the contrary, it becomes bolder and more creative—it raises walls of rock, rugged and perpendicular, it forms beetling crags and wild ravines, till at length these rude steeps again give way, and the finishing outlines are milder and gentler." [3]

[3] *Athens and the Peloponnese*, pp. 199, 200.

Symmetry of the component parts.

Another feature of these mountains which contributes to give them a classical character is the artistic way in which nature has grouped both the component parts of the separate ranges and the various objects in the general views, so as to produce a balance between them, like the skilful arrangement of figures in a picture; so that no one part can be removed without interfering with the effect of the whole. Of the former of these points Mount Mænalus in Arcadia, as seen from Tegea, is a striking instance; the latter has been noticed especially in connection with the mountains that surround the plain of Athens—Hymettus, Pentelicus, Parnes, and Ægaleos,[4] since their bare treeless slopes depend almost entirely on this feature for their picturesqueness; but this same symmetry may be observed throughout the greater part of Greece. Nor must we omit to mention the combination of snow peaks with southern vegetation, which, at certain seasons of the year, is so enchanting. This, no doubt, may also be seen in the Italian valleys of the Alps; but in the Val Anzasca or the valley of Aosta the chestnut groves or vineyards in the foreground are marred by the wild glacier-streams which tear through them, and the boulders which appear at various points, so that we cannot really feel that we are in the "sweet south." This aspect of the country has been little noticed in Greece, but Byron has caught it where he says—

[4] See Mure, *Tour in Greece*, ii. 37.

> "Thy vales of evergreen, thy hills of snow,
>   Proclaim thee Nature's varied favourite now;"

and no one who has seen the olive groves and mulberry plantations of the valley of Sparta in the spring, with the snowy mass of Taygetus rising between 7000 and 8000 feet above it, or the Arcadian slopes that descend towards Olympia, with the white Erymanthus in the background, will be at a loss to understand his meaning. Other peaks, which, either from their position or their inferior elevation, are not thus covered, present a no less beautiful appearance from the tender tints of their marble grain. Pentelicus and Athos in particular, both of which are composed of white marble, possess this feature in perfection, for the effect of the weather on this material is to give it the most delicate grey hue. The latter of these two mountains, which rises like a gigantic watch-tower above the Ægean, and is visible from the coasts on both sides—from the plains of Troy on the one hand, and the slopes of Pelion on the other—when viewed close at hand assumes colours almost opaline, especially as it appears in the light of the westering sun.

Another marked characteristic of Greek scenery is the constant presence of the sea. In consequence of the narrowness of the continent and the numerous inlets, this element usually appears in some part of the view. From Parnassus the Corinthian and Saronic gulfs are visible, and the Euboic and Maliac

Presence of the sea.

seas, as well as the open Ægean. From the heights of Argolis you look, on the one side, over bays and islands to the coast of Attica; on the other, down into the Argolic gulf, at the head of which lies at your feet the plain of Argos, deeply sunk in its rocky cradle. The Arcadian shepherd, if he tends his flocks on Mount Parthenium, looks far over the Ægean, if on the western heights, over the Sicilian sea; while from the upland valleys of the Lycæan range the beautiful curve of the Messenian gulf is visible, and that of Corinth from the sides of Aroanius and Cyllene. Again, these inland seas themselves present you with lake scenery that will bear comparison with any in Europe. As you sail from the straits at Rhium to Naupactus, and from thence to the foot of Parnassus and the Isthmus, you have on the left hand the precipices and steep promontories of the Ætolian and Bœotian mountains, on the right the fertile slopes of Achaia, green with currant vines; while behind these, on both sides, are lofty summits, blue or snow-capt, and in front the ever-shifting tints of the transparent water. Thus, in passing through this wonderful country you are continually exchanging the panorama for the vignette, the ἄπειρον for the πεπερασμένον, and enjoy in profusion the most opposite sources of impressions of beauty. To all this must be added the charm of brilliant colouring. Writers of various countries have vied with one another in describing the glories of an Athenian sunset:—" the flood of fire with which the marble columns, the mountains, and the sea are all bathed and penetrated"—" the violet hue which Hymettus assumes in the evening sky, in contrast to the glowing furnace of the rock of Lycabettus, and the rosy pyramid of Pentelicus."[5]

In thus characterising the leading features of Greek landscape my object has been, not to indulge in picturesque descriptions, but to give you some idea of the country the Greeks inhabited, and the objects which they had continually before their eyes. The question whether the Greeks possessed what we call a taste for the picturesque has been elaborately discussed of late years, and the balance of opinion seems to be in favour of its absence, mainly because of the few indications of it to be found in classical writers. Thus it has been maintained that what they considered a beautiful scene was a pleasant place in which you could enjoy yourself. The subject is not necessarily connected with what we are at present considering, and will not require more than a passing

_{Did the Greeks appreciate scenery?}

---

[5] Stanley on "Greek Topography," in the *Classical Museum*, i. pp. 60, 61 ; compare Bursian, *Geographie von Griechenland*, i. p. 5. In Greece, as elsewhere in the Mediterranean, it is in the winter that the finest sunsets are seen. The characteristic of the summer months is the mistiness of the horizon, which contrasts somewhat strikingly with the distinctness of the nearer objects : this seems to be what Homer intends to express by the epithet ἠεροειδής, which is applied to "the *dim* sea," and is also used of "the *far* distance" (*Il.* v. 770), for objects as much as eighty miles off may be seen notwithstanding.

notice, but cannot perhaps be altogether put aside.⁶ At starting it may be well to understand clearly what we mean by the picturesque, for that term in its proper acceptation means the mode of viewing nature which we get from looking at pictures, and of this there are no traces in Greece before the Alexandrian period, when we occasionally meet with it in Theocritus and Apollonius Rhodius. When Theocritus says—

> ἀλλ' ὑπὸ τᾷ πέτρᾳ τᾷδ' ᾄσομαι, ἀγκὰς ἔχων τυ,
> σύννομα μᾶλ' ἐσορῶν, τὰν Σικελὰν ἐς ἅλα—⁷
>
> But at this rock
> To sing, and clasp my darling, and behold
> The sea's blue reach, and many a pasturing flock—
> *Chapman's Translation.*

he groups his objects with a view to picturesque effect, placing the two figures of the shepherd and shepherdess in the foreground, the flock of sheep in the middle distance, and the sea in the background, in the same way as a word-painter of modern days might do.⁸

⁶ The principal authorities on this subject are Humboldt, *Cosmos*, vol. ii. p. 372 foll. (Otté's Translation); Ruskin, *Modern Painters*, vol. iii. ch. 13, p. 173; Cope, in *Cambridge Essays* for 1856; Clark's *Peloponnesus*, p. 118; *Guesses at Truth*, 1st series, p. 48 foll.; Stanley on *Greek Topography*.

⁷ Theoc. *Idyll.* viii. 55.

⁸ Compare Apollon. *Argonaut.* ii. 729. The Roman poets, as they represent a later period of literature, and were greatly under Alexandrian influence, frequently introduce picturesque descriptions; *e.g.* Catullus, *Nupt. Pel. et Thet.* 271, 287; Virgil, *Æn.* i. 162, iii. 206, 411, 533, 570, vii. 25,

This we may call the third stage in the history of the Greeks' views of external nature, the two others being the early period, and the period of city life. The latter of these may be regarded as the time of neglect. It is true, that both in Æschylus [9] and Sophocles [10] we meet with appreciative descriptions of the sea, and in the *Philoctetes* and *Ajax* there are touches of the feeling of sympathy between man and nature;[11] and still more perhaps in the *Bacchæ* of Euripides [12] and the *Nubes* of Aristophanes [13] there are passages which seem to possess an element of landscape; but in the literature generally these are conspicuous by their absence. It might, indeed, be not unreasonably argued that the dramatic shape in which most of the literature of that time was cast excluded this subject by subordinating everything to the personages introduced; but it seems more likely that the engrossing character of city life, the fulness of enjoyment furnished by literature and the games, and the way in which man was regarded as the centre of all things, left no room for the admiration of scenery. But when

viii. 623, xi. 523; Ovid, *Met.* i. 568. When we come down to the time of Statius, we find the taste further developed, so that he dwells on the charm of the views (*visendi vices*) from the different windows of a villa, and even describes reflections in the water (*Silv.* ii. 72, 48).

[9] Æschyl. *Prom.* 89; *Agam.* 565, 1181.
[10] Soph. *Œd. Col.* 1240; *Ant.* 586; *Trach.* 112; *Aj.* 674.
[11] *Phil.* 936; *Aj.* 412.   [12] Eur. *Bacch.* 1051.
[13] Ar. *Nub.* 324, 279 foll.

we go back to the early period before such influences had set in, we find the case different. The Homeric poems are full of descriptions of natural objects; the mountains, the rivers, and the sea, each in turn furnish subjects of comparison, which are subordinated, as they should be, to human action, but are elaborately and faithfully delineated. The question is whether the early bards and their contemporaries perceived the beauty of what they saw, and felt admiration for it; and this is difficult to answer. Perhaps we shall approach nearest to the truth by comparing them to those who occupy a corresponding position at the present day. Even now, those to whom the changes in the atmosphere are a matter of primary importance, the peasant and the sailor, possess a knowledge of the forms of clouds, and a sympathy with nature's moods, of which we have but a faint conception.[14] Here the appreciation may be unconscious, but it can hardly be said to be wholly wanting; and in comparing them to the Greeks we must not forget that that nation possessed the keenest intellect and the finest sense of beauty of any that the world has seen. They may, indeed, have embodied the objects which they saw with the forms of deities, and so in part removed the vagueness in which much of the charm of landscape consists, but when they spoke of the rosy fingers and saffron robes of Aurora (ῥοδοδάκτυλος, κροκόπεπλος Ἠώς),

[14] On this subject see an essay in the *Fortnightly Review* (No. V. p. 590), on "The Clouds and the Poor."

they can hardly be regarded as deficient in the sense of natural beauty. Moreover, in the succeeding period, when literature was the growth of the cities, we have no reason to suppose that such ideas died out in the minds of the country people; and here we may notice one advantage arising from the study of Greek geography—viz. that whereas the history and the chief authors deal almost exclusively with the urban population, and that too only of the leading States, the geography introduces us to the whole people, dispersed over the face of the country, and inhabiting the mountains and coasts as well as the towns.

The influence, however, that was exercised by the aspect of the country on the character of its inhabitants is an independent matter. Whether they appreciated or not, it is certain that they observed; this we know from the Homeric descriptions just spoken of, from the characteristic epithets which they applied to natural objects, and from the descriptive nomenclature which they employed. This being the case, it was impossible for them to escape from the influence which such surroundings are always liable to exercise. It is easy, no doubt, to exaggerate both this and the effects of the physical conditions of the country, such as climate and soil. The theory of the late Mr. Buckle, who held that these determined entirely, or almost entirely, the character and subsequent development of a people, is an example of the way in which such a theory may be pushed to an extreme. The influence of race is un-

Influence of the aspect of the country.

doubtedly a condition equally powerful, though this again must not be regarded as standing alone. To put the case in the broadest possible way, we may ask, If Greece had originally been peopled by a tribe of Mongols, would they have arrived, by the educating agency of the country, at a high degree of civilisation? And, on the other hand, if the Greeks had found their abode in the plains of Hungary, should we ever have heard of Hellenic culture? Both these questions may safely be answered in the negative; it was the combination of the two elements—of the superiority of race and the excellence of country—and the correspondence between the two, which caused Hellas to occupy the place which she has held in history. It is this which Wordsworth has forcibly, though somewhat quaintly expressed in his famous line—

"The lively Grecian, in a land of hills."

In discussing this subject more in detail, we must endeavour to keep distinct the two influences of a country, which have now been mentioned together—that of its aspect, and that of its physical conditions; though in some instances they seem to run almost inseparably into one another.

The mountains and the sea. In the first place, Greece was destined to be the home of freedom. If it is true, as Wordsworth sings—

"Two voices are there; one is of the sea,
    One of the mountains, each a mighty voice:
    In both from age to age thou didst rejoice,
    They were thy chosen music, Liberty!"—

there never was a country in which they exercised so

strong an influence over the minds of men.[15] It is not merely that a mountain region is easy to defend against an invader, that by its isolation the inhabitants are led to think and act for themselves, that there is none of that uniformity which reduces to one type the cultivators of wide plains; the aspect of the country itself—the magnitude and variety of the objects, their solid mass, ever changing in appearance, sometimes veiled in cloud, sometimes revealing its full proportions—if it is not of a nature to overpower, insensibly elevates the mind, and inspires it with a sense of independence. And the sea, in like manner, while it teaches the mariner a hardy life, and readiness to face the approach of sudden danger, by its vast extent and changeful motion expands the thoughts and inspires the feeling of restless activity. The presence of the mountains was also to the Greeks a school of patriotism. We might almost regard it as symbolical, that the deity who cheered the Athenians before Marathon was Pan, the god of the mountains. The root of this lies in the love of home; and wherever we may choose to seek for the cause, the fact remains, that the mountaineer is of all men the fondest of his home in the midst of his native mountains. The Swiss may speak with envy of the inhabitant of Holland, when he hears that that land is a perfect level, because he knows that it renders him a plentiful

[15] On this subject generally, see Welcker, *Griechische Götterlehre*, i. pp. 40 foll.

return for his labour, instead of yielding it grudgingly to laborious toil; but whatever he may say, or in whatever quarter of the globe he may seek his fortune, he gives the best proof of his affection for his fatherland in coming home to die. And by the same influences the imagination of the people was roused, and a powerful impulse given to the development of their mythology and poetry. From every hill-side and every promontory they saw the sea, which carried their thoughts far away, and suggested ideas of foreign lands, to which the islands that lay at intervals in the view tempted them to emigrate. And by the shore itself, which bordered so large a portion of the country, they became familiar with those different moods of the ocean, which must always have a corresponding influence on the mind of man. It requires no education in sentiment to be awe-struck by the thunder of the breakers, or lulled to sleep by the rippling of the summer waves. The one alarms, the other inspires the feeling of repose ; and these, and a thousand other changes, were not less felt of old than now, and certainly not less by the Greeks than by other races. Similarly, on land, their taste was cultivated by innumerable contrasts, where the cold bald peaks rose above a profusion of luxuriant growths, and the bright sunlight of that translucent atmosphere was exchanged for the gloom of deep ravines. The combination of all these features furnished elements of poetic inspiration such as no other country has ever shown ; and when we thus endeavour to place before ourselves (again to quote Wordsworth's words)

> "The face which rural solitude might wear
> To the unenlightened swains of pagan Greece"—

we can better understand the sources of mythology which the poet has so admirably described in that passage. When the Hebrew Psalmist desired to represent to himself the righteousness and the judgments of God, he compared them to the "strong mountains" and the "great deep." The homes of the beliefs of the polytheistic Greek were, in like manner (as Milton has magnificently expressed it), the "lonely mountains" and the "resounding shore."

Besides this, the *combination* of these two influences greatly affected the Greek mind and character.[16] It is the usual tendency of the mountaineer to be narrow-minded, as his interests and his ideas are enclosed within narrow limits; and this would have been the case with the Greeks had their views not been extended by a counterbalancing element in the sea. On the other hand, the sea, while it widens the range of ideas, is apt to have a denationalising influence, unless qualified, as it was with them, by the love of home, which is engendered by the mountains. Very striking in this respect is the Greek custom, in founding a colony, of carrying the sacred fire from the hearth of the parent city, and the respect paid ever

Their combined influence.

---

[16] *Guesses at Truth*, 1st Series, p. 92.

afterwards in the sacrificial rites to one who had come from thence. Thus, too, the manner in which sea and land penetrated into one another, not forming, as in most countries, two separate elements, but combined into one organic whole, banished all one-sidedness of character from tribes and from individuals, and raised them above the material world by inspiring them with a feeling of command over all the elements alike. This was what was wanting in Egypt and in Hindostan, in both which countries the predominance of one great element of nature had a debasing effect on the civilisation. At the same time, the aspect of so many varied objects by sea and land, and the ever-changing phases that they presented, could not fail to foster that versatility of temperament which has been the characteristic of the Greeks in all ages.

Greek scenery and the Hellenic mind.

We may illustrate this still further by considering the correspondence that may be traced between Greek scenery and the Hellenic mind in some remarkable instances. The principle of moderation and sobriety —μηδὲν ἄγαν—which formed so marked a constituent in the character of the Greeks, and was the great secret of their taste, is equally inscribed on the face of the country. Here the objects are nowhere of colossal magnitude; the mountains, though lofty, do not reach an extraordinary elevation, and none of them is of such a character as to dwarf the rest. The tiny creeks and harbours, the landlocked bays, and the island-studded seas, all suggest the idea of limitation.

The vegetation, though in places rich and luxuriant, never displays the "riotous prodigality" which is seen in Italy. All these features are what we find so constantly illustrated in Greek literature, but especially in the drama, which is distinguished by its evenly sustained dignity and its carefully subdued passion. They are noticeable, above all, in the mythology, where the gigantic and extravagant, which plays so large a part in the legends of other countries, is kept almost entirely in the background. Closely connected with this is another important constituent of the Greek mind—its sense of symmetry, which seems never to have failed them, but was especially conspicuous in their sculpture, which, whether in the manly school of Phidias or in the more luxurious style of Praxiteles and Scopas, depends mainly for its effect on the balance of the parts. This also seems like a reflection of Greek landscape, in which we have noticed not only the harmonious intermingling of sea and land, but the artistic arrangement that may be traced in the forms of the mountains, and the just proportion existing between the component parts in most of the views. To add one more principle, which enters deeply into the Greek conception of nature, and through that into their philosophy, we find constantly inscribed on the face of Hellas the idea that "nature's works are perfect" ($\pi\acute{a}\nu\tau\alpha\ \dot{\omega}\varsigma\ \varkappa\acute{a}\lambda\lambda\iota\sigma\tau\alpha\ \pi\acute{\epsilon}\varphi\upsilon\varkappa\epsilon\nu$).[17] We shall hardly find a more striking illustration of

[17] Stanley on *Greek Topography*, p. 48.

this thorough contentment of the Greek mind with the existing order of things than is supplied by their architecture. If we compare the Parthenon with an Egyptian temple and a Gothic minster, we may perceive this very plainly. The Egyptian temple, with its frowning cornice and enormous pillars, represents depression—the sense of an overwhelming power of destiny. In strong contrast with this, the ascending lines of the Gothic cathedral, which lead the eye up to the roof or the spire, express aspiration, and draw the mind away from earth. The Greek temple does neither of these, it neither looks downward nor upward; it is in perfect repose, the upright lines of the lower part expressing an ascending force, which is counteracted by the superincumbent weight of the horizontal lines above, and its completeness consists in the balance of the two. It is wholly satisfied with its own ideal beauty, and represents the feeling of the perfection of the existing order of things. The same idea was impressed upon the Greeks by the appearance of their country. We have seen how the continent, as it is prolonged towards the south, becomes more and more finely articulated and fitted to be the scene of the development of the Hellenic race, culminating at last in the Peloponnese, an acropolis with marble walls. But beyond this, the places of greatest note on its surface seemed destined beforehand for the purposes which they served. Delphi, with its awe-inspiring chasm, withdrawn from the profane world and encompassed with magnificent surroundings, yet sufficiently near the sea to be accessible to worshippers, appeared the one place fitted to be the central oracle of the race. Helicon, with its graceful form and trickling rills, was especially suited for the abode of the Muses. Athens, on its altar-shaped rock, which forms, as it were, the eye of the plain, in the midst of most classical mountains, and looking out towards the blue sea, seemed the natural home of art, and the seat of maritime dominion. And lastly, to bring this enumeration to a close, Corinth, which from its lofty summit overlooked two seas and commanded the entrance to the Peloponnese, was pointed out as the fitting centre of commercial enterprise. To interfere with an order of things so fitly foreordained, was naturally regarded as an act of impiety; and bearing this in mind, we can understand how Herodotus should regard the cutting of the canal through Athos by Xerxes as prompted by sinful presumption, and how every Greek would approve the answer of the Pythia to the people of Cnidos, when they desired to separate from the mainland the peninsula on which their city was built— that "Zeus would have made it an island had he willed it so."[18]

The correspondences that have thus been traced tend to confirm what has been said before about the influence of the aspect of the country on the mind of

[18] Herod. i. 174.

the Greeks. There is a tendency to ignore this influence, because the subject borders on the region of sentiment, which is a great foe to rational argument; but we may not rightly ignore a set of facts of this kind more than any other facts. We acknowledge the educating power of the eye in other matters; we are aware that the constant sight of ugly patterns and gaudy colours must eventually spoil the taste for beauty; we feel that a different temperament is engendered amongst persons of all classes by living in the presence of the architecture of Paris and of London; and we can hardly refuse to go a step further, and admit the same thing when applied to a larger field of observation. Again I would ask, quite independently of questions of physical and material development, if the Greeks had had no objects presented to their eyes but what they could see in the plains of Hungary, would the world ever have been enriched by Hellenic culture?

Influence of soil and climate. We turn now to the effect on the people of the physical conditions of the country, and especially the soil and climate. Here again we must be on our guard against exaggerating the influence exercised. It is possible for man by strength of will to rise superior to the disadvantages of the land in which his lot is cast; as Strabo remarks that the inclement and mountainous parts of the habitable globe are naturally a bad dwelling-place, but may be brought under cultivation if they fall into the hands of careful occupants.[19] On the other hand, the same author, in another part of his work, quotes the opinion of Ephorus that the Bœotians possessed an extremely advantageous position in Greece from their commanding three seas—on the one side the Corinthian and Crissæan gulfs, which opened towards Italy, Sicily, and Libya; on the other the bays of the Euboic sea, both north and south of the Euripus, which looked towards Macedonia and the Hellespont, and also towards Cyprus and Egypt—but that these gifts of nature had been wasted on them, because they undervalued the civilising influences of education;[20] though he might have added that this boorishness was itself in part a result of the climate. Still, the effect produced by these external causes is very great, and may be especially traced in its permanence. It is not an accident that the women of the vale of Sparta are still the handsomest in Greece, as they were in the days when Homer spoke of "Lacedæmon famed for beauteous women" (Λακεδαίμονα καλλιγύναικα): the cause may readily be discovered in the fineness of the climate and the excellence of the water in that district. In the same way the Bœotian peasant is still distinguished from the rest of his countrymen by his heaviness of temperament and his incivility.[21]

[19] Strabo, ii. 5, § 26.   [20] ix. 2, § 2.
[21] Wyse, *Impressions of Greece*, p. 102; and the author's *Highlands of Turkey*, ii. 205.

Aristotle, in a well-known passage,[22] remarks of the inhabitants of the colder countries of Europe that "they are brave but deficient in thought and technical skill; and, as a consequence of this, that they remain free longer than others, but are wanting in political organisation, and unable to rule their neighbours. The peoples of Asia, on the contrary, are thoughtful and skilful, but without spirit, whence their permanent condition is one of subjection and slavery. But the Hellenic race, he adds, as it is intermediate between them in geographical position, so also combines their qualities; it is at once spirited and thoughtful, and so continues to be free and to have the best government, and would be capable of ruling the world if it had a common political organisation." This was the effect of the climate of Greece, which was temperate and varied, having sufficient warmth to allow the intellect to expand, and sufficient cold to brace the nerves. Aristotle proceeds to remark that these qualities were found in different degrees in different Greek races, and this depended to no slight extent on the character of their atmosphere. The varied surface of Greece also tended to produce the same effect. Its inhabitants, from the nature of the case, had the vigorous constitution and the hardihood of mountaineers, and this sufficed to counteract whatever softness the warmth of the climate might, as in the case of Sparta, have been liable to produce. The physical

[22] *Pol.* iv. (vii.) 7, § 2.

activity thus generated gave a practical turn to the whole life of the Greeks, without disqualifying them for speculation. They might say of themselves at large, what Pericles said of the Athenians—"We study philosophy without being enervated by it" (φιλοσοφοῦμεν ἄνευ μαλακίας).[23]

The soil of Greece was beneficent to its cultivators in what it denied as well as what it gave. The description that Ulysses gave of his island home would apply to the whole country, that it was "rude, but a good nursing mother (τρηχεῖ' ἀλλ' ἀγαθὴ κουρο-τρόφος).[24] "Want has at all times been at home in our land," said Demaratus to Xerxes, "while Valour is an ally whom we have gained by dint of wisdom and strict laws."[25] The ground well repaid cultivation, but required to be carefully tilled, and in many cases to be drained and artificially irrigated. The torrents had to be restrained within their banks, and the subterranean channels, where possible, kept open. It was the opposite of what the Israelites remembered the land of Egypt to be—"a land where thou sowest thy seed, and waterest it with thy foot, as a garden of herbs."[26] It justified the remark of Strabo, that the Greeks inhabited mountains and rocks, but were well off by reason of the attention they paid to politics and the arts, and other forms of economical pru-

[23] Thuc. ii. 40.
[24] Hom. *Od.* ix. 27.
[25] Herod. vii. 102.
[26] Deut. xi. 10.

dence.[27] In some cases the thinness of the soil forced the inhabitants to take to the sea, and thus developed a new form of activity. This was especially noticeable in the case of Athens, which from this cause became a maritime nation at an early period. Another remarkable instance is the island of Ægina, which, from being composed of stony levels and unproductive mountains, became at one time the first maritime power in the Ægean, and, as we see from its famous marbles, a home of the fine arts. But in the cultivation of art, for this very reason, the continent of Greece was for a long time outstripped by its colonies. We have no coins from Greece Proper that will bear comparison with those of Magna Græcia, and by far the finest specimens of early architecture are the temples of Pæstum, Selinus, and Agrigentum. In those countries, and on the fertile shore of Asia Minor, the rapid development of the wealth of the cities offered facilities for the cultivation of refined tastes; but the same cause undermined their vigour and their patriotism, and ultimately deprived them of their independence. In the products of continental Greece, also, there was nothing to minister to indulgence; they provided what was necessary for life, while articles of luxury had to be imported from abroad.

Effect on the language. It should also be noticed that the clearness of intellect which was fostered or rendered possible by

[27] Strabo, ii. 5, § 26.

the purity of the atmosphere, and the vigorous soundness of the temperament of the people, was reflected in their language. When we consider that the Greeks did not, until quite late in the history of their literature, possess any system of grammatical rules, it is a marvel how there could have arisen a vehicle of thought so accurate, so luminous, and so expressive, as the Greek language. To give birth to this, and to bring it to perfection, the most favourable conditions, both internal and external,—both in the mind of the people and in the circumstances under which they lived,—must have been requisite. That a crowd of people should have been able to follow and appreciate the plays of Sophocles and the speeches of Demosthenes is wonderful enough; but that the writer and speaker should have succeeded, without the aid of strict rules, in carrying his thoughts through long periods, containing a multiplicity of clauses, and involving infinite modifications of ideas, without risk of confusion, is an unparalleled phenomenon. But while the language was thus brought to perfection by the agency of one set of causes, it was being divided by other influences into separate dialects, each of which became a perfect instrument to be used in the service of a certain kind of literature. In the broad Doric we see the language of deep-chested mountaineers, fond of strong sounds and concentrated forms of expression. In the soft Ionic the influence of the coasts and lowlands appears, which by their milder air encouraged the multiplication of vowel sounds, and the linking together of flowing periods; while the clear atmosphere of Attica bestowed on that country a dialect of its own, forcible, terse, and logical. These were fittingly employed in expressing respectively simple and solemn lyrics; epic poetry and inartistic narrative; and accurate reasoning and statement.

Greek geography and politics.

But while the physical conformation of the Greek continent tended to form the character of the Greeks, it had an equally powerful influence over their politics. From it arose, in great measure, the different course pursued by the histories of Greece and Rome, the contrast of which causes the co-ordinate study of the two to be so profitable. The history of Rome presents to us a vast, all-absorbing unity, starting from small beginnings, strengthened by continual contests, first with its neighbours in Italy, and afterwards with foreign powers, extending its dominion by gradual stages, and finally embracing the whole of the civilised world. In Greece, on the other hand, we find a number of separate unities, distinct from one another in customs, constitution, and religious rites; never betraying any tendency towards amalgamation, but maintaining their isolation to the last. This phenomenon arose from the narrow valleys and enclosed basins into which Greece is divided; and the marked effect that this exercised on the political system of the Greeks is nowhere more evident than in the fact that Aristotle, with all his wide experience and observation, in describing the best form of state, considered that it should be of such a size that the citizens might know one another, because without personal acquaintance proper persons could not be elected as magistrates.[28] In like manner the country, of which this city is to be the capital, should be easily taken in by the eye; as far as possible self-sufficing in its products; opposing difficulties to the approach of an enemy, while it offered facilities of exit to the natives, and allowing of goods being readily exported.[29] It is only in a country such as we have described that this view could have arisen, where the barriers interposed by nature caused every city to be a political unity, and forced them to depend, as far as possible, on themselves; though this isolation was in some degree qualified by the means of transit the sea afforded, and also by the varied temperature, which caused the time of harvest to be different in different districts, and thus necessitated an interchange of their products.[30] The last-named influence acted more powerfully than we might have supposed; and what we find in Greece at the present day, that the flocks are transferred from one part of the country to another, according to the season, took place also in ancient times. Pausanias tells us that one of the causes of the first

---

[28] *Pol.* iv. (vii.) 4, § 13.   [29] iv. (vii.) 5.
[30] Grote's *History of Greece*, ii. 294, 295.

Messenian war was a quarrel between a man of Messenia and a citizen of Sparta, on account of some oxen which the former had turned out by agreement on the lands of the latter.[31]

Individuality of the states.

It has been remarked of the *Politics* of Aristotle that it has a parochial character, owing to the smallness of scale of the interests which it discusses.[32] The peculiarity thus stigmatised is derived from the character of the country which has been described, and is no more a subject for depreciation than the limited area of Greece itself. The repellent power thus exercised towards external influences was the means of maintaining those special types of character which give peculiar interest to the history of the Greek cities. It was not only between the larger aggregates that these differences existed. We are told that within the area of Bœotia the various cities had their peculiar attributes: that covetousness reigned supreme in Oropus; jealousy in Tanagra; ambition in Thespiæ; insolence at Thebes; selfishness at Anthedon; officiousness at Coroneia; imposture in Platæa; feverishness in Onchestus; and insensibility in Haliartus.[33] This catalogue of qualities, which has the appearance of malicious completeness, is accurate so far as it implies the individuality of character of the separate states, and is thoroughly of a part with the claim of indigenous-

---

[31] Pausan. iv. 4, § 4.   [32] Congreve's *Politics*, Introd. xxiii.
[33] Dicæarchus, quoted by Grote, *History of Greece*, ii. 310.

ness which so many of them put forward.[34] As these local limits had exercised their peculiar influence from the first establishment of the tribe in that district, the special characteristics which belonged to each fraction of it had been more and more deeply impressed, and had gained strength by time, from being guarded by custom, and association, and prejudice. This was at once the strength and the weakness of Hellenic life. Had not Athens been so intensely Athenian, and Sparta so intensely Spartan, the chronicle of Greek history would lose much of its instructiveness. But the want of unity thus engendered was fatal to them at last. It was their inability to combine which rendered them powerless to resist first the Macedonian, and afterwards the Roman, domination. At the same time we must not suppose that bonds of union were wanting to bind together in an organic whole these heterogeneous elements. The foremost of these was the language, which was at the same time the surest test of the difference between Hellene and barbarian. This was supported by Amphictyonic councils, by the worship of common gods, by the responses of common oracles, especially that of Delphi, which kept a rigorous watch over the whole community, by national games, and, after the time of the Persian wars, by national sympathy. We might have expected that these causes would ultimately have produced a federal union, but this was not the

[34] Stanley on *Greek Topography*, p. 45.

case. The nearest approach to it was the Achæan League, but this only embraced a portion of the people, and was of short duration.

<small>Opposition between neighbours.</small> The natural isolation of the Greek communities produced several further results, which modified the course of Greek history, and serve to illustrate certain political principles which have been more fully developed in later times. One of these is the opposition generated by proximity, of which we have the most familiar instance in the relations of Platæa and Thebes. There the smaller state, though lying within the territory of Bœotia, which acknowledged Thebes as its head, was tempted by its position on the lower slopes of Cithæron to assert its independence of its powerful neighbour. And when they looked for aid from without, they had only to mount the ridge behind to gain a view over the plain of Eleusis, which reminded them of their nearness to Athens. Hence arose their alliance with that city, which is associated with their glory and their ruin. Similarly in Arcadia, the relations of Tegea and Mantineia were determined by their jealousy of one another as neighbours, which caused violent contests between them, and when they entered into foreign alliances, drew Tegea into close connection with Sparta, while Mantineia, when she looked abroad at all, was rather attracted to Argos. The conduct of Athens towards her Dorian neighbour Megara was regulated by the same motive. Several of the most important alliances in Greek history arose

from this cause. It was because Bœotia lay between them that Thessaly and Athens were drawn together —a friendship which was of great service to the latter state, because it brought to their aid the Thessalian cavalry, an arm with which they themselves were feebly provided. In like manner, it was the mutual dread of Athens which caused Sparta and Thebes to be closely associated in their politics throughout an important part of Greek history. Thus, by degrees, there arose a feeling of the necessity of the balance of power, which has exercised so strong an influence over the course of modern history. As each of the great states in turn—Athens, Sparta, Thebes—attained to a too commanding position, a combination was formed amongst the others to put it down. And this applied to smaller areas as well as to the whole nation. It was the desire of counteracting the overweening power of Sparta in the Peloponnese, that caused the Argives, after the peace of Nicias, to form a league against her, along with the Mantineians, Corinthians, and Eleians. The same principle accounts for the frequent shifting of sides in Greek politics, which is noticeable in the conduct of all the states, but especially in that of Corinth. That city, which from her central position had more reason than any other to desire the balance of power, from being on friendly terms with the Athenians became their most deadly foe, and continued to be so throughout the Peloponnesian war; but after the humiliation of Athens took

Balance of power.

sides with her against Sparta for some time, until she again found it expedient to return to the friendship of her old ally. Lastly, in the relations of these independent states in war and peace we see the rude beginnings of international law—the holy truce at the time of the games; the rights of neutrals, especially in the matter of refusing a passage to an armed force through their territory,[35] and admitting only a single ship of a belligerent power to their ports;[36] the offer of negotiation, sometimes even of arbitration, before declaring war;[37] the right of suppliants;[38] the exchange and ransom of prisoners;[39] the duty of sparing fruit trees in an enemy's country,[40] and of giving back his dead for burial,[41] with many similar customs.

Varied forms of civic life. Finally, in the individual states themselves we may notice how the physical features of the country gave an impulse to various forms of government or civic life. The remark that Strabo[42] makes concerning Europe in general—that it has the advantage of being everywhere diversified with plains and mountains, so that in each part the agricultural, political, and military elements exist side by side—may be applied with still greater force to Greece. Its varied surface assigned to each narrow district mountains as a training to hardihood, a plain to cultivate, and a

---

[35] Thuc. iv. 78. [36] Ibid ii. 7, iii. 71, vi. 52.
[37] i. 28. [38] iii. 58. [39] iii. 70.
[40] Plato, *Rep.* v. p. 470. [41] Thuc. iv. 98.
[42] ii. 5, § 26.

city as a focus of social and intellectual life. We have seen in a former lecture how the stone of the country, being everywhere abundant, and excellent for building purposes, was at an early period an encouragement to city life; and from this again arose that universal interest in politics which was one main cause of the intensity of action that characterised Greek history. But we must not forget how the fondness for country life was fostered by the other natural features, the mountains and the plains, as we see from the enthusiastic terms in which it is always spoken of by Aristophanes, and the discontent of the people of Attica at being forced to betake themselves to the city at the commencement of the Peloponnesian war. Here was a conservative element of which the oligarchs did not fail to take advantage; and thus we find them, when they were able, encouraging village life in preference to that in the towns, as at Sparta, which was only an aggregate of villages, and did not possess the first constituent of a city in Greece, a wall of circuit. For the same reason the Spartans opposed every attempt to bring their neighbours together from their scattered habitations into a common capital. But the steep places and mountain spurs which are found so commonly in Greece were also, as Aristotle has remarked,[43] an oligarchical or monarchical element, because they afforded so great facilities for building strongholds to command the surrounding district, or

---

[43] *Pol.* iv. (vii.) 11, § 5.

the town that grew up on the hill-side below. Accordingly, the first act of the tyrant is always to make himself master of the acropolis; and the same cause accounts for the long duration of oligarchy in some places where the general influences would seem to tend in the opposite direction. But in the main these causes were more than counteracted by the city life, with its busy discussions and conflicting interests, which encouraged democracy, and in a still greater degree by the maritime pursuits of a great part of the people. This was the nautical mob (ναυτικὸς ὄχλος),[44] so great an object of fear to statesmen and politicians, and above all to philosophers like Plato and Aristotle, as they seemed to them to have caught the nature of the restless element with which they were familiar, and imported a constant succession of new ideas, and were at the bottom of every political change. It is the mixture of all these different elements, brought together in every variety of combination, that gives such a lasting interest to the history of the Greek constitutions, and renders it so permanently instructive.

[44] Ar. *Pol.* iv. (vii.) 6, § 7.

LECTURE VI.

GEOGRAPHY OF NORTHERN GREECE.

Survey of the several Districts—Macedonia—Pelagonia and Lyncestis—Position of Edessa—Pella—Peninsula of Chalcidice—Thessaly : Character of its Subdivisions ; Effect on its History—Phthiotis—Passes leading into Thessaly—The Western Countries—Site of Dodona.

HAVING in the preceding lectures taken a general survey of the features of Greek geography, and having traced their influence on the character and politics of the people, it is time that we should study more in detail the several districts, in order to understand their peculiarities, and the effect of these on their history ; at the same time we may perhaps obtain a more graphic idea of the scenes of some of the principal occurrences. In doing so, we must bear in mind what has been already said about the progressive articulation of the country in proportion as it advances further towards the south, and about the manner in which the water penetrates into the land, and the mountains into the sea. To avoid repetition, also, we must presuppose a knowledge of the general position of the mountains and of those localities which have already been described. As regards method, it may be well for us, besides noticing the natural conformation of each region, to pay attention to the passes and other points of strategic importance, and here and there to study the situation of the leading towns. Let us commence with Macedonia, a country in no sense Hellenic, though its rulers succeeded in claiming that title for themselves, but of great importance to Greece as commanding its entrance from the north.

Macedonia. The determining feature of this country is the river Axius, which formed a line of communication between the barbarous districts of the interior and the sea, the point of demarcation between the uplands and the lowlands being marked by the Stena, or, as it is now called, the Iron Gate (Demir Kapu) of the Vardar. Here the river, flowing from the north, cuts through, at right angles, the mountains that join the Scardus and Orbelus ranges, and forms a deep ravine, through which it rushes in rapids for the distance of a quarter of a mile, beneath the steep cliffs that rise to the height of 600 or 700 feet above. This must always have been an important position, and traces are visible of groovings in the rocks where a passage has been cut through, which may date even from the time of the Peloponnesian war; for Thucydides[1] tells us that lines of road were then made through the country, and these

[1] ii. 100.

must of necessity have followed the natural arteries. The ground to the east of the upper course of the river stretches away towards Thrace, and partakes of the wild and irregular character of that region; but to the west it rises to the great upland plain of Pelagonia, one of the richest districts in the whole Greek peninsula, which lies close under the flank of the Scardus chain, deeply sunk amongst the mountains, and is drained by the Erigon, a confluent of the Axius. This plain—the modern plain of Monastir—which is 40 miles long by 10 wide, and 1500 feet above the sea, was one of the primitive seats of the Macedonian race, and, as Grote has remarked,[2] formed a territory better calculated to nourish and to generate a considerable population than the less favoured home, and smaller breadth of valley and plain, occupied by Epirots or Illyrians. In this way a hardy yet thriving race was developed, which had in it the germs of a great nation. Here is laid the scene of the story that Herodotus[3] has given of the foundation of the Macedonian monarchy, in which the three brothers, supposed descendants of Temenus, make their escape from the service of the king of the country in the midst of numerous fabulous incidents. The southern part of this plain was called Lyncestis; and here it was that Brasidas, as the ally of Perdiccas, encountered the Illyrians, the scene of his masterly retreat being the pass at its south-eastern

Pelagonia and Lyncestis.

[2] *History of Greece*, iv. p. 15.   [3] viii. 137, 138.

extremity, which leads in the direction of Edessa.[4] Between this region and the lowlands is a lake district of somewhat inferior elevation, which bore in ancient times the name of Eordæa. It should further be noticed that there are only two passes through the Scardus chain—one near the head-waters of the Axius, between the modern towns of Prisrend and Calcandele; the other considerably further to the south, leading from the head of the Lacus Lychnitis into the Pelagonian plain—a double pass, for here the Scardus is divided into two branches, and a considerable valley intervenes between them. It was by the latter of these that the Illyrians descended to attack Brasidas on the occasion just referred to; and this, in later times, marked the line of the Egnatian Way, which ran from Dyrrhachium to Thessalonica, connecting the Adriatic and the Ægean.

Position of Edessa.

At the point where the passes from Lyncestis and Eordæa enter lower Macedonia stood the ancient capital, Edessa. The position of this place is remarkable, not only from its strategic importance as commanding the communication with the upper country, but also on account of its extreme beauty, in which respect it is unrivalled in Greece. It is the Tivoli of the Balkan peninsula. At the opening of the valley, which is here about a mile and a half wide, the whole space is filled up from side to side

---

[4] Thuc. iv. 124-8. See my *Highlands of Turkey*, ii. 361.

by a level table of land, from which precipices descend to the plain below, some 200 feet in height. The town lies on the level, and some of its houses overhang the edge of the precipices, which consist of conglomerate rock, and are picturesquely ornamented with bushes. But the most marked feature of all are the cascades; for the clear river, which descends from the upper part of the valley, divides into a number of smaller streams, which pass through the town, and plunge at various points down the steep rocks, forming an exquisite addition to the view, wherever a number of them can be seen together. This place was a magnificent nursery for the great Macedonian kingdom, and at a later period, when Philip of Macedon transferred the seat of government to Pella, it continued to be the national hearth of the race, and the burial-place of their kings. The situation of the city itself seemed to suggest dominion; for whilst it has at its back all the resources of the country, the view from it embraces not only the mighty mass of the snowy Olympus, but the wide plain of lower Macedonia, only bounded, at a distance of sixty miles, by the heights beyond Thessalonica, together with a portion of the Thermaic gulf.

The later capital, Pella, stood in a very inferior position, which has neither strength nor healthiness to recommend it, being on low hills at the edge of an extensive marsh in the middle of the plain: its nearness to the sea must have been its chief recommenda-

Pella.

tion. The situation of Thessalonica, which in Roman times became the chief centre of these parts and was the terminus of the Egnatian Way, is far finer, and recalls the appearance of Genoa, from the way in which the houses rise from the water's edge, and gradually ascend the hill-sides towards the north. It is admirably placed for purposes of communication and trade, as it lies on the innermost bay of the winding gulf, and forms the natural point of transit for exports and imports; besides which it commands the resources of the immense plain, which reaches in a vast arc as far as the foot of Olympus, and receives the waters of three important rivers—the Axius, the Lydias, and the Haliacmon. The mountains which bound this plain on the west, and run from the neighbourhood of Edessa to Olympus, were called the Bermian chain; and the slopes of Olympus, both on the northern side and towards the sea, formed Pieria, the home of the Muses, before their worship was transferred to Helicon. Between the Bermian mountains and Scardus was an extensive but irregular plain, drained by the Haliacmon and its tributaries.

Peninsula of Chalcidice. The maritime district of Macedonia, called Chalcidice, which projects like a trident into the north of the Ægean, has but little claim to be considered part of that country. Its deep bays and long peninsulas, and even the form of its mountains and their vegetation, recall the south of the Peloponnese; and therefore it is to be regarded rather as the result of natural fitness than of accident, that its shores were fringed with Hellenic colonies. These were a continual thorn in the side of the Macedonian monarchs, and it was with a view of getting rid of this that Perdiccas took part against the Athenians in the Peloponnesian war. The easternmost of the three peninsulas, that called Acte, is by far the most conspicuous for its elevation. At the isthmus, where are the remains of Xerxes' canal, its breadth is about a mile and a half, and the ground is comparatively level; but from this point it rises in undulations until it forms a steep central ridge, which gradually attains the height of 4000 feet, and finally throws up the vast conical peak. The peninsula of Sithonia, also, though lower than this, is still distinguished by its lofty broken mountains; but that of Pallene nowhere rises to any height. This last, however, claims our attention, because it possessed the important town of Potidæa. This lay just within the isthmus, which is about half-a-mile wide, and has evident traces of a canal cut through it, which Strabo[5] mentions, though it did not attain to fame like that of Athos, and from its present appearance could hardly have been intended for anything larger than boats. Though the city was rebuilt on a great scale by Cassander, who called it Cassandreia, hardly a vestige of it now remains; but the wall which Thucydides speaks of as towards the isthmus[6] probably ran along from sea to sea, somewhat

---

[5] vii. Fr. 25, ed. Kramer.   [6] Thuc. i. 64.

above the line of the canal. At the present day a plain reaches from beneath the eastern side of the city along the coast as far as Olynthus, but this could not have existed in ancient times, for, both in the retreat of Aristeus,[7] and in the previous destruction of the Persian host under Artabazus, which had been tempted to approach the city by an extraordinary ebb tide,[8] it is implied that the sea on that side flowed under the walls.

Thessaly.   In passing from Macedonia into Thessaly, we leave a non-Hellenic for a semi-Hellenic country; and what is true in this respect of the race of the inhabitants may be said also of the country itself. Though neither maritime nor mountainous to the same degree as southern Greece, it presents a definite organisation, which is not to be found further north. Here the vast plain is bounded on four sides by parallel mountain chains—the Cambunian range on the north, Pindus on the west, and Othrys on the south—while between it and the sea Ossa and Pelion are interposed as a barrier, and at the north-eastern angle Olympus forms the keystone of the whole. This wide area is drained by a single river, the Peneius, which, together with the water of its numerous confluents, passes into the sea through the vale of Tempe. We must not, however, suppose that this extent of country presents one unbroken surface. On the contrary, it is composed of a number of sections which open out into one an-

[7] Thuc. i. 63.   [8] Herod. viii. 129.

other, divided by lower ranges of hills. The principal of these are two, which are called Upper and Lower Thessaly, the former comprising the western and southwestern part, which contained the higher course of the Peneius, flowing from Mount Lacmon, and all those of its tributaries that flow from the south—the Enipeus, the Apidanus, the Onochonus, and the Pamisus; while in the latter, which reaches eastwards to the foot of Ossa and Pelion, the supply of water of that river is diminished rather than increased, for its inundations at certain seasons of the year overflow the lower lands towards the south, and form the lake Nessonis, and when that is full, they again escape and pour themselves into the lake of Bœbe. In Strabo's time these inundations seem to have caused serious injury to the lower plain, for he speaks of the midland of Thessaly as a singularly favoured country, except where it is flooded by the river.[9] He also says that the lake Nessonis was larger than that of Bœbe, which is not by any means the case at the present day; and he regards them both as affording evidence of the time when the whole of Thessaly was under water.

It may convey a clearer idea of the whole country if we take a survey of its different parts from one or two points of view on the neighbouring mountain-sides. First, let us place ourselves on one of the buttresses of Olympus which look towards Thessaly. From here the whole of the plain of Larissa is seen

_{Character of its subdivisions.}

[9] Strabo, ix. 5, § 2.

to the south and south-west, and a long spur runs down from the Cambunian mountains to the west of that city, which may dimly be descried in the midst of its plantations. Behind it lie other hills, which run up from the south, thus forming the line of demarcation between the two great plains. The course of the Peneius is visible as it winds through the level land; and in one place a line of green marshes appears, marking the overflow of its waters from the right bank during the floods of spring. The lake Nessonis, which is formed by this, is a conspicuous object beneath the flanks of Ossa, but that of Bœbe, further to the south, is concealed from view. To the westward lies the valley of the Titaresius, which flows round the base of Olympus on that side, and joins the Peneius shortly before it enters Tempe. From this let us turn to a completely opposite point of view, and suppose that we are entering Thessaly from the side of Malis, through the pass of Othrys, behind the city of Lamia, which was called Cœla, or "the Hollows," in ancient times. When you descend from this towards the north you first enter a soft rich plain of no great extent, on the western side of which appears a small lake, formerly called Xynias, and the peaks of Pindus rise in the distance—the whole composing a scene, which, from its gentle and somewhat tame character, forms a strong contrast to all the views of southern Greece. A low range of hills divides this from the town of Thaumaci, which stands in a commanding position, and overlooks the whole of the upper plain. The scene is described in the following remarkable passage of Livy which relates to this pass :—" When the traveller, in passing through the rugged districts of Thessaly, where the roads are entangled in the windings of the valleys, arrives at this city, on a sudden an immense level expanse, resembling a vast sea, is outspread before him in such a manner that the eye cannot easily reach the limit of the plains extended beneath. From this extraordinary spectacle the place is called Thaumaci ('Wonderland')."[10] Whatever we may think of the etymology, the description is certainly not overdrawn, especially as the snowy summits of Pindus, the Cambunian mountains, and Olympus, are visible in the background. In the same way, if you stand on the western heights of the Cambunian range, an unbroken level stretches before you towards the south for sixty miles, until it is bounded by the distant line of the peaks of Othrys. The plains of Lombardy, as seen from the Alps, hardly present so remarkable a sight, because they are intersected by dykes and hedges, whereas here there is nothing to break up the uniformity of surface. In the spring time the whole extent is of the brightest green, forming a striking contrast to the plain of Athens at the same time of year.

The description thus given will enable us readily to understand the history of the country. The moun- *Effect on its history.*

[10] Livy, xxxii. 4.

tains on the north and south formed successive barriers, which rendered Greece a country difficult of conquest, while at the same time the fertility of the land offered a temptation to invaders, and was thus the primary cause of the early migrations. It was this motive which first induced the Thessalians to leave their home in Epirus, and descend into this district, and from this movement arose the expulsion of the Bœotians from Arne,[11] and their settlement in the country subsequently called Bœotia, involving the division of the Locrian race into two separate parts, together with various other changes. Another wave of the same tide drove the Dorians also southward, whose subsequent migrations changed the face of the Peloponnese. Again, these broad acres were the natural home of a rich aristocracy, whose lands were tilled by a serf population; and this tendency to oligarchy was favoured by the absence of elevated positions suited for the foundation of cities, which might have fostered the spirit of freedom and democracy. Accordingly we find Thessaly from early times under the dominion of a few powerful families, such as the Aleuadæ of Larissa and the Scopadæ of the neighbouring town of Crannon, subject to whom were the various tribes of Perrhæbians, Achæans, and others of the earlier population; while the lowest class was formed by the Penestæ, who were to the Thessalians what the Helots were to the Spartans. Here, too,

[11] Thuc. i. 12.

we trace the same connection that has been already noticed between horses and the oligarchical spirit, for cavalry was the only arm in which the Thessalian nation was strong in war ; and thus the heavy-armed infantry were excluded, who in southern Greece represented the middle class and free institutions. The selfishness engendered by this mode of life, and the luxury resulting from abundant wealth, were unfavourable to the spirit of patriotism, and thus we cannot be surprised to find that, though the majority of the Thessalians sympathised with the other Greeks at the time of the Persian wars, the Aleuadæ made common cause with the enemies of their country. At the same time, when they could put out their full strength, this nation was a very formidable power, as is sufficiently shown by the apprehension they caused to the Phocians, who before the Persian war had built a wall across the pass of Thermopylæ to prevent their incursions. But this was more than counterbalanced by their disunion and want of political character. "When a Tagus is established in Thessaly," observed Jason of Pheræ, "all the surrounding peoples are subject to her ;"[12] and accordingly, when such combinations in government came to pass, as is often the case with such half-organised communities, they were able for the time to make a considerable show, but on the whole they influenced but little the fortunes of Greece. We can hardly find a more instruc-

[12] Xen. *Hellen.* vi. 1, § 9, ed. Dindorf.

tive comment on the correspondence between the people of southern Greece and the country they inhabited than the contrast afforded by the similar adaptation of the Thessalians to Thessaly.

Of the four districts into which this country was divided, Pelasgiotis was that which we have seen in our view from the side of Olympus; Hestiæotis, that about the upper course of the Peneius, over which we looked down from the Cambunian range; and Thessaliotis, that watered by the southern tributaries of that river, over which the eye ranges from Thaumaci.

Phthiotis. The last which remains to be noticed is Phthiotis, a region geographically distinct from the rest of Thessaly, though historically one of its most important divisions. The best conception of it can be gained by looking from the summit of Pelion, a point which commands a view only second to that from Parnassus, embracing, amongst other objects, the greater part of Eubœa, the straits of Artemisium, part of the Maliac and part of the Euboic gulf, and Parnassus itself towering high above the nearer range of Œta. To confine ourselves, however, to the nearer country, the most distinguishing feature is the Pagasæus Sinus (Gulf of Volo), a most beautiful land-locked basin, which lies 5000 feet below you in its whole expanse, with headlands at intervals running out into it, extending from Pagasæ at its head to Aphetæ at its narrow outlet, where the chain of Pelion, turning at right angles to its axis at the end of Magnesia, throws out a projecting line of broken ridges. Opposite to this rise the heights of Othrys, and both from this and from every other quarter the ground slopes down to the gulf, for it must be remembered that there is a watershed between the neighbourhood of the Pagasæan gulf and every other part of Thessaly. Thus, in coming thither from Thaumaci and the south-western district, a bay of the plain is first entered, which gradually narrows as it leads up to Pharsalus, and forms the plain of Pharsalia, intersected by the Enipeus. After this, leaving on your left the scene of another great battle, Cynoscephalæ, and traversing upland plains and wide valleys, you reach a low pass, from which there is a gradual descent to Pagasæ. In the heroic age the region of Phthiotis was of great importance. There, as Thucydides tells us, was the early home of the Hellenic race,[13] and from thence was sprung the great Achilles, as we read in the Homeric catalogue—

οἵ τ' εἶχον Φθίην ἠδ' Ἑλλάδα καλλιγύναικα,
Μυρμιδόνες δὲ καλεῦντο καὶ Ἕλληνες καὶ Ἀχαιοί·
τῶν αὖ πεντήκοντα νεῶν ἦν ἀρχὸς Ἀχιλλεύς.[14]

The Pelasgian Argos, which is mentioned in the same passage, is probably the same town that was subsequently called, from its steep, hanging position, Larissa Cremaste,[15] of which fine remains are to be seen on the southern slopes of Othrys, facing Eubœa, for

[13] Thuc. i. 3.   [14] Hom. *Il.* ii. 683.
[15] Bursian, *Geographie von Griechenland*, i. 64, 82, note.

this district also was included in Phthiotis. The Pagasæan gulf, too, is to be regarded as the cradle of Greek navigation, for it cannot be accident that has placed the fable of the Argonauts in these parts, the pine tree from which the Argo was made being spoken of as cut from the forests of Pelion, and the names of Pagasæ and Aphetæ being supposed to be derived from the building ($\pi\eta\gamma\nu\nu\mu\iota$) and the starting ($\dot{\alpha}\varphi\dot{\iota}\eta\mu\iota$) of that vessel.[16] The site of Iolcos, the centre of so many poetic legends, is on a hill with a rocky summit for its acropolis, which projects towards the head of the gulf from the side of Pelion. The city itself had been destroyed long before Strabo wrote.[17] In the later history of Greece this neighbourhood again rose to importance on account of the foundation of the city of Demetrias by the great Demetrius Poliorcetes, who called it one of the three fetters of Greece, Chalcis and Corinth being the other two. The position of this was within a mile of Iolcos, on a conspicuous mass of rocky ground, which projects into the sea between two small plains, thus commanding the approach to Thessaly from this side.

Passes leading into Thessaly. The passes which lead through the Thessalian mountains were of the first importance, both to that country and to the rest of Greece. On the side of Macedonia the first to be noticed is Tempe, which, from the length and narrowness of the ravine, was a position easily defended, but still offered a practicable

[16] Strabo, ix. 5, § 15.   [17] Ibid.

entrance to an invading force, in consequence of which a number of castles were built at different times at the strongest points. This was the only approach by land from the east, but it was possible, though difficult, for an army landed on the coast at the point of junction of Pelion and Ossa, to force its way over the depression between those mountains; and this explains the importance of the city of Melibœa, the same from which the famous purple came, because that place overlooks the pass, and is thus described by Livy[18] as "conveniently situated to command Demetrias;" (opportune imminens super Demetriadem), that is to say, it was fitted to enable an enemy to turn it and cut off its communications with Macedonia by way of Tempe. On the north there was an important pass from Petra in Pieria by the western side of Olympus, debouching on the Thessalian plain northward of Larissa; this it was by which Xerxes entered, and we learn from Herodotus that when the Greeks discovered the existence of this passage they gave up all thoughts of defending Tempe.[19] It is somewhat strangely described by the historian as entering the plain at Gonnus, whereas that place lies far eastward of the route, and a range of steep mountains intervenes. The only explanation that I know is, that Xerxes had to turn aside in order to occupy Tempe, and that this is loosely described by Herodotus as entering the plain near

[18] xliv. 13.   [19] Herod. vii. 173; cf. 128.

Gonnus.[20] On the side of Epirus the main line of communication passed over Mount Lacmon, and descended the vale of the Peneius to Æginium in the north-west angle of Thessaly, near which place now stand the extraordinary monasteries of Meteora. This was the route by which Julius Cæsar arrived before the battle of Pharsalia. The only other pass through the Pindus chain was that of Gomphi, further to the south; by means of this, which was occupied by the consul Flamininus in the war with Philip, there is communication with the Ambracian gulf.[21] The great southern pass was that of Cœla, already mentioned, which descends from Mount Othrys nearly opposite Thermopylæ; and it was the chief reason of the importance of Pharsalus that it commanded the approach to it.

The western countries. Little need be said of the countries which compose the west of Greece—Illyria, Epirus, Acarnania, and Ætolia—because they were only slightly Hellenised, and being composed of irregular masses of rugged mountains, and possessing few harbours, they presented few opportunities for Hellenic development. The very name of Epirus, or "The Continent," shows how completely that country was regarded as a land apart, since it implies that it was only known through the medium of the outlying islands. On the coast of Illyria, north of the Acroceraunian promontory, we

[20] Heuzey, *Le Mont Olympe*, p. 17.
[21] Livy, xxxii. 14, 15.

find here and there plai 3 near the coast, of some extent, watered by considerable rivers, of which the Aous was the chief; the exports which these afforded caused the prosperity of the neighbouring Corinthian colonies of Epidamnus and Apollonia. These two places, the former of them under the name of Dyrrhachium, became at a later period the two starting-points of the Via Egnatia. Epirus comprised three districts: in the north-west Chaonia, including the country opposite Corcyra, as far south as the river Thyamis; to the east, away from the sea, Molottis; while the whole of the south was called Thesprotia. In this region, otherwise so barren of interest, there was one place of the highest importance, Dodona. But concerning the site of this great oracle we have no certain evidence; no ruins have been found which can be identified with it, and we learn nothing about it from ancient geographers. In the first place, it is to be observed that in the earliest times there were two Dodonas—one in the north of Thessaly, close to Mount Olympus, which is mentioned in the Iliad, in the catalogue of ships,[22] and is described as being near the Titaresius, and in the country of the Perrhæbi; the other, the well-known one in Epirus, which is referred to in the Odyssey.[23] Whether Achilles, when he invokes Pelasgian Zeus from Dodona,[24] refers to the place in Thessaly, is still

<small>Site of Dodona.</small>

---

[22] *Il.* ii. 750.   [23] *Od.* xiv. 327.
[24] *Il.* xvi. 233. Cf. *Dict. Geog.* "Dodona;" Bursian, *Geo-*

doubtful, for we hear of no sanctuary near that spot. The oracle is described by Hesiod as being in a land of meadows and corn-fields,[25] which is an uncommon feature of the country in rugged Epirus; and this, together with other notices in ancient writers from which we can obtain an approximate idea of its position, makes it probable that it was situated near the Lacus Pambotis, the modern lake of Joannina.[26] The features of this spot, at all events,—the huge mountains on one side, the pastoral uplands on the other, and the fine expanse of water—are of that impressive character which the races of this peninsula usually chose for their holy places. The city of Dodona probably stood on a rocky height at the southern end of the lake (hill of Castritza), where ancient walls are found; as to the exact site of the oracle we are left to conjecture. It is, no doubt, an objection to this view, that no lake is mentioned by ancient authors in connection with Dodona, but that there was water near is implied by Strabo's saying that some persons derived the name of the neighbouring region, Hellopia, from the marshes about the sanctu-

graphie von Griechenland, i. 23 ; E. Curtius, *History of Greece*, i. 105, *sub fin.*

[25] Hesiod, ap. Schol. ad Soph. *Trach.* 1167.

ἔστι τις Ἑλλοπίη, πολυλήϊος ἠδ' εὐλείμων,
ἀφνειὴ μήλοισι καὶ εἰλιπόδεσσι βόεσσιν.
ἐν δ' ἄνδρες ναίουσι πολύρρηνες, πολυβοῦται,
πολλοί, ἀπειρέσιοι, φῦλα θνητῶν ἀνθρώπων·
ἐνθάδε Δωδώνη τις ἐπ' ἐσχατιῇ πεπόλισται.

[26] See Leake, *Northern Greece*, iv. 168 foll.

ary (ἀπὸ τῶν ἑλῶν τῶν περὶ τὸ ἱερόν).²⁷ The fact that both the collective names of the Greek people are found in this district, seems to imply that it was an early Hellenic centre. Of the name Hellene we find traces in Hellopia and in Helli, the priests who attended on the oracle and lived in the neighbourhood, and from whom the country seems to have received its name. That of Greeks (Γραϊκοί) is said by Aristotle²⁸ to have been an earlier name for those afterwards called Hellenes, and to have been applied to them in this neighbourhood. It seems to have meant "the old people," a title apparently claimed as an honour by those who used it.²⁹ As the Italian tribes universally applied this name to the inhabitants of the neighbouring peninsula, we must suppose that it was carried from Epirus across the Adriatic, in the course of early communications between the two countries.³⁰ The migration of the Thessalians from their early home on this side of the Pindus, which we have noticed as originating so many movements in Greece, seems to have been the main cause of the wide

---

²⁷ vii. 7, § 10.

²⁸ *Meteor.* i. 14, § 22 ; ed. Ideler.

²⁹ Bursian, *Geographie*, i. 2, *note* (1). The name would thus be connected with γέρων, γῆρας, γραῦς. Bergk has suggested a similar derivation for the name Pelasgian—Πελασγός being for Παλάσιος. (*Literaturgeschichte*, i. 93.)

³⁰ E. Curtius, *History of Greece*, i. 104 ; Bursian, *ubi supra* ; Thirlwall, *History of Greece*, i. 82 (1st ed.)

diffusion of the worship of Zeus of Dodona,[31] and of the respect for his oracle in later times, as well as of the prominent character assumed in the mythology by such features of the country as the Achelous and the Acheron.

[31] Curtius, *Hist.* i. 105.

LECTURE VII.

GEOGRAPHY OF CENTRAL GREECE.

Malis—Pass of Thermopylæ—Northern Locris and Doris—Phocis—Delphi : its Influence ; its remarkable Position ; the surrounding Cliffs—Bœotia : its two Basins—Orchomenus—Thebes—Chalcis and the Euripus—The Passes leading South—Megaris—Attica—Seats of the three Political Parties—Athens : its Site ; the Acropolis ; Areiopagus ; Pnyx ; Dionysiac Theatre ; other Sites.

WE proceed now to the districts south of Thessaly. From the foot of Mount Typhrestus the wide fertile valley of the Spercheius runs eastward to the head of the Maliac gulf, separating by a deep depression the parallel ranges of Othrys and Œta. The south-eastern portion of this, which lies between the cliffs of Œta and the sea, was called by the name of Malis, and Malis. this extended from a little northward of the stream of the Spercheius to the further limit of the pass of Thermopylæ. The three tribes into which, as we learn from Thucydides,[1] the inhabitants were divided—Paralians, Hieres, and Trachinians—seem to have been a territorial division, the Paralians being the inhabitants of the sea-coast, and the Trachinians those of the rude mountain slopes, corresponding to the

[1] iii. 92.

Hyperacrii of Attica. Who the Hieres were is not so clear, but as Callimachus speaks of a sacred city of the Melians,[2] it is likely enough that they were the occupants of this. But the great importance of this region consisted in its containing the key of Greece in the pass of Thermopylæ. In examining the topography of this, we must bear in mind that a great change has taken place in the ground between ancient and modern times, so that the pass does not now exist; for whereas in ancient times the sea washed the foot of the mountains, and the strength of the position depended on the difficulty of the passage between the two, at the present day the alluvium of the Spercheius has so advanced the line of the plain as to allow of leaving the mountains altogether, and traversing the level ground. The river also has changed its course, and has worked towards the south, so as to approach the foot of Mount Œta, the effect of which is that the streams which here descend from the mountains, including the Asopus, and the water from the springs at Thermopylæ, instead of flowing into the sea have become its confluents. The deposit from the hot springs has also tended to render the route more level. To describe the neighbourhood of the pass more accurately—in approaching from the north-west the narrow channels of the Dyras and Melas are first crossed, and then the Asopus is reached,

Pass of Thermopylæ.

---

[2] Callim. *Hymn. in Del.* 287 (ἱερὸν ἄστυ καὶ οὔρεα Μηλίδος αἴης), where, however, Meineke conjectures Ἱρέων.

just below where it issues from a deep gorge. At the foot of the heights to the west of this stream stood the city of Trachis, where Xerxes established his camp,[3] and somewhat higher up is the site of Heracleia, the garrison town founded by the Spartans during the Peloponnesian war.[4] It was by the gorge of the Asopus that Hydarnes commenced his ascent of the mountains, which, when continued through the forests on the upper slopes facing Doris, resulted in his descending on the rear of the Greeks; and not far from the same point is the starting-place of the pass that leads through Doris to the Crissæan gulf. On the further bank of the Asopus a considerable spur is pushed forward from the mountains above, just where a rivulet of red and lukewarm water, strongly tinctured with iron—which for this reason was called the Phœnix—enters the plain. At this point the pass commenced, for the sea then flowed where there are reedy marshes now; but though, as Herodotus[5] remarks, it was narrowest here, yet it could easily be turned by crossing the low heights behind. Further on is a sloping level of considerable extent, the plain of Anthele, lying between the lower plain and the steep precipices of Mount Callidromus, or Anopæa; at the eastern end of this the hot springs gush out from the foot of the mountain. Just beyond these is the true pass of Thermopylæ, where

[3] Herod. vii. 201.   [4] Thuc. iii. 92.
[5] Herod. vii. 200.

a very narrow path runs between a slight precipice and a conical hillock, above which again the ground rises in rough slopes. It was across this path that the wall of defence was built, and the hillock is the reputed burial-place of the Spartans, though in reality it is of natural formation, being the scene of their final resistance, as described by Herodotus.[6] To the east of this the ground opens out, and becomes comparatively level, and there are practicable paths from the heights above, by one of which Hydarnes must have descended.

Northern Locris and Doris. The lofty rugged mountains, which form an easterly continuation of Mount Œta, overlooking the Maliac gulf, bore the name of Cnemis in ancient times, and were the seat of the Epicnemidian Locrians. Their position was important, because through them led the road which connected Thermopylæ with southern Greece, descending into the plains of Phocis at Elateia. When once an invader had crossed this pass, Bœotia and Attica lay open before him, and this explains the consternation felt at Athens when the capture of Elateia by Philip was announced, as depicted in the famous passage of the *De Corona*. Beyond Mount Cnemis again, and facing the Euboic gulf, was the country of the Opuntian Locrians, a people little known in history, but who must have attained a high degree of civilisation, for their silver coins are the most beautiful in execution of the many beautiful

[6] Herod. vii. 225.

coins of Greece. Between them and the Epicnemidian Locrians, and nearly opposite the promontory of Cenæum, in Eubœa, a narrow strip of Phocian territory intervened, giving that people the advantage of communication with the sea at the port of Daphnus. The other branch of the Locrian race — a people " scattered and peeled," for they were broken up at the time of the emigration of the Bœotians from Thessaly[7]—was the Locri Ozolæ, who occupied the southeast of Ætolia, bordering on the Corinthian and Crissæan gulfs. On the eastern border of their territory, in the deep valley which lies beneath the western buttresses of Parnassus, was another important pass, leading from the Crissæan gulf into Doris, from whence a steep track led over Mount Callidromus, descending, as I have already mentioned, to the plain of Malis, near Trachis. It was by this that Demosthenes, the Athenian general in the Peloponnesian war, proposed to march from Ætolia, in order to pass through Doris and join the Phocians, in whose company he was to invade Bœotia.[8] Finally, to mention the last and least of these small territories—Doris, which at one time was the seat of the Dorian race, lay at the back of Parnassus, between that mountain and Œta, a confined upland district, containing the head waters of the Cephisus, and closely connected with Phocis by that river. It possessed only four towns, which were formed into a Tetrapolis.

[7] Niebuhr, *Lectures on Ethnography and Geography*, i. 123.
[8] Thuc. iii. 95.

Phocis. Phocis naturally divides into two parts—the upper valley of the Cephisus, and the mountain region of Parnassus. The former of these interposes between Doris and western Bœotia, being an open and gradually sloping district, surrounded on all sides by mountains, far the most conspicuous being Parnassus, which is distinguished from all other Greek mountains by its mighty mass. This, with its vast buttresses, almost fills up the rest of the country. On its southern side, exactly opposite Delphi, an offshoot, Mount Cirphis, interposes between it and the Corinthian gulf, and between them, running from east to west, the river Pleistus finds its way into the head of the bay of Crissa. This valley was the line of the famous Σχιστὴ ὁδός, which is generally considered to have been so called from the Triodos, or meeting of three roads; but it may have originally received the name from the gash or rent so deeply cut in the mountains. Of the three roads, one led to Daulis, another to Thebes, and the third to Delphi; when Œdipus met and slew his father at this spot, Laius was coming from Thebes, and he from Delphi. As regards politics, the principal source of the power of the Phocians was their influence over the Delphic oracle, which lay within their territories. Hence, at the time of the Persian wars, when we find the Pythia giving doubtful counsels, we may look for an explanation to the views of Phocis; and during the Peloponnesian war, as the Phocians, from enmity to their neighbours the Bœotians, at first sided with the Athenians, it was stipulated by the Spartans at the peace of Nicias that Delphi should be independent of Phocis.[9]

Delphi, in its present state, has been described as "the grave of an extinct religion;"[10] and certainly no place in Greece was so representative in respect of its religious influence. By the Greeks it was regarded as the ὀμφαλός, the navel of the whole world; and undoubtedly it was the most central point of the Hellenic race. "It is in a sense in the middle of all Greece," says Strabo; "both that within and that without the Isthmus, and they called it the earth's navel, adding to this a story which Pindar relates, that the eagles that were let go by Zeus, the one from the west, the other from the east, met at this point."[11] It was, for a time at least, the one power that held the Greek states together, and counteracted the "centrifugal" tendencies of Greek politics. Throughout Greek history, except at certain periods, when it fell under the influence of leading families, or its agents were corrupted by bribes, we see this oracle guiding the helm of affairs; and while the individual states were occupied with their separate interests, it takes thought for them all, endeavours to preserve harmony between them, becomes a referee in dis-

Delphi—its influence.

---

[9] Thuc. v. 18.
[10] Dean Stanley, in Wyse's *Impressions of Greece*, p. 331.
[11] Strabo, ix. 3, § 6.

puted questions, presides over the extension of the Hellenic name in foreign lands, as in the foundation of the colony of Cyrene,[12] upholds a lofty tone of morality in private dealings, as in the answer to Glaucus, son of Epicydes,[13] cheers the spirits of the Greeks when terrified by the prospect of invasion, and diffuses far and wide the practical wisdom of its responses. By means of the position thus acquired, Delphi became much more than an oracle. The sanctity of the place, and its consequent inviolability, caused it to be a place of deposit, where property was left, as in a modern bank; though in the time of Pausanias, and even as early as that of Strabo, this had come to an end owing to the poverty of the country.[14] From being a great place of resort, also, it was a focus of information on all subjects relating to politics, commerce, and foreign relations; so that those who presided over the oracle not only assumed, but possessed, a more far-reaching view than others, and by means of this, and of the experience drawn from a long-accumulated store of precedents, in a great number of instances justified the belief that their god, the interpreter of Zeus, could penetrate the future.

Its remarkable position.

The aspect of Delphi and its vicinity was not less remarkable than its influence. Like others of the most

[12] Herod. iv. 159. Compare what is said of Dorieus, Herod. v. 42.   [13] Herod. vi. 86.
[14] Strabo, ix. 3, § 8; Paus. x. 11, § 1.

important early Hellenic sanctuaries, Dodona and Delos, it would seem to have been chosen for the loneliness and consequent sublimity of its position, in spite of its barrenness. This is implied with regard to Delos by the passage in the Homeric hymn,[15] where Latona is described as visiting all the richest spots in the Ægean before giving birth to her children; but all were afraid to receive her, so that she betook herself to the small and rugged island. In like manner, when the Cretan navigators arrive at Delphi, their first question is how they are to subsist in so unfruitful a spot; but the god answers that they have no need to provide, for where his worship is established, the sacrifices will always be an ample maintenance for his priests.[16] If the traveller approaches, as these its first founders did, according to the legend, from the side of the Corinthian gulf, the snowy peaks of Parnassus will everywhere be in view, acting as a landmark to guide him to his destination. He then turns aside into the narrower Crissæan gulf, which, like so many of the bays in Greece, is bounded by rugged mountains except at its northern end, where a maritime plain, also deeply sunk, extends for some distance inland. On the sea-coast, near the mouth of the Pleistus, lay Cirrha, the port of Delphi; while at the head of the plain, on the side of a buttress of Parnassus, was Crissa, its guardian city. The plain itself,

[15] *Hymn. in Apoll. Del.*, 30 *seq.* Compare Mure, *Tour in Greece*, i. 178. [16] *In Apoll. Pyth.*, 348 *seq.*

which now is covered with vineyards and olive groves, in ancient times was uncultivated, for it was the consecrated land, the subsequent cause of a sacred war, which was forbidden to be devoted to common purposes. When Sophocles speaks of it as "fed by cattle" (βούνομον ἀκτάν), he must refer to its affording pasturage for the oxen used in sacrifice.[17] Near its head, where the gorge of the Pleistus opens out into the level land, was the hippodrome, where the chariot races took place at the Pythian games; and the position of this explains what is meant in the *Electra*, when it is said that "the whole Crissæan plain was filled with the wrecks of chariots."[18] The ordinary approach to Delphi was either by Crissa, or along the mountain slopes ascending from the east, by which way both the Persians and the Gauls arrived on the occasion of the two famous attacks upon the sanctuary. If, however, we follow the Pleistus upwards for a little distance, we find that it is joined by a copious stream of clear water, which descends from the northern heights in a succession of cataracts through an excessively steep valley. This is Castalia.

The surrounding cliffs. At the head of this valley, 1500 feet above the plain, a lofty precipitous escarpment of red and grey limestone runs along facing the south; this in old times bore the name of Phædriades, or the "gleaming peaks," a title which is especially applicable to them at sunrise, when all below is in shadow, according to the

[17] Soph. *El.* 181; see Mure, *Tour*, i. 181.   [18] Soph. *El.* 730.

splendid description in the *Ion* of Euripides:—"The inaccessible summits of Parnassus, brightly shining, mirror to men the car of day"—

> Παρνησιάδες δ' ἄβατοι κορυφαὶ
> καταλαμπόμεναι τὴν ἡμερίαν
> ἀψῖδα βροτοῖσι δέχονται.[19]

The echo from these, we are told, especially when bands of men approached with musical instruments, increased the awe inspired by the spot.[20] At one point in this line of cliffs, just where Castalia rises, the rocks fall back and form an obtuse angle, on either side of which stands up a conspicuous peak, the δίλοφος πέτρα of Sophocles[21]—a title which the Latin poets misunderstood, for when they speak of *biceps Parnassus,* or in other ways enlarge their description of the scene, they suppose these to be the summits of that mountain, whereas Parnassus rises to a single peak, which is many thousand feet above Delphi. At the angle there runs in a deep chasm, only a few feet in width, and at the end of this a cascade, 200 feet in height, falls over the rocks in the winter time; the water from this is joined by the Castalian fountain, which rises at the foot of Mount Hyampeia, the easternmost of the two just mentioned, and the same from which the rocks were hurled by the Delphians on the heads of the Persians. The ground that slopes from this point towards the valley, and is well com-

[19] Eur. *Ion,* 86.   [20] Justin. *Hist.* xxiv. 6.   [21] *Ant.* 1126.

pared by Strabo[22] to the form of a theatre, was the site of the city of Delphi. The description in the Homeric hymn is accurate:—" Above, the rock overhangs, and a hollow rugged gorge runs underneath"—

—— ὕπερθεν
πέτρη ἐπικρέμαται, κοίλη δ' ὑποδέδρομε βῆσσα,
τρηχεῖα.[23]

The position was naturally protected on the two sides, for Mount Hyampeia is continued downwards towards the valley of the Pleistus, while the opposite height, under which the temple and oracle lay, projects westwards for some distance, but then returns at right angles. Thus, from whichever side it is approached, it bursts suddenly into view; and at a time when the whole area was crowded with magnificent buildings, we can easily understand that the effect was overpowering. The temple occupied one of the highest points, close to the foot of the cliffs, and, from the time when it was rebuilt of white marble by the Alcmæonidæ, must have had a splendid appearance. Fragments of columns of that material are still to be seen on the site of the sacred enclosure, those of the Doric order having belonged to the peristyle, the Ionic to the cella.[24] Behind the temple is the fountain of Cassotis. We must, I suppose, regard it as accident that a laurel is now growing on this spot, and a plane-tree, the only one

[22] ix. 3, § 3.   [23] *Ap. Pyth.* 105.
[24] *Dict. Geog.* i. 766*a*.

in the neighbourhood, by Castalia, whereas Agamemnon is believed to have planted one in this region.[25] Near Cassotis was the famous Lesche, decorated with the pictures of Polygnotus; and west of this again were the theatre and stadium, together with the third fountain of this well-watered district, called Delphusa. Not the least striking object in the view is the grand chain of Mount Cirphis, which rises on the opposite side of the Pleistus. Lastly, we must notice the unfavourable climate of Delphi, which is exposed to burning heat in the summer, from the rocks reflecting the sun, and to storms, from the winds drawing up the valley. Both on the occasion of the Persian and Gaulish attack, the invaders were overtaken by a thunderstorm.

Between Phocis and Attica, extending from the Corinthian to the Euboic sea, was the important country of Bœotia. This was composed of two basins or valleys, the chief towns of which were Orchomenus and Thebes respectively; and, accordingly, it is on these two places that the internal history of the district turns, the former having been the more important during the heroic age, the latter in the subsequent period. How powerful Bœotia was, and how great were the resources of this region, may be seen from the names of important towns which it contained; in the neighbourhood of Or-

Bœotia—its two basins.

[25] Theophrastus, *Hist. Plant.* iv. 14. See Ulrichs, *Reisen in Griechenland,* i. p. 50.

chomenus—Chæroneia, Lebadeia, Coroneia, and Haliartus; in the district of Thebes—Thespiæ, Platæa, and Tanagra. The mountains that inclose it are—Helicon, towards the Corinthian gulf; Cithæron and Parnes, on the side of Attica; and a continuation of the Opuntian mountains towards the Euripus; from Phocis it is separated by spurs from the neighbouring chains; and on this side is the most important pass by which it can be entered—viz., the defile through which the Cephisus flows from the neighbourhood of Elateia, entering the basin of the Copais near Chæroneia. It is for this reason that the plain in the neighbourhood of that city was always a famous battlefield. As has been already remarked, the Copaic lake, into which all the rivers of the region of Orchomenus drained, had no outlet for its waters except the catavothras, either natural or artificial. It was in the time of the Minyæ that the chief power in Bœotia was centred here; but they were crushed by the inroad of the Bœotians, who at the same time ejected the Cadmeians from Thebes, and made that place their capital. The position of Orchomenus and its citadel is so characteristic a specimen of the sites the Greeks preferred, and of their military architecture, that it deserves to be described. It is situated on the last spur of Mount Acontium, in a position untenable in modern warfare, because it is commanded by the heights behind, but safe in ancient times, because it was out of bowshot

<small>Orchomenus</small>

in that quarter: at its foot the Cephisus flowed round two sides of the hill, while the third was defended by the marshes of another river, the Melas. The city was widest at its lowest part, and the wall that here ran across formed the base of the triangle, of which the acropolis at the summit was the apex. Between the lower wall and the river was a building called the Treasury of Minyas, of which only a gateway now remains, with two uprights, and an immense slab lying on them. Pausanias[26] speaks of it as one of the wonders of the world. From the lower wall two other walls run along the cliffs on the two sides, with towers at intervals, inclosing a large space of ground, and gradually approaching one another as the hill-side becomes steeper. At last, when they are not more than seventy feet apart, they run parallel to one another for some distance to the foot of the citadel. These walls, like all Greek fortifications, are of the finest stonework, being composed of large squared blocks, fitted together without mortar; and here they are laid in parallel courses. Usually we can discover in the acropolis the original *polis*, as at Athens, to which, at a later time, the lower city was added; but here, owing to the remarkable narrowness and sharpness of the summit, there is only a castle, which, however, is of immense strength. The access to it from the city was by a number of extremely steep steps cut out of the

[26] ix. 38, § 2.

rock; the first forty-four of these run obliquely along the cliff, while the last fifty ascend in a straight line. The castle was defended by strong walls, and divided into towers. From it, as from a watch-tower, the whole of the neighbouring basin could be seen.

Thebes.

The other district of Bœotia, that of Thebes, though composed of irregular plains, and hemmed in by mountains, is not a complete basin in the same sense as the neighbourhood of Orchomenus. The greater part of it is the valley of the Asopus, which flows past Tanagra into the Euboic sea; but Thebes lies in a separate plain of its own. The position of that city, on a low spur of ground projecting northward from the hills behind, and overlooking the plain, is one of the least striking in Greece. The two clear streams which flow on either side of it are those of Dirce and Ismenus. The level ground, which we have noticed as occupying so large a part of the surface of this district, accounts for the importance of the Theban cavalry; and hence, too, it arose that commanders who were strong in that arm selected Bœotia as their fighting-ground. This was the reason why Mardonius retired thither before the battle of Platæa.[27] The political conduct of Thebes, and especially her alliances, were mainly determined by opposition to her neighbour Athens. But, notwithstanding the greatness of her power—for no other Greek

[27] Herod. ix. 13.

state played an equally prominent part during so long a period—her advantageous position between two seas, and on the highroad between northern and southern Greece, seems to have been neutralised by the effect of the heavy Bœotian climate.

One other place should be noticed in this connection, the city of Chalcis, in the neighbouring island of Eubœa. Ephorus remarked that nature might almost be said to have made that island part of Bœotia, because the Euripus was so narrow, and was spanned by a bridge.[28] This bridge was first constructed in the twenty-first year of the Peloponnesian war, when Eubœa revolted from Athens, and was the work of the Bœotians, who thus contrived to make that country "an island to every one but themselves."[29] The power of injuring Athens which they thus obtained was incalculable, because, besides depriving them of the resources of that rich island, they blocked up the line of their traffic from the north of the Ægean, thus cutting off their supplies of gold and corn from Thrace, of timber from Macedonia, and of horses from Thessaly; for by this route the Athenians used to avoid the dangers of Caphareus and the eastern coast of the island. The strait is about 120 feet broad, and is divided in the middle by a rock, on which now stands a castle. The channel towards Bœotia is spanned by

Chalcis and the Euripus.

---

[28] Strabo, ix. 2, § 2.
[29] Diod. Sic. xiii. 47. See Wordsworth, *Athens and Attica*, p. 2.

a stone bridge, that towards Chalcis by one of wood. The latter is by far the deeper channel, and here it is that the extraordinary changes of the tide take place which have excited so much wonder from classical times to the present day, and are not yet explained. Strabo[30] speaks of them as varying seven times in the day, but Livy[31] is more accurate in saying that they are irregular. As you stand on the bridge you may see the water running in one direction like a rapid river, and shortly afterwards it will be taking the opposite course with equal rapidity. These are the "refluent tides of Aulis" (παλίρροχθοι Αὐλίδος τόποι), of which Æschylus[32] speaks; and the "groaning strait" (στονόεντα πορθμόν) of Sophocles.[33] Euripides also mentions the winding eddies of Euripus.[34] From the channel (αὐλός) the neighbouring town of Aulis probably received its name.

It remains now to speak of the country, which, taking for its base the mountains that form the southern limit of Bœotia, projects towards the south-east into the Ægean Sea. The westernmost portion of this, which lies between the Corinthian and Saronic gulfs, was occupied by the district of Megaris, while the remainder, from its length of coast-line, bore the name of Acte or Attica. But, in reality, the entire area forms one geographical whole; and in like manner, in early times, before the Dorian invasion,

---

[30] i. 3, § 12.　[31] xxviii. 6.　[32] *Ag.* 91.　[33] *Ant.* 1145.
[34] *Iph. Taur.* 6-9.

which resulted in the foundation of Megara, it was one politically, being in the hands of the Ionian race. This is proved by the column which once stood on the isthmus, bearing on one side the inscription, "This land is Peloponnesus, not Ionia"—

τάδ' ἐστὶ Πελοπόννησος, οὐκ 'Ιωνία—

and on the other, "This land is not Peloponnesus, but Ionia—

τάδ' οὐχὶ Πελοπόννησος, ἀλλ' 'Ιωνία—

and this, as Strabo remarks,[35] explains the absence of the Megarians from the Homeric catalogue. Of the formidable mountain barrier which extends from the Corinthian to the Euboic sea, the western half is formed by Cithæron, the eastern by Parnes; but Cithæron is also bent round at right angles in the direction of the isthmus, at the northern approach to which it abuts against the mighty transverse block of Mount Geraneia, which occupies the whole country from sea to sea. Three roads lead from northern Greece into the Peloponnese in this direction: one along the shores of the Corinthian gulf, which, owing to the nature of the ground, makes a long detour; the other two starting from Megara, and passing, the one by a lofty though gradual route over the ridge of Geraneia, the other along the Saronic gulf, under the dangerous precipices of the Scironian rocks. Between Bœotia and Attica there were three passes: over Cithæ-

The passes leading south.

[35] ix. 1, § 5.

ron that of Dryoscephalæ, or the "Oakheads," leading from Thebes by Platæa to Eleusis, which we hear of in connection with the battle of Platæa, and with the escape of the Platæans at the time of the siege;[36] a second over Parnes, from Delium and Oropus to Athens by Deceleia, the usual route of the invading Lacedæmonians during the Peloponnesian war; the third midway between the two, and not far from the point of junction of the two mountains—the pass of Phyle, near the summit of which, on rugged heights overlooking the Athenian plain, is the massive fort occupied by Thrasybulus in the days of the Thirty Tyrants.

The conformation of the rest of the country is determined by the mountains, which run down to the sea at right angles to the main chain, thus dividing Attica into a succession of plains. The westernmost of these is the territory of Megara, and is bounded on the one side by the Geraneian chain, and on the other by a line of hills, at the southern end of which rise the two conspicuous peaks called Cerata or "the Horns." The city was built on and between two low hills which rise out of the plain rather more than a mile from the sea; and as it had the port of Pagæ on the Corinthian as well as that of Nisæa on the Saronic gulf, we can at once discover its importance, as it commanded both seas, and all the passes into the Peloponnese. Its early prosperity is attested by its

Megaris.

---

[36] Herod. ix. 39; Thuc. iii. 24.

numerous colonies, amongst which we may notice Megara Hyblæa in the far west, and Byzantium in the far east, and by the encouragement it lent to the fine arts, as being the birthplace of comedy. Its policy was determined by its position between the two powerful states of Corinth and Athens; for, while the latter of these was its hereditary foe, the former often alienated it by its domineering assumptions. At the same time, though the Athenians never forgot that Megaris formed a part of their rightful territory, yet the importance of friendly relations between them was sufficiently great to draw them frequently together. Of this we have ample evidence in the fact, that between the Persian and Peloponnesian wars the Athenians built the long walls from Megara to Nisæa, to facilitate their communication with them by sea; and also in the famished state of the Megarians, when excluded from the ports and markets of Attica, so ludicrously described by Aristophanes in the *Acharnians*.[37]

The position of Nisæa, and of the fortified island of Minoa in its neighbourhood, is a well-known difficulty; but I have little doubt that the island is to be recognised in a conical hill on the sea-coast, about a mile from the city, which would agree with the statement of Thucydides,[38] that the long walls from Megara to Nisæa were eight stadia in length. This, though not now surrounded by water, must once have

[37] Ar. *Acharn.* 729 foll.   [38] iv. 66.

been so, before two streams, which reached the sea at this point, were diverted in another direction. The remains of buildings on the coast to the east of this must mark the site of Nisæa. It is evident from the account in Thucydides[39] that Minoa must have been quite close to the mainland and also to Nisæa.

Attica

Next in order to the plain of Megara came that of Eleusis, the eastern part of which was called the Thriasian plain. Opposite to the seaboard of this, and separated from it by a narrow strait, which forms a succession of graceful bays, was the island of Salamis; and between it and the plain of Athens rose the long ridge of Ægaleos, through a depression in which was the line of the Sacred Way where the torchlight processions used to descend to the coast, the "bright gleaming shores" (λαμπάδες ἀκταί) of Sophocles.[40] The Athenian plain, which was similarly enclosed on the east and west by Hymettus and Ægaleos, presents the same features, especially the light thin soil, which caused Athena's gift of the olive to be so greatly esteemed in Attica. On the western side, towards Ægaleos, the course of the Cephisus is marked by a broad belt of dark green, formed by the groves of Colonus and the gardens of the Academus; and the site of Colonus itself is distinguished by two bare knolls of light-coloured earth, the ἀργῆτα Κολωνόν of

---

[39] iii. 51. See Spratt's plan in the *Dictionary of Geography*, ii. 315.

[40] *Œd. Col.* 1049.

the poet,[41]—not chalky, as the expositors of that passage often describe it to be. On the sea-coast, between the closed harbour of Piræus and the open roadstead of Phalerum, there rises a mass of rocky ground, the hill of Munychia, which forms the acropolis of the town of Piræus. The position of this so commands the approach to Athens from the sea, that it is not far from the truth that he who holds the hill of Munychia must also be master of Athens. The harbour of Munychia was formed by a small bight at the foot of this hill, on the eastern side towards Phalerum; between this and Piræus was another commodious harbour called Zea. The harbour of Piræus itself forms the third of the three natural havens which Thucydides[42] speaks of as constituting the advantage of this port, and is so perfect of its kind, that it is difficult to explain how even the greater nearness of Phalerum to Athens should have caused this admirable basin to be neglected in early times, for it is safe, deep, and spacious, and its entrance is defended by the tongue of land called Eetionia projecting from the northern side to meet the corresponding prominence of the Piræic peninsula, and was still further narrowed by moles, and in time of war could be closed by a chain, in which respects Arnold[43] compares it, and similar harbours in Greece, to the ports of some of the towns on

[41] Soph. *Œd. Col.* 670.
[42] i. 93.
[43] Note to Thucyd. viii. 90.

the Italian lakes. The basin of Piræus was again subdivided into two parts: the great harbour, and the inlet on the southern side called Cantharus, or the "Beetle," which penetrated into the rocky peninsula, and, together with the harbour of Zea on the opposite side, almost divided it in two. It is on this name that Aristophanes plays in the *Pax*, where he represents Trygæus, mounted on his monster beetle, as saying that, in case of his falling into the sea, "there is a beetle's harbour in Piræus."[44] This harbour, together with those of Zea and Munychia, was reserved for vessels of war, while the rest of the Piræus was devoted to merchant vessels. The whole peninsula of Piræus, both on the land and sea side, was defended by fortifications according to the plans of Themistocles, and was connected by a massive wall with the city of Athens, while at the same time another wall was carried from that place to the eastern side of the bay of Phalerum. These were the original Long Walls; the third, which connected the eastern side of the fortifications of Piræus towards Munychia with the city, thus rendering the port-town with its harbours completely a part of the upper town, was added later by the advice of Pericles.

Seats of the three political parties. At the southern extremity of Hymettus, where that mountain projects into the sea, is the promontory of Zoster, on rounding which the traveller who approaches from the direction of Sunium first comes

---

[44] Ar. *Pax*, 145.

in sight of Athens. The northern extremity of that range is not directly connected with Parnes; between them Pentelicus intervenes, and the foot of Pentelicus is separated from Hymettus by an interval of two miles. This level space forms the entrance to the Mesogæa, an elevated undulating plain in the midst of the mountains, reaching nearly to the neighbourhood of Sunium. Between Zoster and that promontory is a line of mountains of lower elevation, and the strip of fertile land interposed between their bases and the sea is the district of the Paralia. At the north-eastern angle of Attica which faces Euboea is a spot of ground the most famous of all, the field of Marathon. That little plain, enclosed on three sides by the rocky arms of Parnes and Pentelicus, while the fourth is open to the sea, is the most characteristic of battlefields. The mountains from which the Greeks descended, the shore along which the Persian ships were ranged, and the marshes at the two sides by which the invader's movements were impeded, and which formed a prominent feature in the picture of the battle on the walls of the Pœcile at Athens, are all conspicuous. High above rises the summit of Pentelicus, from which the shield must have glistened in the sun which, according to the report, was held up by the Alcmæonidæ as a signal to the Persians.[45] The sides of this mountain and the neighbouring Parnes, together with the plain, were the abode

[45] Herod. vi. 115.

of that party in Attica which was most disposed for political change, the Diacrii or Hyperacrii ; and thus, in the course of this brief survey, we have traced the seats of the different political elements ; for while these poor mountaineers had nothing to lose by revolution, the Pedieis, or inhabitants of the well-cultivated plains, were large landholders, whose object it was to retain the chief power in their own hands ; and the Parali, or dwellers on the sea-coast, represented the commercial and mercantile interests, whose moderate views induced them to hold the balance between the two others. The remaining district of Attica was that of Oropus, which, as it lay to the north of Parnes, belonged geographically to Bœotia ; but the Athenians always strove to retain possession of it because of its importance as a means of communication with Eubœa.

Athens; its site. Let us now return to Athens, of which a brief and general account must be given. That city, which in its history was all along the most central point in Greece, was also in its position the most central spot in the Athenian plain; central, that is to say, as a point of attraction to the eye—for there is no such exactness in its situation as might give formality to the view, since it is nearer to the sea on the south than to the foot of Parnes on the north, and nearer to Hymettus than to Ægaleos. But from whatever side you look, the eye rests on the group of craggy hills, in the midst of which stands up conspicuous the altar-rock of the Acropolis. That eminence, which Pindar calls the "navel of the city" (ἄστεος ὀμφαλός),[46] measured, roughly speaking, 1000 feet in length from east to west, by 500 feet in breadth, forming an irregular oval, while its level summit was 350 feet above the plain, with steep bare rocks on every side, except towards the west, where the ascent was least precipitous. On this small table of land, together with a portion of the ground at its foot on the southern side, as Thucydides[47] tells us, lay the original city, and it continued to be inhabited down to the Persian wars, after which time the Acropolis was reserved to be a fortress, a sanctuary, and a repository of works of art. But its original destination as the πόλις explains its having been chosen in preference to other positions, for the height of Lycabettus, which rises at a distance of about three quarters of a mile to the north-east, is far loftier and more commanding, so that Aristophanes[48] classes Lycabettus and Parnassus together as specimens of lofty mountains. On the further side of the Ilissus, which flows at no great distance off to the south-east of the Acropolis, the lower slopes of Hymettus begin to rise gradually; but by far the most important hills are the low heights towards the west, which run from north to south under the names of the Hill of the Nymphs, the Hill of the Pnyx, and the

[46] Pind. *Fragm. Dith.* 3, ed. Boeckh. [47] ii. 15.
[48] Ar. *Ran.* 1056.

Museium. The ridge thus formed was connected with the north-western angle of the Acropolis by the craggy height of the Areiopagus, though between the two there intervened a deep depression, to which, however, the ground rose steeply from the northern side. On and among these hills, and on the Acropolis itself and the ground which reached southward from it towards the Ilissus, the principal public buildings and sites were situated, but the city itself gradually extended towards the north, though the line of the walls in later times ran at a distance of not much more than half a mile from the Acropolis in that direction, and Lycabettus was never included within their circuit.

The Acropolis.

The approach to the Acropolis was on the western side, where, as has been already remarked, the ground was the least steep, and it was from this quarter that it was most exposed to attack. Accordingly the Areiopagus, which, with its crust of rock, resembles a scaly crawling monster[49] advancing towards it, was the position occupied both by the Amazons,[50] when, according to the legend, they besieged the city of Cecrops, and by the Persians under Xerxes.[51] But in the need of defensive works art found its opportunity, and the Propylæa were constructed at this point, to be at once a means of defence and an imposing entrance to the sacred area. As being an independent work of art, complete in themselves, and

[49] Stanley in *Classical Museum*, i. p. 53.
[50] Æsch. *Eum.* 685 foll.   [51] Herod. viii. 52.

yet intended to prepare the mind for another higher and more comprehensive work, they have been well compared to a great musical overture,[52] and the ancients themselves regarded them as equal to the greatest masterpieces of architecture. Here, between the flanking wings of the building, a magnificent staircase of sixty steps led steeply upwards, together with a central road, the scene of the passage of the Panathenaic procession, composed, like all the rest of the structure, of slabs of Pentelic marble, in which the ruts of the chariot wheels are still visible. Facing this was the central portico and vestibule, through which the passage lay into the Acropolis. When the gates were opened and the votary entered, the sight that met his view must at first have been almost overpowering. Two objects especially stood out conspicuous above all the rest—on the left hand the colossal bronze statue of Athena Promachus, the loftiest object in the Acropolis, the point of the spear of which, and the crest of the helmet, Pausanias[53] tells us, could be seen by ships approaching from Sunium; on the right the Parthenon, the grand proportions and harmony of which are even now exceedingly impressive, but can give but a faint idea of what it appeared when it glittered with white marble and brilliant colouring. This was the sight which Aristophanes intends to describe, when in the *Equites*, presenting to the audience the Demus restored to youth, he ex-

[52] Hettner, *Athens and the Peloponnese*, 60.   [53] i. 28, § 2.

claims—"Hark! there is a sound of the Propylæa being opened: then raise a shout at the sight of Athens, the ancient, the wonderful, the renowned in song, where the famous Demus dwells."[54] The effect was increased by there being a rise of about forty feet between the Propylæa and the basement of the Parthenon, and also by that building and the statue of Athena Promachus presenting themselves at an angle to the spectator, and not being parallel to one another—an instance of that ἀσυμμετρία in which the Greeks so much delighted, on account of its multiplicity of effects and the relief it administered to the eye; in which last respect it was still further aided by the absence of hard lines—for it is an ascertained fact that every apparently straight line in the Parthenon is in reality a most delicate curve. Opposite the Parthenon on the north side, also at a different angle, stood the Erechtheium, which contained, among other objects of great antiquity and sacredness, the olive-wood statue of Athena Polias, to which the Peplus of the Panathenaic procession was dedicated. The rest of the area of the Acropolis was occupied with statues and shrines and smaller temples; and when the eye looked abroad, the view on every side was magnificent, including the plain of Athens and the mountains of Attica, with the Piræus and the Saronic gulf, Salamis and Ægina, and the distant mountains of Argolis and the Acrocorinth.

[54] Ar. *Eq.* 1326.

The Acropolis was from early times surrounded by a wall, the "towers that protect the city" (πύργοι μὲν οἳ πόλιν στέγουσιν), which Sophocles represents Antigone as seeing;[55] and from no point of view can they and the other buildings be better seen than from the gardens of Colonus, where the poet places her. But the principal walls were erected after the Persian wars, and those which now remain present us with a most interesting memorial of antiquity, for in those on the north side may be seen embedded drums of columns, the remains of the old Hecatompedon, which was replaced by the Parthenon; thus confirming the statement of Thucydides[56] as to the haste with which the city was fortified at the bidding of Themistocles, and the use of the materials of public as well as private buildings in the construction of the walls. The steep face of rock along this northern side was called the Long Rocks (Μακραὶ πέτραι), the scene of early Athenian legends, which Euripides has worked up in his *Ion;* and beneath them, in the dark shade of the Acropolis, lay the piece of ground called the Pelasgicum, which was left uninhabited in accordance with an oracle, the same feeling which in modern times causes the northern side of churchyards to be avoided, probably combining with the memory of the hateful Pelasgians who had dwelt there to cause it to be regarded as an accursed spot.[57] The rocks themselves

---

[55] Soph. *Œd. Col.* 14. [56] Thuc. i, 90, 93.
[57] Thuc. ii. 17. Comp. Stanley in *Classical Museum,* i. 53.

were honeycombed with grottoes, the most important of which were that of Pan, under the north-west angle, which we have spoken of as connected with the battle of Marathon; and that of Aglaurus, from which a flight of stairs leads upwards close to the Erechtheium, marking the point at which the Persians gained access at the time of Xerxes' siege.[58]

Areiopagus. To turn now from the Acropolis to the other historically important sites of Athens.—The position of the Areiopagus relatively to the other hills has been already noticed; it remains to describe the meeting-place of the famous Council, which had so many hallowed associations in the minds of the Athenians. This was at the south-eastern angle of the hill, towards the Acropolis, and sixteen stone steps cut in the rock lead up to it on the south side from the valley below. At the top of these steps, and facing south, a bench of stone, also excavated, runs round three sides of a quadrangle, like a triclinium, as Wordsworth[59] describes it. These were the seats of the judges, and on the east and west sides is a raised block, the same apparently which Pausanias[60] saw there, and which he speaks of as intended for the accuser and the accused. Here, according to Euripides,[61] at the trial of Orestes, that hero and the eldest of the Eumenides took up their respective stations. The

[58] Herod. viii. 53.
[59] *Athens and Attica*, 75.
[60] i. 28, § 5.
[61] *Iph. Taur.* 962.

sessions of the Areiopagus took place in the open air. Near this spot, and not unconnected with it in the popular mind, under the eastern precipices, were the cavern and fountain and temple of the Eumenides.

Nearly at right angles to the Areiopagus, and facing the western end of the Acropolis, was the hill of the Pnyx, the scene of the assemblies of the Athenian people. On the north-eastern face of this was an extensive space of almost level land, sloping very gently towards the valley below, though in its lower part the ground is banked up and supported by a massive wall. In shape it may almost be called a semicircle, though, as the base-line is not straight but forms a very obtuse angle, it may be still more accurately compared to a semicircular bow with the string partly drawn.[62] The curve of the semicircle is formed by the part which projects towards the valley, while its chord, or the bent string of the bow, is marked by a line of rock vertically hewn, which runs along beneath the crest of the hill. Just at the angle in the middle of this, and facing down the centre of the whole area, there stands a solid rectangular block projecting from the rock, and hewn into steps by which it might be ascended from below. This was the Bema, on which stood the orator, while the space in front, which was capable of containing from 7000 to 8000 persons, was occupied by his audience. From this rocky pedestal the greatest

[62] Murray's *Handbook of Greece*, 186.

masterpieces of Greek oratory were delivered, from Themistocles to Demosthenes; and the surroundings were not unworthy of a lofty eloquence. With the bare ground beneath them and the open sky overhead, the assembled multitude would find an unwonted force in such appeals as ὦ γῆ καὶ θεοί, in which Demosthenes was wont to indulge; and directly opposite to the orator were the glories of the Acropolis, by pointing to which he used to stir the enthusiasm of his hearers.[63] "The Stone," as the Bema was familiarly called, became the symbol of the chief power in the state, and in this sense Aristophanes describes the ruling demagogue as the man who is "master of the stone in the Pnyx."[64] The comfort of the audience was but little attended to, for though the Prytanes who sat in front were provided with wooden benches,[65] the rest of the people either stood or sat on the ground.[66] Hence the sausage-seller in the *Equites*, when he wishes to outbid Cleon in popular arts, provides the Demus with a cushion.[67] So, too, the impossibility of covering so large an area with an awning led to the custom of holding the assemblies at daybreak, and persons who wished to secure good seats went even earlier, as we see from the highly graphic scene at the commencement of the *Acharnians*.[68]

[63] See Wordsworth, *Athens and Attica*, pp. 67 foll.
[64] Ar. *Pax*, 680.   [65] Ar. *Ach*. 25.
[66] Ar. *Vesp*. 43. See Mure, *Tour in Greece*, ii. 62.
[67] Ar. *Eq*. 784.
[68] In a mere sketch like the present it would obviously be

From this great centre of the political activity of the Athenians, let us pass to the scene of their highest intellectual enjoyments, the Dionysiac Theatre. This building, which has been restored to us by excavation within a few years, lay close to the south-eastern angle of the Acropolis, a part of the *cavea* being excavated in the hill-side, as we see also to have been the case with the theatres of Argos, Chæroneia, and many other Greek cities, on account of the economy of labour and material, while the wings and the *scena* were built on in front. From its position it was fitted to be the place of representation of the great achievements of the Attic drama. As its aspect was somewhat east of south, from its upper rows of seats the eye ranged, above the level of the *scena*, over the broad flanks of Hymettus and the blue waters of the

Dionysiac theatre.

out of place to discuss controverted questions of Athenian topography, such as the site of the Pnyx, the line of the walls, and the nature of the remains of ancient buildings beyond the Museium Hill. For these points the reader is referred to Mr. Dyer's *Ancient Athens,* and the German authorities which he quotes, especially the *Sieben Karten zur Topographie von Athen, mit erläuterndem Text* of Professor E. Curtius. In my description I have adopted the generally-received view, except where there appeared to be very strong arguments against it. In one instance, that of the Agora, I have felt the question to be so doubtful that I have resolved, with much regret, to omit all mention of it. The other works to which I am mostly indebted are Wordsworth's *Athens and Attica;* Bursian's *Geographie von Griechenland,* i. pp. 271-324 ; and the excellent article " Athenæ " in Smith's *Dictionary of Geography.*

Saronic gulf, so that it possessed, what Niebuhr has remarked on as a characteristic of Greek theatres, an extensive prospect, including, where this was possible, a view of the sea.[69] Besides this, it was immediately under the protection of the gods of the Acropolis, for both the Parthenon and a statue of Zeus of the Citadel (Ζεὺς Πολιεύς)[70] rose directly above, to which circumstance Æschylus seems to refer in the *Eumenides*, when he addresses the Athenians as "sitting near to Zeus," and "revered by him because they were beneath the wings of Pallas"—

> χαίρετ' ἀστικὸς λεὼς
> ἴκταρ ἥμενοι Διὸς, . . .
> Παλλάδος δ' ὑπὸ πτεροῖς
> ὄντας ἄζεται πατήρ.[71]

Though the size of this building was considerably smaller than that of the great theatre of Sparta, yet in this respect also it was suited for great performances, as it was certainly capable of holding more than 20,000 persons;[72] and there is every probability that at the most flourishing period of the drama the whole number of citizens could be admitted, though the present structure dates from a much later period,

---

[69] Niebuhr, *History of Rome*, iii. p. 311, note 531, and p. 439. See Stanley in *Class. Mus.* p. 52.

[70] Pausan. i. 24, § 4.

[71] Æsch. *Eum.* 997 foll. See Wordsworth's *Athens*, pp. 97, 98.

[72] Dyer's *Ancient Athens*, p. 342.

and even the first stone theatre was not completely finished until B.C. 340. One interesting memorial that remains to us at the present day, forcibly recalling one of the prominent features of the scene, is the line of white marble thrones or stalls which occupied the front row of the *cavea*, being reserved for the chief functionaries, of whom the priests took up the whole of the western half, while a considerable proportion of the seats towards the east were assigned to the civil magistrates.[73] The title of each was inscribed on his stall, and in the centre of the line, facing the Thymele, stood an elaborately carved throne for the priest of Dionysus, who presided on such occasions. This may remind us of an incident in the *Ranæ*, where Dionysus, being introduced on the stage in a state of ludicrous terror, appeals to his priest, sitting opposite, to come to his aid—

ἱερεῦ, διαφύλαξόν μ', ἵν' ᾧ σοι ξυμπότης.[74]

Other sites.

The theatre was situated in the enclosure called the Lenæum, and this again formed part of the district of Limnæ, or "the Marshes," whence the Lenæan festival, the second in order of the Dionysia, was also known as the "festival in Limnæ." To the east of this, on a table of land overlooking the Ilissus, not far from the fountain of Callirrhoë, stood the great temple of Olympian Zeus, which was commenced by Pisistratus, and finished by Hadrian, having thus, in

[73] Dyer, p. 332.   [74] Ar. *Ran.* 297.

the course of its erection, witnessed almost the whole of Greek history. On the rising ground, on the opposite side of the river, was the suburb of Agræ, "the Chase,"—at one time, no doubt, a famous hunting-ground—which contained, among other important objects, the great Panathenaic stadium, carved out in a hollow of the hills. Of the other localities of Athens we need only mention the two remaining suburbs— viz. that of Cœle, to the south-west of the city, beyond the hill of the Museium, and that of the outer Cerameicus, which lay beyond the walls to the north-west, while the inner region of that name followed the same direction within the city, comprehending the Agora. Through the outer Cerameicus led two roads—one the sacred way to Eleusis, the other to the Academy, both of which were flanked at the sides by tombs and monuments to illustrious citizens.

LECTURE VIII.

GEOGRAPHY OF THE PELOPONNESE.

Character of the Peloponnese: its natural Unity—The Isthmus—Corinth—Position of Achaia—Elis: its triple Division—Fertility of the Soil—The Olympian Festival—Description of Olympia—Messenia: its two Plains; its Climate and Soil—Pylos and Sphacteria—Laconia—The Valley-Plain—Sparta and Taygetus—Arcadia: its elevated Position—Plain of Tegea and Mantineia—Character of the Inhabitants—Argolis—Importance of the Argive Plain—Upland Region of Nemea—Sanctuary of Æsculapius.

THE shape of the Peloponnesus is compared by Strabo[1] to the leaf of the plane-tree, and in the breadth of its surface and its deeply indented outline it closely resembles that most beautiful of leaves. A similar idea, in modern times, has given rise to a false etymology of the name Morea, as if it was suggested by the likeness of the country to a mulberry leaf. Another instructive comparison is that to the purse of a net, for the tribes that enter Greece from the north are pressed onward by subsequent waves of migration until they reach this southernmost district, from which they have no means of escape. Consequently, the Peloponnese has always contained fragments, so to

Character of the Peloponnese.

[1] viii. 2, § 1.

speak, of a great variety of races. In ancient times Herodotus[2] enumerates seven as occupying the country; and, at the present day, besides the large admixture of Slavonic blood which flows in the veins of the modern Greek inhabitants, arising from the settlement amongst them, during the middle ages, of various tribes of that stock, we find there Wallachs and Albanians; and, in one instance, that of the Tzaconians, an ancient tribe, seems to have preserved its individuality and its dialect from the hoariest antiquity. But, above all, Strabo[3] is right in calling it the fortress (ἀκρόπολις) of Greece. The mountains which rise on every side of it convert it into a natural fastness. In it were congregated the most Hellenic and the most resolute of the Greek nationalities; and on it the defenders of Greece might fall back when all the outworks had been carried.

Its natural unity. The first place in which the name Peloponnesus occurs is in the Homeric hymn to the Pythian Apollo;[4] in which passage, also, the name Europa is for the first time applied to the continent of Europe. It was by means of the Olympian festival that it obtained universal currency,[5] for Pelops was the reputed founder or restorer of those games, and the meetings at Olympia which were originally intended for the inhabitants of the peninsula, and cemented the union of the several provinces, caused him to be recognised as the epony-

[2] viii. 73.   [3] viii. 1, § 3.   [4] 72.
[5] E. Curtius, *History of Greece*, i. 243.

mus of the land. And the feeling of unity, which is implied by the geographical name, was fostered by other causes. Although after a time the gifts of the soil did not suffice for the increasing population, yet, at first, the variety of products, arising from the different elevation and soil of its separate parts, tended to render the country independent of foreign supplies, and caused communication among its occupants. And though here, as in Spain, both the natural position and the interests of the provinces are so distinct as to render almost hopeless any attempt at centralisation, yet the community of race and local contiguity formed a sufficient bond to unite them against a mutual enemy. Thus it was that Sparta, as the strongest state, arrived by successive stages at the hegemony, and was able to make war with Athens in the character of leader of the Peloponnesians.

The isthmus by which this peninsula, the culminating point of the peninsular formation of the Greek continent, is approached, is about three and a half miles wide in its narrowest part, and rises but little above the level of the sea. We cannot, therefore, be surprised if the idea suggested itself of cutting a canal through it from sea to sea; and this, though contrary to the feelings of the Greeks, was actually attempted by Nero; and the traces of his work remain, though it was left unfinished. Usually, in ancient times, vessels used to be drawn across on a sort of roadway called

The Isthmus.

the Diolcos, to which process Thucydides applies the expression ὑπερφέρειν or διαφέρειν τὸν ἰσθμόν.[6] On the isthmus was situated the sanctuary of Poseidon, the scene of the Isthmian Games, and the wall of the sacred enclosure formed part of the line of defence which was designed to impede the approach of an enemy to the Peloponnese. The first occasion on which we hear of such a wall being constructed was at the time of the invasion of Xerxes;[7] but this was hurriedly built, bricks and timber as well as stone being used as materials, and must have soon fallen out of repair, for we do not hear of it during the Peloponnesian war, and therefore the massive walls, parts of which now remain, must belong to a later period. But any such fortification was uncalled for, since the true line of defence of the peninsula was formed by the Oneian mountains, whose rugged heights rise immediately within its entrance, with Corinth as their forepost.

Corinth. That famous place possesses all the conditions which Aristotle[8] considers to be desirable for a city. It faces the north and east, which, according to him, is the most favourable aspect. It is well supplied with good water by the fountain of Peirene. Its towering acropolis is one of the strongest positions in Greece. From that height, the *bimaris Corinthi mœnia*, it commands the isthmus, the two gulfs,

[6] viii. 7, 3.   [7] Herod. viii. 71.
[8] *Pol.* iv. (vii.) 10.

and an immense extent of country, from the summit of Parnassus in one direction to the Parthenon of Athens in the other. It is always fanned with fresh breezes. It possesses two ports—that of Lechæum on the Corinthian, and that of Cenchreæ on the Saronic gulf, and thus occupies the finest commercial position in Greece as the point of communication between the far east and the far west. In like manner, from commanding the entrance of the Peloponnese, the Corinthians were able to impose duties on all the imports and exports of that district.[9] At this point the lines of road met, which led from Argolis, Arcadia, and Achaia, towards northern Greece; and no other station was so convenient for shipping to foreign parts the produce of the interior. It was a strong argument which the Corinthians urged at the commencement of the Peloponnesian war,[10] that those states which were less on the line of traffic than themselves, if they declined to assist them, would find increased difficulties in bringing their saleable articles down to the sea, and receiving in return what the sea had to supply them with. Thus it was that Corinth, though less able than most to brook a maritime rival, had always the interests of peace at heart as favourable to trade; and thus too, from her extended communication with foreign countries, and larger views of political questions, she

[9] Strabo, viii. 6, § 20.   [10] Thuc. i. 120.

obtained that cosmopolitan character which distinguished her from other Dorian states.

Position of Achaia. About nine miles to the north-west of Corinth, and two from the Corinthian gulf, in a strong but not striking position on an elevated table of land, lay another city of first-rate importance, Sicyon, which, besides its early political influence, long continued to be one of the chief homes of the fine arts. Where its territory comes to an end that of Achaia begins, and reaches along the southern shore of the gulf as far as the straits at Rhium, and from thence to the promontory of Araxus, on the confines of Elis. Its character is easily described, for it occupies the fertile sloping land that descends in a long and narrow strip from the lofty precipitous mountain chain of north Arcadia to the sea. Both its rivers and its promontories have already been described — the former being universally winter torrents, which rush down from the mountain gorges, the latter being formed by the alluvium which these carry with them into the sea. Accordingly, the name of the country, as we find it in Homer,[11] is Ægialus, or the coastland. But, notwithstanding its long shore-line, this country was not destined to be a great maritime power from its want of harbours. In this respect the opposite coasts of the gulf form a complete contrast; for whereas that of Achaia is straight and unbroken by headlands of sufficient

[11] *Il.* ii. 575.

magnitude to form a safe roadstead, the northern shore is deeply indented by bays, one of which, that of Crissa, gave its name to the whole gulf, even as late as the time of Thucydides. The difference of the two is forcibly expressed by the modern Greek saying—" The coast of the Morea has the water, that of Rumelia the harbours;" and when a storm is approaching the sailor will immediately run across and make for the northern shore.[12] As might be expected from its safe but unobtrusive position, though itself a prosperous land, Achaia had little influence on the fortunes of Greece. During the early part of the Peloponnesian war it continued on friendly terms with Athens;[13] and having no Dorian sympathies, it must have been against their will that they were ultimately forced to take sides with the Lacedæmonians. As their country was divided up into a succession of valleys and small plains, a federal union was the most natural political system by which they could be held together; and thus their early confederation of twelve cities became the germ of the important combination which bore the famous name of the Achæan league.

Following the coast southwards from the extremity of Achaia, we enter the country of Elis, which occupies the north-western portion of the Peloponnese. Its shore-line is sandy and interspersed with lagoons; and its two promontories of Chelonatas and Ichthys

Elis—its triple division.

[12] E. Curtius, *Peloponnesos*, i. 407, 408.   [13] Thuc. ii. 9.

are merely outlying rocky islands joined to the mainland by belts of sand. The political divisions of the district—Hollow Elis, Pisatis, and Triphylia—correspond to the geographical. The first and northernmost of these, which is Elis proper—for that name signifies "the vale," being the same as the Latin *vallis*, and being found in the form ΕΑΛΕΙΩΝ, in the inscriptions on coins—was composed of the valley and plains of the river Peneius, together with the slopes of Mount Erymanthus, whence it flows, which bore the distinctive appellation of Acroreia. That mountain is the determining feature in the geography of this neighbourhood, as it stands, like a huge boundary stone, at the meeting-point of the three provinces of Achaia, Elis, and Arcadia, just as the still loftier Cyllene, at the eastern extremity of the chain, holds the same position between Arcadia, Achaia, and Argolis. The central division, Pisatis, which is separated from Hollow Elis by the spurs of Mount Pholoe, an offshoot of Erymanthus, consisted of the environs of the lower valley of the Alpheius, which river flows from southern, as its principal tributaries, the Ladon and Erymanthus, flow from northern Arcadia. Triphylia, the third division, which stretches along the coast as far south as the confines of Messenia, is of less importance, being only a narrow strip between the mountains and the sea, and, from its outlying position, it was easily dissevered from the rest of the country.

From its situation, Elis was a country not easily defended, both because the upper courses of its rivers and the mountains from which they flow were in the hands of another people, and in consequence of its want of natural harbours, and the exposed character of its level coast-line. Its one port, where the Eleians had considerable docks, was Cyllene, situated on a bight on the northern side of Mount Chelonatas. But these disadvantages were more than compensated by two circumstances—one natural, the other accidental—the fertility of the soil, and the possession of the sanctuary at Olympia. Of the former of these we have evidence from a variety of sources. Thus, in the story of the conquest of Peloponnesus by the Dorians, we are told that Oxylus, whom they had chosen, in obedience to an oracle, as one of their leaders, avoided conducting them into the country by way of Elis, lest the sight of that good land, which he had reserved for himself, should tempt them to grudge him the possession of it.[14] Here, too, was the kingdom of Augeias, whose name (derived from αὐξάνω) implies his immense wealth, and whose stables, which it required a Hercules to cleanse, signify the presence of innumerable herds of cattle. In like manner, in the Odyssey, we hear of rich proprietors in Ithaca, like Noëmon, sending their herds across to Elis to pasture there;[15] and in the Iliad Nestor has a very long story to tell about his

Fertility of the soil.

---

[14] Paus. v. 4, § 1.   [15] *Od.* iv. 635.

raid into that land in hopes of plunder, and of the vast flocks and herds that they drove off.[16] In connection with the last passage, we may notice that in Homer the country is described as being inhabited by two tribes, the Epeians and Pylians, the former occupying the northern part, the latter the south, extending some distance along the coast of Messenia.

<small>The Olympian festival.</small> The second cause of the prosperity of the Eleians was the establishment in their land of the festival of Olympian Zeus, which brought immense wealth into the country, and gave them to some extent a sacred character, which, though it was not always respected—for, owing to the jealousy of Sparta, they were among the greatest sufferers from the Peloponnesian war—yet, on the whole, guaranteed them immunity from invasion. How great a place of resort Olympia was, is proved by the innumerable votive offerings of all nations that were stored up there, so that some forty chapters of Pausanias' work are devoted to the description of them and the buildings that contained them. That writer speaks of the Eleusinian mysteries and the Olympian games as the two most sacred things in Greece,[17] and in the case of the latter that very sacredness was the source of immense political influence. Nowhere else could it be seen so conspicuously how powerfully Greek religion and Greek art acted as a uniting force to hold together the separate

---

[16] *Il.* xi. 671 foll.   [17] v. 10, § 1.

states which formed the Hellenic community. The holy truce itself at the time of the games exercised a humanising influence by limiting the severity of war, and teaching the tribes to recognise a higher and more merciful law than that of the god of arms. At Olympia all the Greek races met together, without distinction of dialect or political affinities, whether their homes were on the continent or in distant colonies, and competed with one another in amicable rivalry. Thence arose the true Pan-Hellenic feeling, which imparted a sense of unity to the whole people, and made them feel that those who had the privilege of meeting there occupied a different position from the rest of mankind. Thus, when Alexander of Macedon desired to show that he was of Hellenic lineage, he entered himself to compete at Olympia,[18] and when his claim was admitted there his family were thenceforward acknowledged as genuine Greeks. The intensity of the feelings that were aroused by the contest can hardly be better illustrated than by the remark of Thucydides concerning the enthusiastic reception of Brasidas by the people of Scione, that "they crowded round him, and encircled his head with garlands like a victor in the games."[19] Mr. Grote speaks of the sympathy felt towards a victorious athlete as not merely an intense sentiment in the Grecian mind, but perhaps of all others the most

---

[18] Herod. v. 22.
[19] Thuc. iv. 121. See Grote, *History of Greece*, vi. 596.

widespread and Pan-Hellenic, being connected with the religion, the taste, and the love of recreation common to the whole nation. At such a time a conspicuous individual was felt to be the representative of his country; when, along with his own name the name of his fatherland was proclaimed, it caused exultation in the breasts of all his countrymen; when poets like Pindar celebrated his praises in their verse, the title of his native land was always mentioned, and frequently its ancestral glories were entwined with his own. Accordingly, when Alcibiades boasted before the Athenians that the splendour of his display at Olympia and the magnificence of his victory had dispelled the idea which before prevailed among the Greeks, that the resources of Athens were exhausted,[20] he may have excited ill-will by his overweening arrogance, but he certainly stated the truth with regard to the effect of such shows upon the Greek mind. At first, as has already been said, this festival had a specially Peloponnesian character, so that the Mytilenean envoys made it the occasion of appealing to the powers confederated against Athens; and so the remark is true that Sparta attained her position as a representative capital, not on the Eurotas, but on the Alpheius;[21] by the protectorate which she exercised here in conjunction with the Eleians, she came to be regarded as the presiding power in the peninsula. But it became also a thoroughly national

[20] Thuc. vi. 16.   [21] E. Curtius, *History of Greece*, i. 242.

celebration, and thus exercised an influence over every part of the community.

The scene of this remarkable festival was singularly in accordance with its character. Its aspect has been characterised as "cosmopolitan." Instead of the sharply-cut mountains, bare hill-sides, and narrow torrents which are commonly found in Greece, we find here gentle rounded hills covered with abundant and beautifully grouped pine-trees, in the midst of which the copious river sweeps along in numerous windings. The valley opens towards the sea as if to welcome visitors, and yet is sufficiently retired to appear enclosed within the neighbouring declivities. The general direction of the valley is from east to west, and on the northern bank of the stream, between it and the base of the hills, are two levels, the upper of which is separated from the lower by steep slopes. Towards the west the area is bounded by the river Cladeus, which descends from the north through a lovely glade clothed with magnificent plane-trees, and joins the Alpheius at right angles. Not far from their junction, on the upper level, stood the temple of Olympian Zeus, behind which rises a conspicuous conical hill about 200 feet high, which is frequently mentioned by Pindar as Mount Cronius, or the hill of Cronos. East of this, and partly enclosed by the mountain spurs, is the position of the stadium; and on the lower level, between that building and the river, was situated the hippodrome. On the banks of

Description of Olympia.

the stream in former days the white poplar used to grow, which was said to have been first brought hither by Hercules from the Acheron in Thesprotia.[22] A short distance to the east is the site of the city of Pisa, which was originally to Olympia what Crissa was to Delphi,—a guardian city; but in the year B.C. 572 it was so completely razed by the inhabitants of the rival city of Elis on the Peneius, that Strabo informs us that some persons even at that time doubted whether the place had ever existed.[23] Among the wooded hills to the south lay the country seat of Xenophon,[24] an excellent retreat for an old sportsman.

The boundary between Triphylia and Messenia was formed by the Neda,[25] a river which was famed in antiquity for its numerous windings,[26] and the picturesque gorges of which, with their luxuriant growth of plane-trees, present some of the most beautiful scenes in Greece. On its banks occurred an incident worthy of so romantic a spot, which marks the approaching end of Messenian history, towards the close of the second Messenian war. At that time, we are told, "the gods turned their faces away from Messenia." The eleventh year of the siege of Eira brought with it a sure sign that the end of the contest was approaching. "When a goat shall drink the water of the Neda," so the oracle had spoken,

---

[22] Paus. v. 14, § 2.   [23] viii. 3, 31.
[24] Leake, *Morea*, ii. 213.
[25] Paus. iv. 20, § 2.   [26] Ibid. viii. 41, § 3.

"the destruction of Messenia is at hand. But in the dialect of Messenia the same word (τράγος) signified a goat and a wild fig-tree. One of these trees overhung the stream, and at length stretched its boughs down to the water. When Theoclus, the seer, saw this, he knew that the oracle was accomplished, and that the fated term of resistance had arrived, and he warned Aristomenes to resign himself to the loss of his country."[27]

The mountains of Messenia take their origin in Mount Lycæum, the vast mass that occupies the south-west corner of Arcadia, and form two branches— the one running through the western side of the country as far as Cape Acritas, the westernmost of the three promontories that project southwards from the Peloponnese; the other along the eastern side until it attaches itself to the mighty chain of Taygetus. Midway between their starting-point and the Messenian gulf a spur is thrown out from either side, and the valley formed by their meeting divides the level country into an upper and a lower plain, in the former of which flows the Balyras, in the latter the Pamisus, of which that river is a tributary, though, for convenience sake, they are often called the upper and lower valley of the Pamisus. The lower plain, which stretches along the shore of the gulf, and for about ten miles inland, is watered, in addition to the

Messenia— its two plains.

[27] Thirlwall, *History of Greece*, i. 365 (1st ed.); and Paus. iv. 20, § 2.

Pamisus, by numerous springs, and from its fertility was called, in ancient times, Macaria, or "the Blessed."[28] The upper was the famous plain of Stenyclerus, or the "Confined Territory" (στενός, κλῆρος), a name it well deserves from being closely hemmed in by mountains. This was the original Messenia, and hence arose the name of the country, as being the "Midland" (μέσσος), shut off from the surrounding districts.[29] In this is concentrated the real history of the land; within it lay Andania, the capital of its early kings, and at its two extremities rise the two mountain fastnesses which were occupied during the two great wars with Sparta. That at the southern end, which advances from the western mountains, is Ithome, the scene of the protracted defence by Aristodemus, on the broad summit of which, 2600 feet above the plain, crops might be sown and reaped, and which, from its conspicuous position, commands the whole country, being at the same time almost detached from the neighbouring heights, except where a depression in the ridge connects it with Mount Eva, its southern continuation towards the gulf. Again, at the northern extremity, high above the plain, and far retired among the steep mountains in the neighbourhood of the Neda,[30] rises the rocky peak of Eira, for ever associated with the name of Aristomenes; a

---

[28] See however, below, p. 350.
[29] Bursian, *Geographie von Griechenland*, ii. 156.
[30] E. Curtius, *Peloponnesos*, ii. 152.

natural citadel, fitted to be the scene of a final struggle.

The climate of Messenia was the softest and warmest in Greece, more resembling the enervating air of Ionia than that of the European shores of the Ægean. In this, and in the extraordinary fertility of its soil, we see the secret of its misfortunes. The story of the lot of Cresphontes, who at the Dorian partition of the Peloponnese cast into the urn a clod of moist earth (ὑγρᾶς ἀρούρας βῶλον),[31] to secure to himself the possession of this country, typifies its entire subsequent history. It was a goodly land, but its inhabitants did not possess the robust vigour which could enable them to hold their own. In this we see the difference of the fortunes of Laconia and Messenia. Had the vale of Sparta been open to the sea, and fanned all the year round by its temperate breezes, it might perhaps have met with the same fate as its neighbour. But that district, though scorched by the heat of summer, is yet braced in most seasons by fresh winds, and demands of her sons the active life of a mountaineer. The contrast between the two is well expressed by Euripides in a passage of the Cresphontes, which Strabo has preserved. There he speaks of Laconia as being—

Its climate and soil.

πολὺν μὲν ἄροτον, ἐκπονεῖν δ' οὐ ῥᾴδιον·
κοίλη γὰρ, ὄρεσι περίδρομος, τραχεῖά τε
δυσείσβολός τε πολεμίοις.

---

[31] Soph. *Aj.* 1286.

But, on the other hand, Messenia is—

καλλίκαρπον
κατάρρυτόν τε μυρίοισι νάμασι,
καὶ βουσὶ καὶ ποίμναισιν εὐβοτωτάτην,
οὔτ' ἐν πνοαῖσι χείματος δυσχείμερον,
οὔτ' αὖ τεθρίπποις ἡλίου θερμὴν ἄγαν.[32]

Far spreads Laconia's ample bound,
With high-heaped rocks encompassed round,
　　The invader's threat despising;
But ill its bare and rugged soil
Rewards the ploughman's painful toil;
　　Scant harvests there are rising.

While o'er Messenia's beauteous land,
Wide-watering streams their arms expand,
　　Of nature's gifts profuse;
Bright plenty crowns her smiling plain;
The fruitful tree, the full-eared grain,
　　Their richest stores produce.
Large herds her spacious valleys fill,
On many a soft-descending hill
　　Her flocks unnumber'd stray;
No fierce extreme her climate knows,
Nor chilling frost nor wintry snows,
　　Nor dog-star's scorching ray.

In addition to this, the relative position of the two countries rendered almost unavoidable the subjugation of Messenia. For, whereas the summits of Taygetus rise immediately above Sparta, on the western side that mountain descends in gradual slopes to the

[32] Strabo, viii. 5, § 6. The translation is from the English edition of Muller's *Dorians*, i. 80.

plain; so that, though from the summit of Ithome its snowy peaks are visible, from the level ground below they are hidden from the view. Accordingly, when the Spartan climbed to the ridge behind his city, and cast his eyes westward, he saw a tempting possession outspread beneath him, and felt at the same time that the passes leading into it—both the easy one which Strabo notices,[33] from the north of Laconia to the Stenyclerian plain, and the more difficult ones across the lofty summits—were in his own hands.

But the Messenians, though subdued and expelled, were not denationalised. They have rightly been called the Poles of antiquity.[34] From first to last, wherever dispersed, they maintained the idea of nationality, and became a constant thorn in the side of their conquerors. At the time of the great earthquake they profited by the misfortunes of Sparta, and again occupied Ithome, which was conquered only after a ten years' siege. Those who capitulated at that time, being established by the Athenians at Naupactus, became of the greatest service to that power during the Peloponnesian war, and were employed on special occasions against their hereditary foe, as at Pylos, where we are told their speaking the Laconian dialect gave them a great advantage.[35] At last, by the agency of Epaminondas, whose policy it was to establish strongholds in the neighbourhood of Sparta, and

[33] viii. 5, § 1.
[34] Bursian, *Geographie*, ii. 160.　　[35] Thuc. iv. 3.

keep that power in check by means of enemies on her immediate frontier, the Messenians were restored to their native country. It was at this time that the city of Messene was founded, on the western side of Ithome, with the summit of that mountain for its acropolis; for it should be remembered that during the earlier period no city of that name existed. To this belong the famous walls, which are the finest specimen of Greek military architecture, especially the gateway towards Megalopolis, which encloses a circular space of ground sixty-two feet in diameter, with an outer and an inner gate, the lintel of the latter of which is formed by a block of stone eighteen feet in length. The stadium also is perhaps the finest specimen of that kind of building in Greece. But the prosperity of the country did not revive. During the Spartan occupation tillage was so neglected that a great part of the land became a desert, and it never recovered from its early depopulation.

In contrast with the otherwise harbourless coast of western Peloponnesus, Messenia possesses the two harbours of Methone and Pylos. The former of these, which is small but a safe anchorage, though not unimportant in ancient times, assumed much greater prominence in the middle ages, when Modon became a strong fortress, and often changed hands between the Venetians and Turks. But it sinks into insignificance in comparison with the harbour of Navarino, which has always been accounted one of the finest in

Greece. In approaching from the land side, the eye is first struck by the length of the island of Sphacteria, which stretches in front of the harbour, forming a low flat ridge at its southern extremity, then rising about its centre to the height of nearly 300 feet, while its highest point is at the northern end, where it reaches from 400 to 500 feet. Its length is somewhat less than three miles, and consequently is underrated by Thucydides, who estimates it at fifteen stadia.[36] On the side facing the harbour there are two landing-places —one about a mile from the southern end, at which one party of the Athenians must have landed before the final attack, as they at once fell in with the Spartan outposts, who would be stationed in that quarter;[37] the other, and most important, somewhat north of the centre of the island, where a passage through the cliffs leads directly into the interior. Just opposite this, on the western side, is the most level plain in the island, with a very deep well in the centre, which must have been the main station of the Spartans.[38] The island all along shelves from east to west, and the coast towards the sea, though rough, is low, and landing there is easily practicable in fair weather. At the northern end the ground rises steeply, and is difficult even to clamber over, owing to the sharpness of the points of rock of which it is composed. In ancient times, when the soil was less worn away, it may have been less rough, but at any

[36] Thuc. iv. 8.   [37] iv. 31.   [38] Ibid.

time it must have been excessively awkward fighting ground. When Thucydides says that this part of the island was ἐκ θαλάσσης ἀπόκρημνον καὶ ἐκ τῆς γῆς ἥκιστα ἐπίμαχον,[39] he must not be understood to mean that it was precipitous on the sea side, for it is so only towards the harbour, but that the shore in that quarter was steep and rocky so as to prevent landing, while the roughness of the ascent was a sufficient defence on land. The path by which the Messenians got into the rear of the Spartans[40] must have started from the centre of the island, otherwise they could not have escaped observation. From thence there is a sort of ledge by which they could pass along near the sea under the precipices on the harbour side until they reached some close gullies, by which they could scramble to a narrow rough plateau on the north and east of the peak, about thirty feet below its summit.

To the north of this, and separated from it by a narrow and shallow channel, stands the height of Coryphasium or Pylos, which is precipitous on all sides, though least so on its southern face. At this point, accordingly, the attacks of the Spartans were made:[41] that of Brasidas from the sea, near the south-western angle, where there is a beach and shelving rocks; the other on the opposite side, towards the harbour. At present a lagoon bounds the eastern side of this rocky height, but as there has been a tendency for such pieces of water to form all along this

[39] Thuc. iv. 31. [40] iv. 36. [41] iv. 9.

coast since classical times, there is reason to believe that the area was formerly covered with sand. There can be no doubt that this height was the position occupied by the Athenians. The idea, suggested by Arnold, that Sphacteria was here, is overthrown by the absence of any level place with a source of water such as Thucydides describes in that island; by our finding traces of ancient Hellenic walls there, whereas there never was a town on Sphacteria; and, above all, by the circumstance that in that case there would have been two islands off the coast, and that the Athenian squadron would certainly not have retired to the island of Prote for shelter[42] if they could have betaken themselves to an unoccupied island close at hand. One difficulty still remains—the breadth of the two entrances to the harbour at either extremity of Sphacteria, which is represented by the historian as far less than it is at the present day.[43] The only satisfactory explanation of this is to suppose that a great change has taken place in that respect since he wrote. On the north side of the height of Pylos, under the steep cliffs, is a large and picturesque cavern, the same which Pausanias speaks of as existing in Coryphasium, and as being the reputed stable of Nestor.[44] The question whether this place was the Pylos of Nestor was much debated even in classical times. On the whole, the probabilities seem to be in its favour, and many difficulties in respect of

[42] Thuc. iv. 13.   [43] iv. 8.   [44] iv. 36, § 2.

the distance of the Homeric Pylos from Elis will be removed, if we understand that that name belonged as well to the country of the Pylians as to the chief city.[45]

Laconia—the valley-plain.

We turn now to Laconia. In ancient times the usual route from northern Greece to Sparta was by way of Tegea, from which city a road led through the difficult upland district called Sciritis, then, as now, covered in parts with fine forest trees, the highest part of which is formed by a plain between 3000 and 4000 feet above the sea. It is from this side also that the modern traveller usually approaches Sparta; and when at last he suddenly comes in sight of that place and its environs from the heights which overhang its eastern side, descending from the flanks of Mount Parnon, the name of the country, its epithets, and its history, become at once intelligible to him. The valley or plain—for it may be called either—a plain, because of the level expanse of a great part of its area; a valley, because of the rocky walls in the midst of which it is deeply sunk, extending eighteen miles in length by four or five in breadth, is the original Laconia, the κοίλη Λακεδαίμων of Homer, so called from its deep basin or λάκκος—a term which at the present day is applied for the same reason to Messenia,[46] and is not unfrequently used for a valley by the modern Greeks. Through the whole length of this flows the

[45] *Dict. Geog.* ii. 685, *b.*
[46] Wyse, *Excursion to the Peloponnesus,* i. 258.

Eurotas, a river in size and appearance resembling the Dart in Devonshire; but for some distance above Sparta it is confined in a gorge at the foot of the heights from which we are supposed to be looking by a low irregular spur of ground, which projects across from Taygetus, thus forming an upper and a lower plain. Emerging from this, its fertilising waters wind for ten miles through plantations of mulberries and olives, until they enter the Aulon, or narrow defile, at the southern end, through which they pass to the sea. In the same way as the general aspect of the district explains the Homeric epithet κοίλη, so that of κητώεσσα[47] becomes clear from the appearance of the spur just mentioned, which, like the lower buttresses of the neighbouring mountains, is seamed in an extraordinary manner with rifts and fissures, the result, in all probability, of numerous earthquakes. This word, Strabo tells us,[48] was sometimes written καιετάεσσα, and was then derived from the rents in the ground—ὅτι οἱ ἀπὸ τῶν σεισμῶν ῥωχμοὶ κάιετοὶ λέγονται—one of which was the well-known Καιάδας of Sparta, the pit into which criminals were thrown. Whether or not there is any authority for this form of the word, the more usual form, κητώεσσα, according to Buttmann, has the same etymology and the same meaning.[49]

Just where the last outlying hills of this spur sink down into the level ground, stood the city of Sparta, thus forming the eye of the plain. It occupied four

Sparta and Taygetus.

[47] *Il.* ii. 581.   [48] viii. 5, § 7.   [49] *Lexilogus*, 381.

of these low heights, and received its name from the rich tilled land (σπαρτή) which lay outspread in front of it. On the opposite side lies the magnificent Taygetus, the most imposing of all the Greek mountains, which attains its greatest elevation, 7900 feet above the sea, directly above Sparta. At first it rises from the plain in steep buttresses, of the average height of 2000 feet, which break into abrupt peaks, and are so conspicuous from below, that they seem to have given the whole mountain its modern name of Pentedactylon, or the Five Fingers. Then follows an extensive tract of forest land, famed at the present day as a resort of wild animals,[50] and where, in ancient times, wild goats, boars, deer, and bears, were found in abundance.[51] Part of this was called Theræ, or the Chase, and to the hunting which this supplied is to be attributed the famous race of dogs of Taygetus, and in part also the hardy vigorous character of the Spartans. Above the woodland tract, again, rises the long line of steep summits, which during the summer present the appearance of a mass of grey limestone, but for two-thirds of the year are deeply covered with snow. The loftiest of these was called Taleton, while the next in height bore the name of Euoras or "Belvedere."

It has been remarked by Professor Curtius in his admirable book on the Peloponnesus,[52] that the state which possesses both sides of Taygetus has it in its

[50] E. Curtius, *Peloponnesos*, ii. 308.
[51] Paus. iii. 20, § 4.   [52] i. 69.

power to be master of the peninsula. It is the acropolis of the Peloponnese, as that country is of the rest of Greece. It lies back, sheltered by the countries in front of it, a natural stronghold, from which the inhabitants can issue forth at will, to conquer or take command of their neighbours. Thus the hegemony of Sparta was a natural one, arising from her position, not artificial, like that of Athens, which depended on the circumstances of her fortune. In like manner, it is easy to understand from this view how it came to pass that Sparta had no need of walls. Though the city itself was undefended, the district had the strongest of ramparts in the rugged mountains that hem it in on every side, so that there were only two passes by which it could be entered. Of these the one led from the Stenyclerian plain and from south-western Arcadia into the upper valley of the Eurotas, which was easily defended; while in the other, a still more difficult route, the roads from Tegea in south-eastern Arcadia, and from Argos through Thyrea, met at Sellasia in the valley of the Œnus, from whence they descended on Sparta. At Sellasia it was that the Spartans met with their greatest and final defeat, when their country was invaded by Antigonus Doson in B.C. 221. The same causes tended to keep external influences at a distance, and rendered possible such a system as that of Lycurgus, which could not have been maintained without the utmost exclusiveness, and without a certain unexpansiveness of character. Hence also arose the timid foreign policy of Sparta, and her clumsiness in dealing with other nations, arising from want of knowledge of the world. But her political strength also arose from the concentration thus given. It would be hard to conceive a position better adapted for the maintenance of an aristocratic commonwealth. The plain itself and the best land in its neighbourhood was in the hands of the ruling race, who dwelt together in Sparta, leaving their properties to be cultivated by their serfs, the Helots; while the rest of Laconia, a mountainous and for the most part unproductive country, was left to the Periœci, who, though they retained their freedom, had no share in the government.

Of the buildings of Sparta little need be said. The prophecy of Thucydides[53] has been remarkably fulfilled, that if the city of the Lacedæmonians were to be deserted, and only the temples and the foundations of its buildings were to be left, after the lapse of a long period of time it would cause great disbelief in its power, in comparison of its fame, in the minds of posterity; whereas, if the same thing happened to the Athenians, persons would conceive their power to have been twice as great as the reality, judging by the appearance presented to the eye. What the remains of Athens are there is no need to remind you: of Sparta there exists a large theatre, which

---

[53] i. 10.

however, dates from Roman times; after this a tomb, a sarcophagus, and a few other objects, constitute all the antiquities.

Arcadia is accurately described by Strabo [54] as lying in the middle of the Peloponnese, bordering on, and neighbouring to, all the other provinces. Environed on all sides by mountains, and greatly elevated above the surrounding country, so that even the plain of Mantineia is more than 2000 feet above the sea, it nowhere touches the coast of the peninsula, so that it is completely enclosed within its own boundaries. Its whole area, however, is not of a uniform character. The eastern portion is composed of the closed valleys which we have already noticed, containing either lakes or marshy plains, and drained by subterranean channels—viz. those of Pheneus, Stymphalus, and Orchomenus, in the north, and the great double plain of Mantineia and Tegea in the south. On the other hand, the western portion is an irregular hilly plateau, with scenery in many places resembling that of an English park, intersected by the upper course of the Alpheius and by its tributaries. The forests of oak and pine, with which the country in ancient times was densely covered, were the resort of numerous bears,[55] and from them the district seems to have received the name of Arcadia, or the "land of bears" (ἄρκος, ἄρκτος).[56] So, too, according to the

Arcadia— its elevated position.

[54] viii. 2, § 2.
[55] Paus. viii. 23, § 9.   [56] Bursian, *Geographie*, ii. 181.

Arcadian legend, Callisto, the daughter of Lycaon, was metamorphosed into a she-bear, and became the constellation of the bear in heaven, so that Propertius says—

Callisto Arcadios erraverat ursa per agros :
Hæc nocturna suo sidere vela regit.[57]

In consequence of this, Artemis, the goddess of the chase, was held in especial honour there, so that the two lofty mountains which form the eastern boundary of the country, Artemisium and Parthenium, received their names from her. The other deities that especially presided over Arcadia were the sylvan Pan, the god of shepherds, whose pipe of many reeds is represented on the coins ; and the primitive Lycæan Zeus, to whom human sacrifices continued to be offered even down to the Macedonian period.[58] The prevalence of the oak also caused the Arcadians to be an acorn-eating people (βαλανηφάγοι ἄνδρες),[59] and added pork to their meals, where fish would have been the diet of the Athenians.[60] The other animal besides the pig that was most successfully reared in this country was the ass, whence Persius says "Arcadiæ pecuaria rudere dicas."[61] Great numbers of these were exported to all parts of Greece.

[57] Propert. iii. 20, 23.   [58] *Dict. Geog.* i. 191, *a*.
[59] Herod. i. 66.
[60] Grote, *History of Greece*, ii. 300. Grote, however, cannot be right in speaking of their " diet of sweet chestnuts," for that fruit-tree was not then introduced.   See above, Lect. iv. p. 159.   [61] Pers. iii. 9.

Owing to the simplicity, not to say rudeness, of the manners of the Arcadians, village life prevailed amongst them longer than amongst any other of the Greeks, and consequently but few of their ancient cities are known to fame. The principal exception is formed by the two great strongholds which occupied the extremities of the most extensive plain. The name of the southernmost of these, Tegea, signifies the "place of defence" (τέγος, στέγω, Lat. *tego*),[62] an appellation which is highly suitable because it commands the exit of the pass from the south through the district of Sciritis, and thus formed an outpost to guard the country from the attacks of Sparta. In the northern part of the plain lay Mantineia, a not less important position from its commanding the passes on the side of Argolis. Five great battles were fought in its neighbourhood; the first, which is described by Thucydides, between the Spartans and the Argives and their allies;[63] the second, of which Xenophon has left us an account, which has been rendered famous by the death of Epaminondas;[64] the third, in which Demetrius Poliorcetes defeated the Spartans; the fourth, in which the same power was overcome by Aratus, with the loss of their king Agis; and lastly, the fifth, which is narrated by Polybius, in which the Spartans were again defeated in a great engagement by the army of the Achæan

[62] Bursian, ii. 218.
[63] Thuc. v. 64 foll.   [64] Xen. *Hell.* vii. 5.

League under Philopœmen.[65] The scene of Epaminondas' death was a place called Scope, where a spur from Mount Mænalus advances into the western side of the plain, and this, together with a corresponding projection from Mount Artemisium on the opposite side, marks the point of demarcation of the Mantineian and Tegean plain. From the former of these, two passes led to Argos;[66] the most direct, called Prinos, was through Mount Artemisium, immediately to the east of the city, while the other, called Climax, or "the ladder," from the steps in one part cut in the rock, took a more circuitous route further to the north. A third, further to the south, led from Argos to Tegea through Mount Parthenium: this formed the high road between northern Greece and Sparta, and was that taken by the courier Pheidippides on the occasion of his memorable journey.[67]

Character of the inhabitants. There is reason to believe that the Arcadians were, as Herodotus tells us,[68] Pelasgians, and the heavy climate of their closed valleys, which, as we have seen, resembled that of Bœotia, was not an influence calculated to counteract their original boorishness. Still, their patriarchal life seems to have secured for them among the other Greeks, not without reason, the character of simplicity, piety, and hospitality. It may have been for this reason that the Pythia, when applied to by the Cyrenæans to suggest to them

---

[65] Polyb. xi. 11.   [66] Paus. viii. 6, § 4.
[67] Herod. vi. 105.   [68] i. 146. Cf. Bursian, ii. 188.

a good form of government, referred them to an arbitrator from Mantineia.[69] But the position of Arcadia, though it developed the physique of its inhabitants, did not tend at the same time to awaken their energies, or provide them with a career in life. Being removed from the sea, it had no traffic of its own, and thus all those enlivening influences were cut off which arise from communication with foreign nations. At the same time it was necessary to provide for the surplus population, and the youth of the country, when from the sides of their native mountains they looked out upon the sea, felt that there, if anywhere, a career lay open before them. Thus it was that the Arcadians became the mercenary soldiers of the Hellenic world, as we find them on various occasions, but especially at the time of the Syracusan expedition, where they are mentioned as serving on both sides.[70] In like manner as the Messenians were the Poles, so the Arcadians were, both in their geographical position and their occupation, the Swiss of antiquity. At home they had no common history: the story of Arcadia is the annals of her several towns. The foundation of Megalopolis by Epaminondas to command the pass which enters Laconia by the valley of the Eurotas, was a final attempt to give this people a national unity; but this, like other attempts at συνοιχισμός in Arcadia, signally failed. The subsequent history of that city

[69] Herod. iv. 161.   [70] Thuc. vii. 57.

was described by a comic poet in the words: "the great city is a great desert" (ἐρημία μεγάλη 'στὶν ἡ Μεγάλη πόλις).[71]

Argolis. The district which, taking for its base the eastern part of Achaia and Arcadia, projects towards the south-east into the Ægean, bore the collective name of Argolis. It slopes in different directions to three seas—the Corinthian, the Saronic, and the Argolic; and this, together with the circumstance of its being a separate peninsula, advanced in front of the rest of the Peloponnese, and more closely connected with the outer world, is sufficient to account for what in itself is a subject for wonder, the fact that Argos was so long able to dispute with Sparta the hegemony of the country. *Importance of the Argive plain.* But it was in the Argive plain that the real power was concentrated. This is sufficiently proved by the whole territory receiving its name from the capital, the earlier title of Acte being forgotten, whereas in most Greek states the district and the capital had independent names. The Phœnicians, too, seem early to have discovered its importance; and their colony at Nauplia, on the low rocky tongue of land that projects sidewards into the head waters of the bay, was of the utmost importance to the development of the country. Here is localised the story of Palamedes, the son of Nauplius, "the seaman," and brother of Œax, "the rudder," whose name is still attached to the impregnable rock behind the town of

[71] Strabo, viii. 8, § 1.

Nauplia, the Gibraltar of Greece, which is called the Palamedi. He is said to have invented lighthouses, measures, scales, the discus, the dice, and the alphabet, and is an evident embodiment of civilisation imported from abroad. The same early influence of this neighbourhood is implied by the numerous ancient towns congregated in so small an area, for nowhere else in Greece can we find such remarkable specimens of primitive military architecture as the walls of Tiryns, Mycenæ, and the Larissa of Argos. Tiryns, on its crust of rock, forming an excrescence from the level plain, can boast now, as in the days when Homer called it " well-walled " ($\tau\varepsilon\iota\chi\iota\delta\varepsilon\sigma\sigma\alpha$),[72] the huge rude blocks composing its masonry, which caused the Greeks to regard it as the work of the Cyclopes, and the wonderful galleries within the walls themselves, by which the defence was intended to be protracted. On the opposite side, Argos, from the name of its castle-crowned citadel, Larissa, betrays its Pelasgian origin, for Larissa in the legends is the daughter of Pelasgus. And at the head of the plain, overlooking its whole arid length, in a position which once was the most favourable of all, when the swamps of the sea-coast rendered the lower part unwholesome,[73] Mycenæ, by its parallel courses or closely-fitted polygons of gigantic stones, the rude carving of its gate of lions, and its immense subterranean treasuries, testi-

---

[72] *Il.* ii. 559.
[73] Curtius, *Peloponnesos*, ii. 341.

fies to the reality of that wealth and power which is celebrated in early story.

<small>Upland region of Nemea.</small>

Between the plain of Argos and the neighbourhood of Corinth and Sicyon, lies an upland region, divided into a number of small plains or valleys, such as those of Phlius, Cleonæ, and Nemea. Through these led the two passes that formed the line of communication with Argos from the north, one of which was a mountain path, being intended, so Pausanias tells us, for "well-girt men" (ἀνδράσιν εὐζώνοις);[74] while the other, which, though rough, was passable for carriages, was that called the Tretos, which, after traversing deep ravines, enters the plain close under Mycenæ. The position of Nemea deserves further notice for its having been the scene of one of the four festivals common to Greece. It is described by Pindar as "deeply sunk," and lying "beneath shadeless mountains of dread antiquity."[75] At the present day it is a most solitary spot. The little green plain, from two to three miles long by half a mile broad, is destitute of trees, as also are the surrounding heights. The most conspicuous object is Mount Apesas, the flat summit of which resembles an altar, and was known in ancient times as the place where Perseus first sacrificed to Zeus Apesantius.[76] The marshy state of the ground justifies the epithet "well-watered" (εὔυδρος) which Theocritus[77] applies to it; and here

---

[74] ii. 15, § 2.   [75] Pind. *Nem.* iii. 30, vi. 74.
[76] Paus. ii. 15, § 3.   [77] xxv. 182.

must have grown the parsley with which the victors in the games were crowned. The remains of the temple of Zeus are among the most picturesque in Greece, consisting of three slender columns, which rise above a mass of scattered fragments. We cannot be surprised at finding it a ruin, when Pausanias tells us that in his time the statue was no longer there, and the roof had fallen in.[78]

There remains yet one more place in Argolis to be mentioned, which is even more interesting as illustrating the life and feelings of the Greeks. This is the sanctuary of Æsculapius, near Epidaurus, the most fashionable resort of invalids in Greece. The city of Epidaurus, lying on a small peninsula on the neighbouring coast, served as an advanced guard to protect the Hieron, in the same way as the town of Rhamnus stands on the shore in front of the temple of Nemesis, near Marathon.[79] Here the pilgrims used to land, and crossing the little plain at the back of the city—which, from its fitness for the growth of vines, obtained for that place its Homeric epithet of "vine-clad" (ἀμπελόεντ' Ἐπίδαυρον)[80]—would enter a deep valley clothed with fragrant and beautiful

<small>Sanctuary of Æsculapius.</small>

---

[78] ii. 15, § 2.

[79] These are excellent specimens of the maritime towns built on the small peninsulas of the Greek coast, of which Thucydides tells us that at an early period ἐπ' αὐτοῖς τοῖς αἰγιαλοῖς τείχεσιν ἐκτίζοντο καὶ τοὺς ἰσθμοὺς ἀπελάμβανον (i. 7).

[80] *Il.* ii. 561.

shrubs, such as the myrtle, arbutus, and oleander, which, if they arrived in the spring time, would be then in full blossom. From thence they would ascend for many miles, sometimes having peeps of the sea behind them, sometimes losing it from view, while the valley became a gorge, and the path led sometimes through the torrent-bed, sometimes along precipices high above it, until at length, passing through a narrow defile, they emerged into a large basin in the midst of the mountain-tops: at the further end of this was the sanctuary. If the imagination has something to do with the cure of invalids, we may well suppose that the impression created by the surroundings of the place, and the *religio loci* connected with the presence of the god of healing, would tend to promote their recovery. Beyond this, and good mountain air, this retreat (for we can hardly call it a watering-place, as it possessed neither baths nor mineral waters) seems to have had little to recommend it. At the same time, we must not judge its ancient condition by its present appearance. Now the mountain-sides are bare, the soil is dry, and, with the exception of the splendid theatre, the work of Polycletus,[81] the seats of which are almost perfect, though half hidden by bushes of golden cytisus, the buildings are all in ruins. But in former times the heights must have been wooded, and the

---

[81] Paus. ii. 27, § 5.

temples and other beautiful edifices must have risen from the midst of groves and gardens. We need not doubt, also, that in such a place of public resort the means of recreation and amusement were amply provided.

LECTURE IX.

ON THE CONNECTION BETWEEN GREEK GEOGRAPHY AND GREEK MYTHOLOGY.

Origin of Greek Myths—Greece suitable for Polytheism—Myths connected with the Geography—Local Myths of Thessaly—Sacred Centres of Mythology—Haunts of Deities—Birthplace of Music—Local Worship of Poseidon—Mythical Genealogies—Descent derived from River Gods—Myths suggested by Water—Myths of the Catavothras—Local Legends of Theseus—Myths of Observation—Etymological Myths—Ancient Legends in Modern Greece—Story of the Copaic Lake.

Origin of Greek myths

It will, I suppose, be generally allowed that one main source of Greek mythology was figurative language. There seems to have been a period of development in the history of the Indo-European races, when large classes of ideas were expressed by means of personification. Of this we find clear evidence in the Vedas, which contain the metaphorical language out of which myths were formed, though as yet no mythical element existed in them. The language of the other Aryan races must have passed through the same stage. In the course of time these expressions were misunderstood, and they became myths, the persons being conceived of as real

LECT. IX.]   GEOGRAPHY OF GREECE.   299

persons, and their acts as real acts; and these myths were afterwards further corrupted by being supplemented for purposes of explanation.[1] In a few instances, though, as it appears to me, in only a few, we are able at present to trace with tolerable certainty the correspondence of myths in Sanscrit and Greek. As the science of comparative mythology progresses, we shall probably be able to identify others; and in the end many will remain which have descended from a common original, though we may be unable to discover it. But the mythopoeic power was not limited to this early period, but continued to exist among the Greeks long after they

[1] An instance may serve to illustrate this process. Among the early races the sun was spoken of as a powerful hero; the bright days were his herd of cows—350 in number, as they are described in the Odyssey (xii. 127 *seq.*), thereby representing approximately the days of the year; the winter was a wild, misshapen, furious giant, dwelling in the west— the land of sunset, and so of darkness; the pale light and short days of winter are described as the concealing of the cows by the giant in his cavern—an idea found in the Vedas. Accordingly, the return of spring would be expressed in the following way:—The hero brings back the cows from the cave of the giant in the west. When the original significance is lost, this appears as the Greek myth of Hercules and Geryon. Hercules (the sun-god) carries off the oxen (the long bright days) from the cave of the monster Geryon (their concealment during stormy winter) at Gades (in the region of darkness). This simple outline is afterwards filled in by numerous additional facts, to explain the reason for Hercules' visit to the west, and to help out the story in other ways.

had established themselves in their permanent home. It was not merely that the deities whom they brought with them, or imported from without, had new functions attributed to them, or were regarded as the moving agents in a variety of phenomena, though legends were constantly arising from this cause; but the use of figurative language still peopled the world with mythological beings, and gave birth to innumerable stories. As I am not lecturing on mythology, I must refrain from pursuing this subject further; but it was necessary to premise thus much before proceeding to show its connection with the geography. In the case of the older myths this connection came to pass from their being localised in certain places, as in the instance of the infernal rivers — the Styx and the Acheron — which were identified with the Arcadian and Thesprotian streams; or from the powers of nature and physical changes being associated with the earlier deities, as in the myth of Hercules and the Achelous; while the later legends arose from the facts of geography being expressed in figurative language, as where a river issuing from Mount Erymanthus is called the Erymanthian Boar, and its inundations on the lands of Psophis are described as the ravages committed by that animal.

Greece suitable for polytheism. Greece was a land specially adapted to the development of polytheism, both from the variety of the country and the tendency of the inhabitants to break up into separate clans.² Each district had its own distinctive features and its own associations; and when these had given birth to a group of mythological ideas, they were fostered within that area by the isolation of those into whose belief they had entered.³ Afterwards, when they had been brought to maturity, and forms of worship had grown up round them, they passed beyond their original limits, and became part of the common heritage of the Hellenic race. Besides this, the varied pursuits of the people, arising from the configuration of the country, and differences of soil and climate, introduced various interests and subjects for thought, all of which were accompanied by their respective deities. The occupations of hunting and tending cattle on the mountains associated them with Pan and Artemis, and the other sylvan gods; in the valleys, agricultural pursuits and the cultivation of the vine caused them to worship Demeter, Silenus, and Dionysus; while sailing and fishing on the sea brought them into contact with the whole family of marine deities. Nor must we forget the aspect of the country, which was eminently fitted to nourish poetical superstitions. It was beyond all others a

---

² Preller, *Gr. Mythologie*, i. 7 foll.

³ Bergk remarks (*Literaturgeschichte*, i. p. 965) that " in the remote parts of Greece old beliefs continued to exist which were not influenced by the Hesiodean theogony as the ordinary beliefs of Greece were."

land of mystery. Its deep ravines, and dark caverns, and strange disappearances of rivers; the contrast between the sunny brightness of the maritime plains and the thunder-storms and snow-falls which are frequent in some of the highland regions; the solitude of the mountains; and the sound and motion of the restless sea—all tended to suggest innumerable fancies with regard to the powers of nature. These the realistic spirit of the Greeks, who saw nothing doubtfully or vaguely, invested with definite forms, which were constantly present to them, and formed a world, independent of, but yet in communication with, their own.

Myths connected with the geography.

In some countries the mythology is not connected with particular localities, either because the ground itself does not present sufficiently salient features, or because the mind of the people does not naturally associate the two. The latter of these two causes is especially noticeable in the myths of the Latin races, which, from the impalpable character of their divinities, were very little identified with places. But this, as we have seen, was not the case in Greece. To the Greeks Aphrodite was Cytherea and Hermes Cyllenius. Every thread in that intricate web which we call the history of the gods and heroes had its local colouring. In not a few of the legends the occurrence is related with slight variation in more than one place. And further, a large amount of mythology actually had its source in geography. It is hardly necessary here to prove this, as many instances of the connection of the two have been adduced in former lectures. Besides those just referred to of the Erymanthian boar, and the contest of Hercules and the Achelous, we have noticed the legends of Alpheius and Arethusa, of Boreas and Orithyia, and of Hercules dragging Cerberus to light at the hot springs of Mount Laphystium. We have seen how caverns were associated with Pan and the Nymphs, how fountains on mountain summits were ascribed to the hoof of Pegasus, and how Poseidon was regarded as both the holder and the shaker of earth; lastly, we have observed the position held by trees and flowers in the worship of the gods, and the story of the origin of the poetic art from the reeds of the Copaic lake. In fact, this connection was traced in some instances by the Greeks themselves. In a passage already quoted, Strabo has pointed out, with great clearness, the mythological significance of the fable of the Achelous, and elsewhere he has offered interpretations of other myths, either his own or from other writers, which, though not always felicitous, show that such views were not uncommon. Thus, when speaking of the excellence of volcanic soil for the growth of vines, he says that some persons, with a refinement of criticism, regard this as the explanation of the story of the destruction of Semele by fire at the birth of Dionysus,[4] the wine-god, being, as it

[4] Strabo, xiii. 4, § 11.

were, the son of brimstone. This graceless interpretation is worthy of Pausanias, who frequently rationalises the old myths. The following is a specimen of his method, being his explanation of the story of Narcissus, the locality of which was a fountain near Thespiæ. "At this place," he says, "is Narcissus' fountain, and they say that Narcissus looked into this water, and not perceiving that it was his own reflection that he saw, fell in love unawares with himself, and died of love at the fountain. Now, this is absolutely ridiculous, that a person who had reached an age to fall in love should be unable even to distinguish between a living being and the reflection of one. There is, however, another account of him, which, though less known than the former, is also reported —namely, that Narcissus had a twin sister who closely resembled him in appearance, and wore her hair like him, and was dressed in the same way, and that they used to go out hunting together. Now, Narcissus fell in love with his sister, and after the girl's death, on going to the fountain, though he was aware that he saw his own reflection, yet he felt it to be a solace to his love when he fancied that he was not looking at his own reflection, but at the image of his sister."[5]

Local myths of Thessaly. The land in which the earliest Greek mythology found its home was Thessaly. With it are associated the battle of the Gods and Titans, the flood of Deucalion, and the building of the Argo and departure of

[5] Pausan. ix. 31, § 7.

the Argonauts. Of these the story of Deucalion, though it is found amongst most of the Aryan races, can hardly be dissociated from local geographical features, and the same is the case with the Titanomachy. It is true that in this, as in so many other Greek myths, we may not confine ourselves to one interpretation; and this is one main cause of the difficulty of explaining Greek mythology — viz. that myths from various sources are interlaced with one another so as to become almost indistinguishable. It was a peculiarity of the creative Greek mind, that it recast, in a crucible of its own, whatever materials were presented to it. This took place in its mythology; and so the characters of gods and heroes grew up, and mythical events took place, with the details of which we are perfectly familiar, but which nevertheless represent no one original conception. Thus, the struggle of the Gods and Titans embodies the idea of the wild forces of nature, such as the winds, storms, and torrents, being checked in their work of ruin, and subdued by the order which prevails in the cosmos. It is also an ancient philosophic myth of the old order giving place to new, of a lower civilisation opposing itself to a higher, and forced to give way to it. Further, it contains an element of historical reminiscence of the deities of the earlier inhabitants of the soil being driven off the field by the Hellenic gods; and this accounts for the old-world character of this order of deities, it being the almost universal rule, that where invaders have conquered the natives of a country and settled among them, the gods of the conquered race have become the demons of the conquerors. But, in addition to all this, it represents violent movements of the earth's surface, especially the changes by which Thessaly assumed, or was thought to have assumed, its present aspect—the earthquake which rent Olympus apart from Ossa, and changed Thessaly from an inland sea into a plain.[6] The description in the *Theogony*, where the gods take their stand on Olympus, the Titans on Othrys, may almost be regarded as a picture of this change. There the whole world is represented as rocking, even to the depths of Tartarus; Olympus reels to its base as the armies close in the encounter, until Zeus comes forth with his omnipotent might, launching lightnings and thunderbolts, by which the surface of the earth is set on fire, and the forests roar in the conflagration.[7] Here again the ancients had anticipated the modern interpretation, for Strabo tells us concerning the peninsula of Pallene in Chalcidice, that by some it was called Phlegra, and was considered to have been the abode of the Giants, implying that it was associated with the workings of some great forces of nature.[8]

Sacred centres of mythology.   The same local character which we have thus seen to belong to some of the oldest Hellenic legends was

Preller, *Griechische Mythologie*, i. 37, 48.
[7] *Theog.* 678-694.
[8] Strabo, vii. *Fragm.* 25 (Kramer).

imprinted on much of the Greek religion by the prominence of the sacred centres of mythology. Olympus, from having been regarded as the home of the gods at the time when the Dorian race was settled at its foot, continued to be so esteemed even when Thessaly was separated from the rest of Greece.[9] Owing to the same cause, Tempe was the seat of the worship of Apollo on the continent of Greece before Delphi, whence arose the custom in later times of sending a procession from the latter place to gather the sacred bay on the banks of the Peneius. In like manner the sanctuary of Dodona in Epirus was from the earliest times dedicated to Zeus, and continued to be the most famous centre of the legends relating to him; and the mysteries of the great goddesses found a home at Eleusis, and above all, the later worship of Apollo was established at Delphi. Nor were the Greek heroic myths less local in their grouping. It is at Argos that we find the stories of Inachus and Io, of Danaus and his daughters, and Prœtus and the Prœtides, of Perseus, and at a later period of the Pelopidæ, who furnished such a fruitful subject to the Attic stage. At Thebes grew up the numerous legends of Cadmus, of Amphion and Zethus, of Œdipus and the Epigoni. Corinth had to tell of Sisyphus, Glaucus, and Bellerophon. And so, too, Athens, Sparta, Orchomenus, and others of the principal cities, had a fund of mythical lore, which, however widely its fame

[9] Curtius, *History of Greece*, i. 114.

might be spread, had in each case arisen on the spot, or at least had been permanently associated with that locality.

<small>Haunts of deities.</small> A similar result was produced by the association of certain forms of worship and traditional beliefs with particular features of the country. The lofty mountain summits were especially dedicated to Zeus and Helios, and here we trace the influence of the Pelasgic religion, for that people, like the ancient Persians and Germans, made no use of temples and images, but kept alive their reverence for spiritual things by worshipping in the midst of impressive surroundings.[10] Thus we find in later times an altar to Zeus on the summit of Athos,[11] and Æschylus[12] calls that mountain "the Athoan height of Zeus" ('Αθωον αἶπος Ζηνός): on one of the peaks of Mount Lycæum was a sacred grove and altar of Zeus Lycæus, which formed a centre of the ancient Arcadian worship of that deity; and the principal summit of Taygetus was consecrated to the sun, and horses and other victims were sacrificed there in his honour.[13] The springs have been already noticed as offering a home to innumerable legends, so that Pausanias is for ever recurring to them on account of their mythological interest. The promontories also have a peculiar importance in this respect, not only because of the temples that were erected there—as that of Athena at Sunium, and

---

[10] Curtius, *History of Greece*, i. 51.   [11] Mela, ii. 2.
[12] *Ag.* 285.   [13] Paus. iii. 20, § 4.

those of Poseidon at Tænarum and Geræstus—but on account of the strange rites that were attached to them, and the fables associated with their weird forms. The voluntary death of Sappho by casting herself from the Leucadian headland, and the custom which Strabo[14] mentions as existing in Cyprus of casting from a promontory such persons as violated the altar of Apollo, do not seem to have been isolated instances, but rather a form of expiation dating from the earliest antiquity.[15] The grottoes and hollows in their neighbourhood were regarded as the resort of the sea nymphs and marine deities and monsters, the brood of Nereus; or as sheltering malevolent beings, such as Scylla, who represented the dangers of navigation. In some cases they were consecrated as the places of burial of deified sailors, like Misenus and Palinurus; in others, the towering headland itself, as that of Mimas opposite Chios, seemed the embodiment of the huge giant whose name it bore; or else its shape or name caused some ancient story to be located there, as when the promontory of Drepanum in Achaia is regarded as the place where Cronos cast the sickle with which he had maimed his father Uranus,[16] or when that of Zoster in Attica is said to have been the scene of Latona loosing her girdle.[17]

In speaking of the Copaic lake, we have seen how *Birthplace of music.*

[14] xiv. 6, § 3.
[15] E. Curtius, *Beiträge zur geographischen Onomatologie*, p. 147.
[16] Paus. vii. 23, § 4.   [17] Ibid. i. 31, § 1.

the poetic art was thought to have originated there, because of the reeds which fringe its shores. In Arcadia also, where music was supposed to have had an independent development, we find the myth of the nymph Syrinx, who, being pursued by Pan, fled into the river Ladon, and at her own request was metamorphosed into a reed, of which Pan then made his flute. The scene of this, which was evidently chosen from being appropriate to the story, is described in the following manner. The Ladon, "on account of its clear stream, is regarded as the most beautiful river in the peninsula. Its water is distinguished by abundance of fishes, its banks by picturesque variety of scenery. The configuration of its long valley has not the same definite character as those of the Helisson and the Alpheius. At one moment it contracts to a ravine, at others it expands into small plains, where the river has reedy banks and affords nourishment to fine groups of plane-trees. Here there is no lack of corn-land and pasturage. This is why the native stories of this river-district tell of the herds of horses of King Onkos, of the pursuit of Daphne, the nymph of the woods and fountains, and of Syrinx, who expires in the reeds."[18] So too the Styx and the Achelous are regarded as the eldest daughter and eldest son of Ocean; and as the ocean in the Greek cosmogony is regarded as the origin of all things, so Styx represents the primeval darkness from which

[18] Curtius, *Peloponnesos,* i. 368.

arose the beginnings of life, while Achelous is the emblem of organic life itself which spreads over the earth in innumerable streams.[19] The former of these was identified with the Arcadian waterfall, which we have already described. The latter was represented by the Acarnanian river, because it was the most important stream in Greece, and had its source in the neighbourhood of the oracle of Dodona. Hence it came to be regarded as the representative of all rivers, so that Virgil could rightly describe the element of water as "draughts of the Achelous" (*Acheloia pocula*).

Local worship of Poseidon.

The manner in which the worship of one of the great deities became localised, and his functions afterwards extended, may be seen in the worship of Poseidon. He was one of the great divinities which were common to the whole Greek race. He exercises a part of the functions which once were supposed to belong to the one supreme God who ruled all creation; and thus he is sometimes called Ζεὺς ἐνάλιος, in the same way as Hades is called Ζεὺς χθόνιος. But nevertheless, though he continued to be venerated elsewhere, yet it was the Peloponnese that became the great focus of his worship. That country, from its being girdled by the sea, and penetrated by numerous bays, appeared to be dedicated, as it were, to the "holder of earth" (γαιήοχος); and from being frequently exposed to shocks of earthquake was called to revere the great "earth-shaker" (ἐνοσίχθων). Conse-

[19] Preller, *Gr. Mythol.* i. 28-30.

quently at the isthmus, where both these functions were in the highest degree apparent, he had his sanctuary, which held the position of Propylæa at the entrance of the peninsula. Besides this, at Corinth, at Nauplia, and especially at Trœzen and on the neighbouring island of Calauria, he held a pre-eminent position; in Arcadia also, where he was the god of springs and rivers, on the southern promontories of Malea and Tænarum, at Pylos in Messinia, and at several places on the coast of Elis, especially on the promontory of Samicon, we find his worship established: but the most famous of all the seats of his worship were those on the Achæan coast, at Ægæ and Helice, at the former of which places, according to the Homeric description, was his palace in the depths of the sea—

ἔνθα δέ οἱ κλυτὰ δώματα βένθεσι λίμνης,
χρύσεα, μαρμαίροντα τετεύχαται, ἄφθιτα αἰεί.[20]

But after this district had thus been made the special abode of the god, his functions came to be enlarged to suit the local phenomena. For throughout historical times the land has been gaining on the sea in the Peloponnese, and the shore line advancing in places, especially on the west coast; and hence Poseidon came to be regarded as the giver of land, not merely because he retired to make way for it, but because the sand and shingle that he cast up

---

[20] *Il.* xiii. 21. See Preller, *Gr. Myth.* i. 448.

helped to form the alluvium. This is what is meant by the title of Prosclystius, under which that god was worshipped at Argos.[21]

To turn now to the myths that arise from features of geography being expressed in figurative language —we are met first by a remarkable group, in which the peculiarities of a country are presented in the form of a genealogy, seldom complete from this point of view, but containing names derived from other sources. Thus, in the list of the early kings of Attica we find Actæus or Actæon, who represents the ἀκτή or sea-coast that bounds so great a part of Attica and gave that country its name;[22] later on occurs Cranaus, a personification of the rocky soil of the mountain-sides, and indeed of the greater part of the surface of the land, whence both Pindar[23] and Aristophanes[24] apply the epithet κρανααί to Athens: and further we meet with Erichthonius, who is probably identical with Erechtheus, but whose name in this form seems intended to express the fruitful soil of the plains.[25] In the genealogy of the early kings of Sparta we find similar features. "The first king of the land," we are told,[26] "who was himself indigenous, was Lelex, and after him the people whom he governed were called Leleges. From him was sprung Myles, and at Myles'

Mythical genealogies.

---

[21] Paus. ii. 22, § 4 ; and Curtius, *Peloponnesos*, i. 48.
[22] Preller, *Gr. Myth.* ii. 139.
[23] *Ol.* vii. 151.   [24] *Av.* 123.
[25] Preller, i. 159.   [26] Paus. iii. 1, § 1.

death his son Eurotas in turn inherited the kingdom. This man, by means of a dyke, carried off into the sea the water that formed a lake in the plain, and when this had run off, as what remained was the stream of a river, they called that Eurotas." Here we have the description of a real or supposed change, resembling that which took place in Thessaly at the opening of Tempe. " Eurotas, however, having no male children, left the kingdom to Lacedæmon, the son of Taygete, a reputed descendant of Zeus, from whom also the mountain received its name. Now Lacedæmon took in marriage Sparta, the daughter of Eurotas, and when he came to the throne, he first changed the name of the country and people and gave them his own, and at a later period built a city and called it after his wife, the same which is called Sparta down to our time." The perverse ingenuity of this narrative is almost equalled by the following account of the country round the famous temple of Hera in the Argive territory.[27] " The temple itself is in the more level part of Eubœa. For they call this mountain Eubœa, saying that the river Asterion had three daughters—Eubœa, Prosymna, and Acræa—and that they were the nurses of Hera. And they name the mountain opposite the Heræum after Acræa, and the ground about the temple after Eubœa, and the region below the temple of Hera they call Prosymna. Now this Asterion flows above the Heræum, and then

[27] Paus. ii. 17, § 1.

falls into a chasm and disappears." Here we have a tolerably transparent description of the features of the district. The river, from the fostering power of its water, is regarded as the parent of the surrounding region; the name of the first of his three daughters, Eubœa, like the island of the same name, signifies "good grazing ground;" that of Prosymna, apparently, the route by which processions in honour of the goddess approached; that of Acræa the mountain peaks above. These, from their neighbouring position, seemed to guard the temple, and consequently were spoken of as the nurses of Hera. Of the same kind as this, though more finely veiled and far more graceful, is the myth of the Acrocorinth which Pausanias[28] has recorded. According to this, that fortress-peak was described as a present from Briareus to the Sun, and again from the Sun to Aphrodite. The first of these figures represents its towering proportions, the second the brilliancy of the surrounding natural features, the third the lovely city which was extended at its foot.[29]

In the collection of statuary in the Vatican there is a celebrated colossal figure of the Nile, in which *Descent derived from river-gods.*

[28] ii. 4, § 6.

[29] See also the allegorical description of the physical geography of the district of Tegea in the story of the contention of the two sons of King Tegeates, Skephros and Leimon—*i.e.* the rugged uplands and the meadowland—as given by Pausanias (viii. 53, § 1-3); and compare the detailed interpretation of the myth in Curtius, *Peloponnesos*, i. 253.

that deity is represented in a recumbent attitude, with sixteen children grouped in different positions about him. The number sixteen is said to represent the sixteen cubits which the river rose at the time of the annual inundation, but the idea which the group is intended to embody is the fertilising and generative influence, that we have just seen in more than one instance attributed to streams, and their power of sustaining human life. This is what is meant in the *Theogony*,[30] where Hesiod describes Tethys as bearing to Oceanus a sacred race of daughters, the water-nymphs, three thousand in number, whose office it is to foster the human race (ἄνδρας κουρίζουσι). On this principle, almost every city in Greece that was situated on the banks of a stream was described as descended from it; or rather, as in the case of Sparta, the river was said to have received the name of a god or hero, while the city was called after his daughter. To the later Greeks the mythological genealogies seem to have been so familiar, that they failed to trace the meaning of them; but we, in order to arrive at the interpretation, have simply to invert the order of ideas, and to say, for instance, that the city of Sparta was represented by a nymph, and that the river Eurotas, from which the city drew its subsistence, was regarded as her father. The conception, however, which here lies before us in such a simple form, was at the root of much of Greek mythology,

[30] Hes. *Theog.* 346 foll.

and passed into stories much less easy of explanation. Thus it is that numerous clans traced their origin up to a great river-god,[31] and that the gods themselves in their early years, according to the local traditions, had been brought up by the fountain-nymphs of a certain district, as Zeus by those of Crete or of Arcadia, and Dionysus by those of Nysa or Dodona. Thus too arose the frequent stories of the amours of the rivers and other water deities, which, when woven together and further supplemented, became a fruitful source of elaborate legends.

The myths that were suggested by water in Greece are so numerous, that they deserve to be treated by themselves. From its changeful character, and the variety of forms in which it appeared, as well as its importance to man, that element was certain to attract the attention, and to be suggestive to the imagination. At the same time we must beware of exaggerating its influence on the mythology, as Forchhammer has done in his *Hellenica*, a work of true genius, which, without word-painting or picturesque effect, presents the country in all its minutest features, as in a raised and coloured map, but is marred by the wild mythological theories that are worked into the physical geography. Foremost among these stories was that of the Danaides. The scene of this is the Argive plain, where, according to another legend, there had been, as in Attica, an early struggle

Myths suggested by water.

[31] Preller, *Gr. Myth.* i. 28.

between the gods of sea and land for the patronage of the country, and in this instance also the sea-god had to retire vanquished.³² Enraged at this, Poseidon commanded the fountains, which were subject to his dominion, to cease to flow, and from that time the soil of Argos became thirsty. Thus, as we have seen in the case of the Asterion, the streams that descend from the mountains soon disappear beneath the surface, sucked in by the arid ground long before they reach the lower part of the plain. Under these circumstances, at a time when several populous cities— Nauplia, Tiryns, and Argos—existed in the neighbourhood, it was necessary to have recourse to artificial irrigation. Of this Danaus is the representative, and so Hesiod describes him as having furnished water to the parched country—

Ἄργος ἄνυδρον ἐὸν Δαναὸς ποίησεν ἔνυδρον.³³

But for all that, the task was a laborious and thankless one. No sooner was the water conducted in carefully-constructed channels over the land, than it filtered through, and thus arose the story of the fifty daughters of Danaus, who were condemned perpetually to pour water into a tub full of holes. The name of one of these maidens is Asteris, and thus closely corresponds to that of the river Asterion; and

---

³² Curtius, *Peloponnesos*, ii. 340.

³³ Hesiod, quoted by Eustathius on *Il.* iv. 171. Cf. Strabo, i. 2, § 15 ; and see Curtius, *Pel.* ii. 558.

the interpretation is still further confirmed by the history of Amymone, the only one of the fifty who was exempted from the task.[34] This nymph granted her favours to Poseidon, and in return received from him the gift of the perennial source of water, which flows from the southern extremity of the Argive plain into the marsh of Lerna. The contrast between this plentiful spring and the general dryness of the country gave birth to this part of the legend; and another account says that this privilege was conferred on the maiden, because of the service she had rendered the city of Argos in bearing water thither during a season of drought.

The torrents, which flow during the winter, and leave their channels dry during the summer, are described in the following graceful myth, which is related by Pausanias.[35] The scene is laid in Achaia, where almost all the streams are of this character. "After passing the Charadrus," he says, "you come to the insignificant remains of the city of Argyra, and a fountain of the same name on the right hand of the high road; here the river Selemnus descends to the sea. Now what the people of the country say about it is, that Selemnus was a handsome youth who used to tend his flocks there, and Argyra was one of the sea nymphs, and that as she fell in love with Selemnus, she used to rise from the sea to visit him. But after

[34] Mure, *Tour in Greece*, ii. 181. Preller, *Gr. Myth.* ii. 51.
[35] vii. 23, § 1, 2.

the lapse of no long time Selemnus began to lose his beauty, and the nymph ceased to visit him. So when Selemnus was deserted by Argyra and died of love, Aphrodite changed him into a river. I tell the story as it is related by the people of Patræ." Here the love of the shepherd of the river bank and the sea maiden represents the torrent reaching the sea; the cessation of their love and the death of the shepherd signifies the drying up of the water and its no longer flowing in the summer months.[36]

Next let us examine the fable of the Lernean hydra, which was supposed to inhabit the marsh near Argos. The hero of this is Heracles, who is one of the most compound in his origin of the Greek divinities, representing at least three elements—the great Phœnician deity, as in the story of Iolaus, whose companionship with Heracles signifies the Ionian people acting in concert with the Tyrians—the Aryan sun-god, as when he throttles the snakes at his birth, *i.e.* destroys the powers of night by his rising—and the beneficent force by which the powers of nature are subjugated to man. The place is thus described:—" Along the sea-shore is a strip of firm gravel; but between this and the foot of the hills, quaking paths and ditches brimful of stagnant water remind us that we are crossing the Lernæan marsh. At the edge of *terra firma* a copious source gushes from under conglomerate rock, and close by is a still deep pool. These

[36] Curtius, *Peloponnesos*, i. 405.

features of nature remain unchanged, while the groves, temples, and statues, which abounded hereabouts, have left not a wreck behind."[37] Here it was that Hercules struggled with the water-snake, and ultimately overcame it, notwithstanding that it had fifty heads, and as soon as one of these was cut off, two others sprang up in its place. We have already seen how the name of snake was applied to rivers in Greece on account of their serpentine windings, and thus we shall have less difficulty in understanding the meaning of this fable. The Lernæan hydra is the sinuous water finding its way through the marshy ground; and the destruction of it by Hercules is the process of draining and confining it within a channel, the numerous and ever-growing heads being the springs and watercourses ever bursting out afresh. In the same way, the Nemean lion, who is the son of Typhon —that is, the storm—probably symbolises a violent mountain torrent. Its abode is in the Tretos, as the deep ravine is called through which the pass leads from Nemea to the head of the Argive plain. Its destruction by Hercules is the banking of the stream, by which it was prevented from committing other ravages.[38] In other feats of prowess also of that hero, such as the contests with the Erymanthian boar, with the Achelous, and with Nessus, we have noticed his close connection with changes in the face of the country.

[37] Clark, *Peloponnesus*, 96.   [38] Curtius, *Pel.* ii. 506.

In all these instances the transition from figurative language to myth is sufficiently apparent. From saying "The pioneer of civilisation checks the serpentine stream, and restrains its sources," it is only one step further to say, "Hercules overcomes the hydra, and cuts off its heads."

Myths of the catavothras.

The water systems of the Arcadian valleys, with their strange subterranean outlets, were, as might be expected, a source of a variety of myths. In the first place, it was conceived that all the water of the country was originally hidden beneath the soil, so that it nowhere emerged to the surface. This strange notion is brought prominently forward by Callimachus in his hymn to Zeus,[39] where he describes Rhea, when she brought forth the infant god, as searching in vain for water to wash the babe; for "as yet the great Ladon did not flow, nor Erymanthus, the whitest of rivers, but up to that time Arcadia was waterless. At that time," the poet continues, "the moist Iaon supported above it many hollow oaks, and the Melas bore many cars, and many deadly beasts made their lairs above the Carneion, though it was a liquid stream, and a man would go on foot over the Crathis and the pebbly Metope with nought to quench his thirst, for the mass of water lay beneath men's feet." At last the goddess in her perplexity invokes the earth, exclaiming, "Dear earth, do thou too bring forth; thy birth-pangs are easy," and then,

[39] 15 foll. See Curtius, *Pel.* i. 157.

raising aloft her staff, smites the mountain-side, which opens and emits a mighty stream. The draining of the valleys by means of catavothras gave rise to other stories, for the hand of Hercules had to be called in to effect this beneficent change : to his agency was attributed a vast dyke, of great antiquity, by which the river Aroanius was conducted through the plain of Pheneus,[40] and also the subterranean outlets of the lake, which the people of the city affirmed to be not natural, but artificial.[41] The passage of the water underground, when the obstruction is removed, and the consequent overflow of the Ladon, which joins the Alpheius, and descends to Olympia in flood, was described in the mythology of that district as an invasion of Elis by Hercules; and in the neighbourhood of Pheneus were shown the tombs of the heroes who perished on that occasion.[42] The story of a confluent of the Ladon, which flowed by the city of Onca in northern Arcadia, was further narrated in the following manner :—When Demeter, who was wandering in search of her daughter, came to that place, she was pursued by Poseidon, who desired to ravish her : to avoid this, she changed herself into one of the mares of Oncus, the king of the country, and grazed in company with the herd. But Poseidon, perceiving this, assumed the form of a horse, and after a while she bore him a son, who was

[40] Paus. viii. 14, § 3.   [41] Ibid. § 2.
[42] Ibid. viii. 15, § 5.

called Arion.⁴³ Now, as Demeter signifies the earth, while Poseidon is the god of water, and the horse is a frequent symbol of running water in Greek mythology, and consequently is closely associated with the last-named deity, this simply means that a stream issued from the earth near the town of Onca. Then the story goes on to say that Hercules, when on his expedition against Elis, asked this horse as a present from Oncus, and was mounted on him when he conquered the Eleans. In other words, this stream joins the water which comes from Pheneus and floods the plain of Olympia.

<small>Local legends of Theseus.</small>

Another set of legends relating to improvements in the country is grouped round Theseus, a hero who in many ways is connected with Hercules, though his sphere is narrower, being limited to the Ionians of Greece Proper.⁴⁴ The principal achievements attributed to him refer to the coast-line between the sanctuary of Poseidon at the isthmus, which was originally Ionian, and Athens, and we seem to see described in them the establishment of a safe means of communication between the two.⁴⁵ His first engagement is on the Isthmus itself, where he destroys the robber Sinis, that is the "ravager," and on the same spot he subsequently founded the Isthmian games. The other name of this monster is the "pine-bender" (Πιτυοκάμπτης), and this leaves little doubt

---

⁴³ Paus. viii. 25, § 5. See Curtius, *Pel.* i. 371-2.
⁴⁴ Preller, *Gr. Myth.* ii. 285.   ⁴⁵ Ibid. 289, foll.

that he is the embodiment of a violent wind, though by mistaken etymology a story grew up of his having fastened his victims to the bent branches of two pines, by the rebound of which they were torn in sunder. His next exploit is near Crommyon, in a woody neighbourhood full of ravines, where he destroys a wild sow, called Phæa, or "the dusky." After what we have already seen of the names of rivers, we have no difficulty in recognising this as a mountain torrent. Then comes the most important of all, the struggle with Sciron, the brigand that gave his name to the Scironian rocks, by whom all the passers by were forced to wash his feet, whereupon, as they knelt before him, he cast them as a prey to a huge sea-tortoise. We learn from Strabo [46] that the violence with which the north-west wind blew over the Scironian rocks caused it to receive the name of Sciron at Athens; so that here again we can see that the brigand is the wind that causes such danger to those who pass those cliffs, now, as of old, a perilous transit. The washing his feet is their creeping round the base of the precipices close to the sea, while the sea-tortoise is discovered in a rock called Chelone, from a supposed resemblance to that animal.[47] Finally, between Eleusis and Athens he overcomes Procrustes, or "the racker," whose proper name was Damastes, the "subduer," or Polypemon,

---

[46] ix. 1, § 4.
[47] Bursian, *Geog. von Griechenland*, i. 368, *note*.

the "injurer." As we are told by Diodorus[48] that the scene of this was the part of Mount Ægaleos called Corydallus, which corresponds to the ridge where the modern pass of Daphne leads from Eleusis to Athens, we may conclude that Procrustes represents the dangers of that pass, and possibly his famous bed may be the narrow passage through which all alike were forced to go.

<small>Myths of observation.</small> Let us now turn our attention to another class of Greek legends, which are not necessarily connected with language at all; I mean those that are called Myths of Observation—a name which, if I mistake not, was first given by Mr. Tylor in his *Primitive History of Mankind.* These arise from the mind noticing remarkable phenomena, either natural or artificial, and then either inquiring into their origin or in some other way speculating about them. Thaumas, according to the allegory, is the mother of Iris: wonder is the cause of many-coloured invention, and so from this source numerous stories have sprung up. The eye measures the width of a narrow chasm, and the mind speculates on the possibility of leaping across it; thence arises a story that under extraordinary circumstances it has been accomplished, and this is embellished with numerous details. At Lydford, in Devonshire, it is a drunken farmer who returns from market, unaware that the bridge over the ravine has been broken, and whose horse leaps across with

[48] Diod. iv. 59, quoted by Preller, ii. 291, *note.*

him unconscious on its back. On the St. Gotthard pass in Switzerland it is a priest, who, to escape his pursuers, leaps across with a girl in his arms. Similarly, the basaltic columns in the north of Ireland, from their artificial appearance, coupled with their immense scale, have suggested the idea that they were the work of some superhuman power, and thus have obtained the name of the Giant's Causeway ; and similar fancies have arisen from Druidical remains. A Greek legend of this character is that connected with the plain of the Crau, in the south of France, which originated with the people of Massilia. This plain, which extends over an area of several square miles, is entirely covered with large pebbles; and when the Greeks sought an explanation of it, they connected the phenomenon with Hercules, the great western traveller ; so the story arose, that in his combat with the Ligurians, when his arrows failed him, Zeus showered these stones down from heaven to serve him as missiles against his enemies. This story is embodied in a fragment of Æschylus, which Strabo has preserved for us : —

ἰδὼν δ' ἀμηχανοῦντά σ' ὁ Ζεὺς οἰκτερεῖ,
νεφέλην δ' ὑποσχὼν νιφάδι γογγύλων πέτρων
ὑπόσκιον θήσει χθόν', οἷς ἔπειτα σὺ
βαλὼν διώσει ῥᾳδίως Λίγυν στρατόν.[49]

Markings on rocks have been a fertile source of

[49] Æschyl. *Fragm.* 196, ed. Dind. ; cf. Strabo, iv. 1, § 7.

such myths. Thus Cicero[50] tells us, that in the basaltic rocks near the lake Regillus, was seen a mark like that of a horse's hoof; and as this could have been made by no earthly horse, it was attributed to the horse of one of the great Twin Brethren after the battle of the Lake Regillus—a story which Macaulay has introduced with great effect in his *Lays of Ancient Rome*.[51] The same story arises from the same cause in many other places. At the convent of Mount Sinai, in Arabia, a similar mark is said to have been made by Mahomet's mule;[52] and in the north of Spain, in the valley that leads up to Covadonga, the scene of the great defeat of the Moors by the Spaniards, may still be seen the footprint of the horse of Pelayo, the Christian hero on that occasion. At Athens we have a very peculiar instance of this kind of myth. In the rock beneath the northern portico of the Erechtheium, in the Acropolis, three holes are visible, which were said in ancient times to have been made by the trident of Poseidon, and to be connected with a salt well hard by, which gave forth the sound of waves when the south wind blew.[53] Now these objects, together with an ancient olive-tree near them, were regarded as evidences of the contention between Poseidon and Athena for the patronage of Attica.

Similarly narrow straits of the sea suggest the idea

---

[50] *De Nat. Deor.* iii. 5; see Arnold, *Hist. of Rome*, i. 120.
[51] p. 98.   [52] Stanley, *Sinai and Palestine*, 54.
[53] Paus. i. 26, § 5; cf. viii. 10, § 4.

that the shores on the two sides were once united, and afterwards separated by a violent disruption. This idea existed among the Greeks with regard to the straits of Messina, whence arose the name Rhegium, " the rent." The story is given by Virgil in the 3d Æneid :—

> Hæc loca, vi quondam et vasta convulsa ruina
> (Tantum ævi longinqua valet mutare vetustas)
> Dissiluisse ferunt, cum protenus utraque tellus
> Una foret : venit medio vi pontus, et undis
> Hesperium Siculo latus abscidit. [54]

> These lands, they say, by rupture strange
> (So much can time's dark process change)
> Were cleft in sunder long agone,
> When erst the twain had been but one :
> Between them rushed the deep, and rent
> The island from the continent.
>   (*Conington's Translation.*)

Again, if Tempe is derived from τέμνω, "to cut," as C. O. Müller suggested, the depth and narrowness of the gorge seem to have originated the idea that it was broken open by the trident of the earth-shaking god, whence its name arose. Openings in the ground, too, from their appearing to lead down into darkness beneath the earth, were supposed to be entrances to the infernal regions, as was the case at Tænarum; and hot springs, from their seeming connection with

[54] *Æn.* iii. 414 foll.

a subterranean fire, suggested the same idea, as at Laphystium, where, as we have seen, Hercules brought Cerberus to the light of day. So also the volcanic phenomena at Lemnos were the source of the legend of Hephæstus having fallen on that island when cast by Zeus out of heaven; and similar appearances at Bathos, in the valley of the Alpheius, in Arcadia, caused the neighbouring people to maintain that the battle of the Gods with the Giants took place there and not in Pallene; so that they offered sacrifices to the lightnings, storms, and thunder, in that spot, as having been the weapons of the heavenly warfare.[55]

Etymological myths.

A few words must also be said about that class of myths which are called etymological. The process by which these is formed is as follows :—At an early period a name is assigned to an object in the ordinary course of nomenclature; but in the course of time the meaning and derivation of this name are forgotten. Then, from the unwillingness of the human mind to rest satisfied without a derivation, a new and erroneous one is found; and afterwards a story arises to explain this. Legends that arise from mistaken etymology are extremely common in Greek. In Pausanias we are constantly meeting with them; but they have an inferior interest from being usually the product of a later age, and we are now concerned with them only so far as they are connected with

[55] Paus. viii. 29, § 1.

geography. We may take as an instance the story of the foundation of Mycenæ. The derivation of this name which is usually given is from μυχός, "a recess," this being especially applicable to the place, as it lay in the inmost recesses of the Argive plain,—μυχῷ Ἀργεος ἱπποβότοιο, as Homer describes it.[56] This, however, was forgotten, and afterwards a new etymology suggested itself, from μύκης, "the cap of a scabbard," and to account for this the following myth arose, which is recorded by Pausanias.[57] When Perseus returned to Argos after the murder of Acrisius, being ashamed on account of the fame of it, he persuaded Megapenthes, the son of Prœtus, who held sway in the northern part of the Argive plain, to exchange his kingdom with him, and on receiving the dominion of Megapenthes he founded Mycenæ. His reason was that the cap of the scabbard of his sword fell off in that place, and he regarded the occurrence as an omen of the planting of the city.

It may be noticed, in conclusion, as illustrating the local character of Greek mythology, that in some cases the connection between certain beliefs and certain places has continued up to the present day. We must not expect, except in very rare instances, to find the same legend existing in modern as in ancient times; the changes that have passed over the coun-

Ancient legends in modern Greece.

[56] *Od.* iii. 263.   [57] ii. 16, § 3.

try have been too great for that. It is enough if we find corresponding ideas reproduced in the same locality. The extraordinary number of sacred springs in modern Greece—ἁγιάσματα, as they are called—has often been noticed as a point of resemblance between the modern inhabitants and their forefathers ; but in one case the same belief is attached to a spring that existed respecting it in antiquity. This is the source, on the side of Mount Hymettus that faces Athens, the water of which is drunk by the Athenian women as a remedy for unfruitfulness, and a preventive of hard labour in childbirth. In ancient times this was sacred to Aphrodite, and was called Κύλλου πήρα, and had the same qualities attributed to it, since we are told that it was κρήνη ἐξ ἧς αἱ πιοῦσαι εὐτοκοῦσι καὶ αἱ ἄγονοι γόνιμοι γίνονται.[58] So, too, the Nereids, who in modern times exercise all the functions of the ancient Nymphs, find a favourite place of abode in the Corycian cave, which was an accustomed haunt of the Nymphs in classical times.[59] But it is most remarkable that Olympus, which was the great centre of mythology in ancient times, continues in some ways to be so at the present day. It seems hardly accidental, that while this mountain was regarded as the especial abode of the supreme heathen god, every one of the convents on its sides

[58] Schmidt, *Das Volksleben der Neugriechen*, pp. 79, 80.
[59] Ibid. 103.

should now be dedicated to the Holy Trinity, a thing unknown in any other district in Greece. The Fates also, which were formerly described as sitting near the throne of Zeus, are now constantly associated with Olympus in the minds of the people, especially in the exercise of one of their ancient functions in presiding over marriage and childbirth; so that in many parts of the country it is customary for women to invoke them to come from the summits of that mountain.[60] So, too, while Pliny tells us that no wolves were to be found in any part of Olympus, at the present day there is a similar legend about the complete absence of bears.[61]

The following curious myth of the Copaic lake is told by the Bœotian peasants at the present day :— "An old king formerly ruled over the whole plain, which was completely dry, as the waters ran off through the catavothras. He possessed innumerable herds, and two hundred flourishing villages, where now reeds grow in the marshes, and in winter a broad lake extends. When he felt his end approaching, he divided his possessions between his two sons. To the one he gave his lands, to the other his herds. After a time it came to pass that a severe frost and snowfall suddenly destroyed all the cattle. The brother who was thus reduced to poverty came to

Story of the Copaic lake.

[60] Schmidt, p. 211; and my *Highlands of Turkey*, ii. 24, 25.
[61] Schmidt, p. 44; and my *Highlands*, ii. 12.

his rich brother, and begged for a share in his superfluous wealth ; but the other turned him scornfully from his door. The shepherd then devised a fearful vengeance. He secretly stopped up the catavothras, and when the winter rains came, the water could no longer escape. So the lake rose, and the fair villages were all submerged by the waves." [62]

[62] Ulrichs, *Reisen in Griechenland*, i. 212.

LECTURE X.

ON THE ETYMOLOGY OF GREEK NAMES OF PLACES.[1]

Principles of Nomenclature—Names derived from the Vegetation—Names derived from Animals—Caution required—Doubtful Etymologies—Non-Hellenic Names—Vagueness of the Greek Terminations—Peculiarities of Form—Sources of Names: Relative Position; Elevated Position; Enclosed Situation; Maritime Character; Environs, etc.; Water; Pasturage and Tillage; Colour; Resemblances to Men and Animals; Resemblances to Inanimate Objects; Worship of Deities—Names containing Numerals—Names from Occupations, etc.—Political Names—Names evidencing Geographical Changes—Pelasgic and other Names—Phœnician Names—Ancient Names in Modern Greece.

IN endeavouring to investigate the meaning of the names of places in Greece, the principle we have to start from is this—that no place, under ordinary circumstances, receives a name arbitrarily or without

Principles of nomenclature.

[1] The principal works that have helped me in finding the etymologies of individual names are G. Curtius' *Grundzüge der griechischen Etymologie* (2d ed.), a work distinguished by its philological caution as well as its masterly treatment of the subject; E. Curtius' *Peloponnesos*, from the notes to which a large amount of valuable material may be gleaned; and that model of compendious learning, Benseler's 3d ed. of Pape's *Wörterbuch der griechischen Eigennamen*, in which

some assignable reason. In modern times, when, from want of exercise, the onomatopoeic faculty is less quick than it used to be, the name attached to a locality is in some cases a mere symbol, possessing no connotation whatsoever; and this is especially the case when the place to be designated is devoid of salient features. Thus it is with some of our modern streets, which, after the ordinary sources of nomenclature have been already exhausted, are called after some large town for the sake of distinction. Thus

it has been attempted with great ingenuity to render the Greek names, both of persons and places, by corresponding proper names in German—a heroic task, but one which, to the English reader at all events, hardly conduces to intelligibility. To these writers I am deeply indebted. Some help I have also obtained from Bursian's *Geographie von Griechenland*. But the only considerable attempt that has been made, as far as I am aware, to classify the Greek names of places according to their etymology, is in E. Curtius' admirable essay already referred to (p. 71), *Beiträge zur geographischen Onomatologie der griechischen Sprache*, in which the names of promontories are treated of. The subject had not wholly escaped the ancient lexicographers, as may be seen from the *Etymologicum Magnum*, where (*s. v.* Ἐλεεῖς) the names of the Attic demes are classified under the heads of locality, local features, vegetation, employments, and male or female inhabitants; and it is somewhat surprising that it has not attracted more attention in modern times. I have not felt myself bound in all instances to mention the authority, where there is one, for any particular derivation, but have done so mainly in the case of important names, and those whose etymology is open to question.

it is especially in the United States of America, where we meet with such barbarisms as towns bearing the names of Troy, Athens, Memphis, and Cairo. But at the early period in the history of a country at which such titles are usually assigned this cannot happen; and names are for the most part given on account of some attribute of the place, or some feature sufficiently characteristic to distinguish it from others. It will readily be seen how large an opening is thus left, to those who impose these names, for the exercise of observation, ingenuity, acuteness, and imagination. Where an unobservant people will leave unnoticed all but the most ordinary objects, those that are quick in observation will select in each spot those that are the most distinctive. Where a dull people will fix on names of a commonplace character, the ingenuity of a clever people will be shown by the varied and almost recondite sources from which they draw their titles. Where a heavy people will represent their impressions by inexpressive terms, the clear-sightedness of an acute people will be reflected by the well-marked stamp and clear ring of the words they employ. Where an unimaginative people will see only a rock or a cavern, those that are gifted with fancy will trace a resemblance to an animal, a part of the human body, or some other object, or will otherwise veil the baldness of the reality by means of association. All these contrasts may be illustrated by comparing the ancient and the modern names of places in Greece. No doubt the early settlers in a country have always the advantage of finding a virgin soil, whereas those that follow them inherit many of their names after they have lost all trace of their original meaning. But, making allowance for this, the difference of nomenclature is sufficiently striking. Instead of the varied and expressive names of rivers, promontories, and mountains, we now find in many cases such general terms as Potámi, Acrotíri, Voúno,[2] in the same way as Ouse, Usk, and Avon recur as river-names in England, though to a far greater degree. Not unfrequently a river, the old name of which has been lost, possesses no name of its own, but is called after the principal town on its banks—thus the Arachthus in Epirus is called the "river of Arta;" the Peneius in Elis the "river of Gastuni." The names themselves are vague and inexpressive: the Achelous has become the Aspropotamo or "White River;" Karadagh, the Turkish for "Black Mountain," and its modern Greek equivalent, Mavro Vouno, recur so frequently as to be quite confusing; Vathy, or "Deep," is the title of innumerable harbours. Thus local names will be found a valuable test of the intelligence of those who assign them.

Names derived from the vegetation.

As a specimen of the way in which the names of places and features of the country may be grouped,

[2] E. Curtius, *Peloponnesos*, i. 89.

let us first take those that are derived from the vegetation. This is a large class in most countries, and usually comprises some of the most ancient names; but in Greece, as we have already remarked,[3] the titles derived from this source are remarkably numerous, testifying to the great variety of the vegetation in early times, which was a natural result of the marked difference of elevation and climate in different parts of the country. This is confirmed by our finding that many of the modern names in Greece have the same origin;[4] but it is especially remarkable in the ancient nomenclature that the recurrence of the name of the same tree or plant is comparatively infrequent, which implies that the Greeks possessed an ample vocabulary and a fondness for special titles at the time when they occupied the country, as well as an extensive flora. It may be well in this enumeration to confine ourselves mainly to Greece Proper, as we have done in the case of the mountains and rivers, only introducing other names for purposes of comparison. For a complete investigation of the subject, it would be necessary to examine all Greek local names, wherever found; but the present attempt does not aim at completeness, and, by so doing, we should be prevented from arguing in the same manner from the meaning of the names to the character of the country.

The following names are derived from forest trees:

[3] p. 154.   [4] See my *Highlands of Turkey*, ii. 107

—From the oak, Drymodes in Arcadia, Drymos in Bœotia and Eubœa, Drymæa in Phocis, Dryoscephalæ in Bœotia, and the territory of Dryopis; from the esculent oak, the Attic demes of Phegûs and Phegæa; from the evergreen oak, Prinos, the pass between Mantineia and Argos; Ascra in Bœotia is also called from a word signifying "oak;"[5] from the cork-tree perhaps Phelloe in Achaia, in which country that tree is still found; from the fir, Elateia in Phocis, and Elatos, the old name of Mount Cyllene; from the pine, Pityûssa, an island off the coast of Argolis; from the elm, Ptelea in Attica and Thessaly, and Pteleon in Phthiotis and Triphylia; from the plane-tree, Plataniston, the name of two rivers, in Arcadia and Messenia, Platanistas, a suburb of Sparta, and Platanius, a stream in Bœotia; from the poplar, Ægeira in Achaia; from the willow, Itea, a deme of Attica; from the hazel, Caryæ in Laconia and Arcadia; from the cypress, Cyparissus in Phocis, Cyparisseis in Triphylia, and Cyparissia in Messenia and Laconia; from the cornel, Craneium,[6] a suburb of Corinth, and Craneia, mountains in Epirus; from the arbutus, Comarus, a harbour near Actium; from the wild pear, Acherdûs, a deme of Attica, the other form of which, ἀχράς, gives the etymology of Achradina at Syracuse; from the wild fig-tree, Erineos, a harbour of Achaia, and places in Doris, Phthiotis, and Attica; from the sumach,

---

[5] ἄσκρα· δρῦς ἄκαρπος.—Hesych.
[6] E. Curtius, *Peloponnesos*, ii. 592.

Rhûs in Megaris.[7] From the smaller trees and shrubs come the following:—From the thorn-bush, the Attic deme of Bate; from the myrtle, the deme of Myrrhinûs; from the bay-tree, Daphne in Arcadia and Laconia, and Daphnûs, the Phocian port on the Euboic sea; from the palluria (ῥάμνος, Lat. *paliurus*), a shrub with hooked thorns, well known to the traveller in Greece, the town and deme of Rhamnûs in Attica; from the agnus castus (ἄγνος), the deme of Agnûs; from the pomegranate (σίδη), the town of Side, on the Laconian coast, that of Sidûs near the Isthmus, and Sidûssa, a fort near Erythræ in Ionia. There is also a city called Side in Pamphylia, on the coins of which Athena is represented holding a pomegranate in her hand.

Turning now to cultivated trees, we find, as we might expect, that names derived from the vine predominate. From this source come Ampelos, a promontory of Sithonia in Chalcidice; Thriûs in the west of Elis; Œnoë, in two places in Attica, in Corinthia, Argolis, and Elis; Œnophyta, in Bœotia; Œneôn, in the Ozolian Locrians; Œniadæ, at the mouth of the Achelous; Œnûs, a river in Laconia; and the Œnûssæ islands, off the south-west point of the Peloponnese. There are also islands of the same name off Chios, which we may notice in connection with the famous Chian wine. From the olive are derived Mount Elaïon, on the borders of Arcadia and

[7] Bursian, i. 376, *note*.

Messenia; Elæûs, a deme of Attica, and towns of that name in Epirus, and near Lerna in Argolis; and the island of Elæûssa, off the coast of Attica. From the fig, Sycurium, a town under Mount Ossa, and from another sort Olynthus. From the chestnut, Castanæa or Casthanæa, in Thessaly, might seem to be derived, but this is not the case, for that city is mentioned by Herodotus,[8] and the chestnut was not introduced until much later; some ancient authorities say that the tree received its name from that place,[9] but this also is doubtful. In Epirus, opposite the north of Corcyra, we find a place called Phœnice. This name might signify merely that it was a Phœnician settlement, but its situation some little distance inland is against this, and it is more probably derived from the date-palm, which may well have grown there, from the warmth of this part of the western coast and the sheltered position of the place at the foot of the mountains.

Cultivated plants also contribute a considerable number of names of places. Crommyon, near the Isthmus of Corinth, was the "onion-bed" ($\varkappa\rho o\mu\mu\upsilon\acute{\omega}\nu$), and Sicyon, the "cucumber-bed" ($\sigma\iota\varkappa\upsilon\acute{\omega}\nu$). The neighbouring Cenchreæ is called from millet ($\varkappa\acute{\varepsilon}\gamma\chi\rho o\varsigma$); Phacion, in Thessaly, from the lentil ($\varphi\alpha\varkappa\acute{o}\varsigma$), as also Phacûsa, an island in the Sporades; Prasiæ, a deme of Attica, and a city on the east coast of Laconia, from the leek ($\pi\rho\acute{\alpha}\sigma o\nu$). The promontory of Crithote, in

---

[8] vii. 183.   [9] See Hehn, *Kulturpflanzen*, p. 286.

Acarnania, is from barley (κριθή); and the town of Siphæ, on the southern coast of Bœotia, is called by Pausanias[10] Tipha, and signifies "spelt" (τίφη). In like manner the Attic deme of Leucopyra represents "white wheat" (πυρός). Opûs, in Locris, and again in Elis, is probably from silphium (ὀπός); Selinûs, the name of rivers in Achaia and Triphylia, from parsley (σέλινον); and the saffron crocus gives its name to Croceæ in Laconia, Crocion Pedion in Phthiotis, and Crocyleia in Acarnania and Ætolia.

The following, again, are derived from wild plants:—Acanthus, from the plant of the same name; Marathon, from the fennel (μάραθος); the town of Bolbe, in Macedonia, on the lake of the same name, from some kind of bulb (βολβός); Rhizûs, on the coast of Magnesia, in Thessaly, from some kinds of roots; Scillûs, in Triphylia, from the squill (σκίλλα); Anagyrûs, a deme of Attica, from the bean trefoil (ἀνάγυρος); Ericeia, another deme, and Ericûsa, a small island near Corcyra, from the heather (ἐρίκη); Lapathûs, in the neighbourhood of Tempe, from sorrel (λάπαθον); Narthacion, a mountain in Thessaly, from the ferula (νάρθηξ); Calamæ, in Messenia, from stubble (καλάμη); and from various kinds of reeds and rushes, Thryon, a town in Elis, on the Alpheius (θρύον), Donacon, in the territory of Thespiæ (δόναξ), and Schœneus, a river in Bœotia, with Schœnûs, a place in Arcadia, and a harbour in Corinthia (σχοῖνος). To these we may add

[10] ix. 32, § 4.

a few names of places derived from wild flowers :—
Minthe, a mountain in Triphylia, from mint (μίνθη);
Mecone, the earlier name of Sicyon, from the poppy
(μήκων); the fountain of Cissûssa in Bœotia, from ivy
(κισσός); and Rhodûssa, a town in Argolis, Rhodûntia, on
Mount Œta, and Mount Rhodope, from the rose (ῥόδον).

This enumeration, large as it is, containing about
one hundred names and sixty different kinds, might be
considerably increased if we were to include the
names of places, and especially of islands, along the
fertile shore of Asia Minor. Indeed, the islands, if
we take their earliest titles, seem more commonly
than not to have derived their names from this source.
Any one who studies the Homeric catalogue will be
struck by the great predominance of this mode of
nomenclature, and in Attica at least seventeen of the
demes are called from trees and plants. With regard
to the terminations, we may notice that by far the
most common are those in οῦς, οῦσσα, signifying abundance, and agreeing with τόπος or χώρα understood.
Next to these comes the termination in ών, signifying
a bed, or garden, or collection of plants; and that in
αία is not uncommon.

Names derived from animals. The fauna of the country is not so fertile a source
of names as the flora, but still supplies a considerable
number, and these are not without their interest.
Proper names so soon become mere symbols that we
often fail to notice the meaning which lies on their
very surface; and so it is with some of these. When

we speak of the Bœotians of Arne, we hardly realise, perhaps, that we are saying, almost in as many words, the "cattle-grazers of lambtown," by which we imply, at all events, that they were a pastoral people, living in a pastoral country. To begin, however, with the wild animals :—From the lion are derived Leon, a promontory of Eubœa; Leontion, a town in Achaia; and Leontarne, "the lion and the lamb," a place in Bœotia. Lyncestis in Macedonia is called from the lynx. The wolf is for the most part confined to the highlands of Arcadia: there we find Lycæum and Lycone as names of mountains; and Lycoa, Lycosura, Lycuria, and Lycæa (in two forms, fem. and neut.) for places; but there is also a place called Lycoreia on Parnassus, and a river Lycormas in Ætolia. The bear is only found in the name Arcadia in continental Greece; but an island near Halicarnassus is called Arconesus, and the names Arctonnesus and Arctonoros occur at or near Cyzicus on the Propontis. The stag gives its name to the Elaphus, a tributary of the Alpheius, and to Elaphonnesus and Elaphitis, islands off the coast of Asia Minor. From the boar are called the two rivers Sys, in Achaia and on the side of Olympus. From the fox the Attic deme of Alopece, and Alopeconnesus, a town of the Thracian Chersonese.

Next, to take the domesticated animals :—The ox, of course, furnishes a large number of names, of which we need only mention a few. Eubœa, the coin of which is an ox's head; Bœotia, Boium in Doris, probably Bœbe[11] in Thessaly, and Buthrotus in Epirus. From the bull is called the river Taurius in Argolis. From the goat, the river Tragos in Arcadia; Polyægos, an island in the Cyclades; Ægium in Achaia; Ægiplanctus, a mountain in Megaris; Ægaleos in Attica; and perhaps Ægilia, Ægina, and others; though several names which might seem to be derived from this source are doubtful, for some are probably derived from αἶγες, in the sense of "waves;" and some, perhaps, as Ægæ, the old name of Edessa in Macedonia, from ἀΐσσω, with the meaning of "springing water." From the ram the river Crios in Achaia. From the sheep, the territory of Malis; the mountain range Œta; the places called Œum[12] in Attica and Locris; and the river Probatia in Bœotia. From the lamb Arne in Thessaly and Bœotia; Arnissa in Macedonia and Illyria; and the island of Rheneia. Hardly any names seem to be derived from the horse, except the fountains of Hippocrene and Aganippe, which have a mythological origin. From the dog come Cynoscephalæ in Thessaly; Cynuria, the district between Argolis and Laconia; and Cynosura, the name of promontories in Salamis and near Marathon. The two latter names became, according to Hesychius, general terms for rough and rocky places. From swine are derived Sybota, the

---

[11] Pott, *Personennamen*, 437.   [12] Ibid. 436.

name of the harbour and islands on the coast of Epirus; and Chœreæ, near Eretria in Eubœa: and from the ass the Oneian mountains near Corinth, and the promontory of Onugnathos near Malea.

It remains to speak of names derived from the smaller animals, birds, insects, reptiles, etc. From the owl ($\beta\tilde{v}\zeta\alpha$) is derived Byzantium;[13] from the cuckoo, Mount Coccygium in Argolis; from the raven, Mount Corax in Ætolia; from the crane, Mount Geraneia; from the tufted lark, Mount Corydallus in Attica; from the goose, a place called Chenæ ($\chi\tilde{\eta}\nu\alpha\iota$) on Mount Œta; from the sparrow, Struthûs, a promontory of Argolis; and from the quail, Ortygia, the early name of the island of Delos, which is also found belonging to a place in Ætolia, and to the island at Syracuse; from the mouse, Myonnesus, a small island off the coast of Thessaly; from the tortoise, Mount Chelydorea in Arcadia, the promontory of Chelonatas in Elis, and a place called Chelone, beneath the Scironian rocks; from the seal, which animal is still found about the coasts and islands of the Ægean, the district of Phocis, perhaps so called from their appearing in the Crissæan gulf; Phocæ, a place on the coast of Bœotia, and Phocæa in Ionia, on the coins of which place the figure of a seal is represented. From the ant, the rock Myrmex, near Artemisium; and from the spider, Mount Arachnæum in Argolis. From the

[13] G. Curtius, *Gr. Etym.* 263.

sea-urchin, Echinus, a town and promontory in Phthiotis; and Echinades, the islands off the mouth of the Achelous. From the cuttle-fish (σηπία) the rocks of Sepias on Mount Pelion; while Sepia in the north of Arcadia is from the vipers (σήψ), which Pausanias [14] describes as being found there. From other snakes the rivers Ophis and Ladon in Arcadia receive their names; and from the water-snake perhaps Hydrûssa, an island near Attica, the derivation of which is confirmed by the island Tenos having been once called both Hydrûssa and Ophiûssa. It will have been noticed, in the course of this enumeration, that we cannot in all cases argue from a name to the abundance of the corresponding animal, because in some instances it is assigned on account of a supposed resemblance in form.

Caution required.   In the preceding lists of names the derivations are for the most part clear, and do not admit of much question. But with a large number of local names, from the nature of the case, such certainty is not attainable. For, as G. Curtius has remarked,[15] whereas, in the case of ordinary words, the problem of etymology is, with two factors given, the sound and the meaning, to find the third, the origin; in the case of proper names the problem is, with one factor given, the sound, to find the two others, the origin and the meaning. It is true that, in the case of local names, we possess a peculiar help to identifica-

---

[14] viii. 16, § 2.   [15] *Gr. Et.* 111.

tion, in being able to compare the name with the features of the locality, and also that the analogies, according to which such names are imposed, are of a limited order; but, on the other hand, even when the name is descriptive, the peculiarity which has suggested it is frequently either not permanent, or not sufficiently distinctive to decide the question. It is evident, therefore, that great caution is required before we decide on any particular etymology. Thus, the river-name Alpheius is derived by G. Curtius [16] from the same root as the Latin *albus*, whence comes Albula, the ancient name of the Tiber; and this etymology would seem to be confirmed by the whitish colour of its slightly turbid water; but, notwithstanding the plausibility of this, it seems more likely, from the analogy of such words as ἀλφεσίβοιος, that it was named from the productive character of its fertilising waters (ἀλφάνω).[17] Again, Sparta is derived by Bursian [18] from its "scattered" character, because that city grew up from the combination of a number of villages, and was not enclosed by a wall. But this etymology, though perfectly reasonable, appears less probable than that which derives it from the "sown land" (σπαρτή, sc. γῆ) in front of it, as it stood at the edge of the plain; and at that early period the inorganic character of the city would not have been so unusual, and therefore so distinct-

Doubtful etymologies.

---

[16] *Gr. Et.* 264.   [17] See above, p. 91.
[18] *Geographie*, ii. 119.

ive, a feature as at a later time.[19] The same writer explains Othrys, the mountain, as another form of ὀρθός, "steep;"[20] but this, though quite according to the analogy of other mountain-names, is perhaps hardly as satisfactory as that from ὀφρύς, "the brow." Lastly, to take one more instance, the city of Eretria, in Eubœa, from its maritime character, seems naturally to be explained as the "rower's town;" but then we find a town near Pharsalus, in Thessaly, and another place in Athens, called by this name, neither of which was near the sea, or in any way connected with that in Eubœa, so that the name could be explained as derived from it. Now, Strabo[21] tells us that Eretria in Eubœa was once called Arotria, and this fact, taken together with the inland position of some of the places so called, makes it probable that the name was derived, not from the oar, but from the neighbouring "ploughed land."

Non-Hellenic names. These instances of doubtful etymologies are sufficient of themselves to suggest caution, and the necessity of it is still further impressed upon us by other considerations. Thus, we have to be on our guard against mistaking for a genuine Greek name one of foreign origin. Nothing can appear simpler than the derivation of the name Macaria, which occurs in many places in Greece. We find it as the early title

[19] Aristophanes (*Av.* 816), playing on the name, derives it from σπάρτη, "a rope" (made from the shrub σπάρτος).
[20] *Geographie*, i. 42.   [21] x. 1, § 10.

of the islands of Cyprus, Rhodes, and Lesbos, and as the name of a fountain in Attica, near Marathon, and of places in Cyprus, Messenia, and Arcadia. It would seem to mean "the blessed," and the Arcadian town was even called in Latin Beata.[22] But it is certain that in most, and perhaps in all of these instances, the name is derived from Makar, the name of the Phœnician Hercules. Not to enter further into the arguments by which this is proved,[23] we may notice in passing, that in the last book of the Iliad Lesbos is called Μάκαρος ἕδος, "the abode of Makar;"[24] and that the well in Attica was said to have been called from Macaria, a daughter of Hercules.[25] But though, on all these grounds, we have need to be on our guard against hasty derivations, it would be a mistake to confine ourselves to those which can certainly be shown to be true. Every advance in etymology has to be made by ventures, it being however required that such ventures be made on true philological principles, and with due regard to the circumstances of the case. In this way the ventures of one generation become, in many instances, the certainties of the next. Only it must be understood, that many of these are, for the time at least, of a tentative character. If we possessed the great work of Ste-

[22] Steph. Byz. *s. v.* Μακαρέαι.

[23] See J. Olshausen in the *Rheinisches Museum* for 1853, p. 329.

[24] *Il.* xxiv. 544.   [25] Paus. i. 32, § 6.

phanus of Byzantium, we should probably be able to speak with far greater confidence on the subject, for the author seems to have paid special attention to the names of places, and had collected a large amount of information on the subject, and on the topography as connected with it, from ancient writers. As it is, only a bare epitome of the work has come down to us, though even this furnishes us with much valuable matter.

<small>Vagueness of the Greek terminations.</small>
In a language like Greek, which is accustomed to express modifications of an idea by means of inflections, the want of specific meaning in the terminations cuts us off from one important source of information with regard to names of places. In English the syllables *ton, by, ham, hurst, croft, dale, ea, cester,* and innumerable others, at once reveal to us the nature of the place to which the name they are appended to was given. The meaning of Appleton, Thornycroft, Anglesea, Bicester, is as evident as if the titles *town, enclosure, island, camp,* were written separately. But in Greek this is not the case, both on account of the vagueness of the original terminations, and because the same termination is employed for different objects. Here and there terminations are found to have a specific meaning, as the ων of Κρομμυών, and the ους of Δαφνοῦς; but even here we have no means of deciding on the character of what is described, for while Κρομμυών is a town, Πλατανιστών is a river; and while Δαφνοῦς is a city, 'Αγνοῦς is a

deme; and in the vast majority of instances, the terminations, such as εια, αια, ιον, αιον, ηνη, convey to our minds the vaguest possible notion. Thus, while Mr. Taylor, in his excellent book on *Words and Places*,[26] is able to show the absence of bridges in early times in England by the fact, that where the great lines of road were intersected by rivers, we constantly meet with the names of towns bearing the suffix *ford*, in Greece, on the other hand, no such argument would be possible, because no such definite idea is expressed by the terminations. Besides this, there is some reason for believing that a certain number of these terminations date from a pre-Hellenic period. Professor Pott, in his great work on the *Names of Persons*,[27] has pointed this out with regard to two classes of endings—viz. (1) where ν is followed by a dental, but especially by θ, as in Κήρινθος, Ἀμάρυνθος, names of towns in Euboea, and Τίρυνς, gen. Τίρυνθος; (2) where σσ or ττ are found, as in Βριλησσός, Ἰλισσός, Λάρισσα, and Ὑμηττός, Μυκαλαττός. For an enumeration of such names, which occur very frequently, I must refer you to his book; but their peculiarity of form, their frequent appearance out of Greece, as in Thrace and Asia Minor, and the fact that very many of the roots with which they are joined have no explanation in Greek, lead him to the conclusion that they are the legacy of some earlier, perhaps Pelasgic race. This consideration may throw doubt on the derivation,

[26] p. 267.   [27] *Personennamen*, pp. 451 foll.

otherwise probable, of Zacynthus from $ζα$ ($= διά$) and ἄκανθος, the name being thus considered to correspond to the Homeric epithet ὑλήεσσα:[28] but when we consider the recurrence of the form κυνθος in connection with mountains and mountainous islands—as Cynthus,[29] Cythnus, Berecynthus, Aracynthus—it seems probable that it is an old word signifying "a height," and that the derivation of Zacynthus also is to be drawn from that source. It has been suggested also that ασσος means "town," and is found in that simple form in the town of that name in the Troad; but this, though it would suit many names, such as Halicarnassus,[30] is rendered impossible by its being applied indiscriminately to mountains and rivers also, as in the instances already given. We may notice also, that the interchange of σσ and ττ is not confined to the Attic dialect, for it is found also in the Bœotian; and so Strabo[31] remarks that Mycalessus is called Mycalettus in that dialect.

Peculiarities of form. It is important to remark that, as most proper names are originally appellatives, the change from the one to the other is usually marked by a corresponding change of accent.[32] This is found in names of persons, as where from the adjective διογενής we get the name Διογένης, from the participle τισάμενος the

---

[28] G. Curtius, *Gr. Et.* 544.
[29] So Aristophanes (*Nub.* 596) speaks of Κυνθίαν ὑψικέρατα πέτραν. [30] See above, p. 53. [31] ix. 2, § 11.
[32] Pott, *Personennamen*, p. 2.

name Τισαμενός; and the same thing constantly occurs in names of places, as where the adjective αἰπύ becomes the town in Elis Αἶπυ, and the participle ἑλίσσων the river Ἑλισσών, κλαζόμεναι the town Κλαζομεναί, and in like manner Ὀρχομενός, Ἀλαλκομεναί, and numerous other cases. We should also notice, what Strabo[33] has remarked, and a very superficial survey of Greek names suggests, the variations of gender and number in the name of the same place. The difference in gender is to be accounted for by the substantive understood, with which the word in its adjectival form agrees, as τόπος, γῆ, χώρα, χωρίον, etc. The use of the plural number does not admit of so simple an explanation. In names of towns, as Θῆβαι by the side of Θήβη, Κεγχρεαί by the side of Κεγχρέα, and in numerous other instances where the singular does not exist, the plural seems to express a collective force. In other features of the country the variation arises from peculiarities which enable them to be regarded either as one or as more than one. Thus, Malea is the extreme point of the promontory, Maleæ that and the neighbouring headland of Onugnathos: Sphagia is the island of Sphacteria, Sphagiæ that island together with two neighbouring rocks.[34] So, Paxi represents the two islands of Paxos and Antipaxos; Pisa is the water meadows on the banks of the Alpheius; Tempe is perhaps the succession of ravines of which the pass is formed. In some cases the name of a city in

[33] ix. 2, § 25. [34] Pape, s. v. Sphacteria.

the masculine plural signifies the inhabitants or tribe, as Parapotamii; but this is far less common in Greece than in Italy.

<small>Sources of names.</small>

<small>Relative position.</small>

To return now to the classification of names of places, let us first consider those which are derived from the nature of their position. The following are named from relative position:—Amphipolis, from its being surrounded on three sides by the Strymon; Amphissa, from the plain in which it lies being hemmed in by the mountains at the head of the Crissæan gulf; Ambracia, from the bend which the river Arachthus makes round that city; Amphilochia, perhaps from the secluded position of that district among the mountains near the innermost angle of the Ambracian gulf. Antirrhium, the Ætolian promontory, from its being opposite the headland of Rhium; Antiphellus, on the coast of Lycia, from its being opposite the town of Phellus; Antissa, the town in Lesbos, which Strabo[35] tells us, on the authority of Myrsilus, was once an island, and was so named from being off Lesbos, which was formerly called Issa. Methydrium, in Arcadia, as Pausanias[36] tells us, gets its name from its situation on a hill between the rivers Malœtas and Mylaon; Mesogæa is the midland district of Attica; Messene is the Stenyclerian plain, enclosed by mountains;[37] Messa lies in the inmost recesses of a safe harbour on the west coast of Tænarum;

[35] i. 3, § 19.   [36] viii. 36, § 1.   [37] See above, p. 274.

Mesola, a town of Messenia, is so called, according to Strabo,[38] because of its position near the bay which separates that country from the district of Taygetus; and Mesoboa, a town on the banks of the Ladon, and the fountain of Messeis at Therapne in Laconia, from some similar cause. Add to these Peiræum, a town of the Peræa, as the part of Geraneia was called which projected into the Corinthian gulf, in consequence of its being opposite Corinth, and being the district to which the Corinthians used to send their flocks across for pasturage during the summer months;[39] Peræa, also, as a name for the strips of land which the islands off the west coast of Asia Minor possessed on the mainland; Peiraïce, a district of Attica, over against Oropus; and probably also Trœzen, which, like Taras, is derived from the same root as τέρμα[40] and the Latin *trans* and *terminus*, and signifies "a place beyond or opposite." Mount Anchesmus was named from its neighbourhood to Athens; and Dyme in Achaia stands for δυσμή, "sunset," being the westernmost of all the Achæan cities.[41]

In examining the names of mountains we have noticed a number of places which are called from their elevated position, such as Corinthus, from the root of κορυφή, and its earlier name, Ephyra, "the look-out place."[42] Other places which have received

Elevated position.

[38] viii. 4, § 5. [39] E. Curtius, *Peloponnesos*, ii. 552.
[40] G. Curtius, *Gr. Et.* 201. [41] Bursian, *Geog.* ii. 319.
[42] See above, pp. 51-54.

their names from the same cause, are—perhaps Thebæ, which, according to Varro,[43] in the old Greek and old Italian languages signified "hills;" Colonus in Attica, Colone in Messenia, and Colonæ in Thessaly and Phocis, meaning "mound;" the Epicnemidii, from their position on Mount Cnemis in Locris; Las, *i.e.* "rock," a town in Laconia; the Homeric towns, Orthe in Thessaly, and Æpeia in Messenia, both meaning "steep," similar to which is Acragas in Sicily. Larissa Cremaste in Phthiotis was called "hanging," from its rising steeply above the sea of Artemisium; Stymphalus, in Arcadia, is probably another form of στυφελός, "rugged;" Scope, the scene of Epaminondas' death, is the "look-out place;" and Panopeus, in Phocis, means the "conspicuous." From the strength of their position are called Alalcomenæ, in Bœotia, the "warder-town," from ἀλαλκεῖν, "to ward off;" Erymanthus, from ἔρυμα, the bulwark of the land; Tegea, the place of defence;[44] the Arcadian town Gortys, which was also called Cortys, and is thus connected with κάρτος, κράτος;[45] and a number of

[43] *De Re Rustica*, 3, 1, 6. "Lingua prisca et in Græcia Æoles Bœoti sine afflatu vocant colles Tebas: et in Sabinis, quo e Græcia venerunt Pelasgi, etiam nunc ita dicunt." This does not seem quite safe authority: Hesychius says, θῆβος = θαῦμα, in which case it may mean "wonderful." See Liddell and Scott's *Lex. s. v.* Θῆβαι.

[44] See above, p. 289.

[45] Hesychius says:—" Κορτύνιοι· οἱ Ἀρκάδες· ἡ γὰρ Κόρτυς τῇ, Ἀρκάδων :" and again, " κορτερά· κρατερά, ἰσχυρά."

LECT. X.] GEOGRAPHY OF GREECE. 359

other places signifying "fort," or "tower," such as Phylace in Phthiotis and Arcadia, Pyrgi in Triphylia, Teichos in Achaia, and Teichiûs near Thermopylæ.

From their narrow or enclosed situation, or their circuit of walls, the following are named :—Orchomenus, both the town in Bœotia and that in Arcadia, derived from εἴργω, ἕρκος, ὄρχος;[46] Cleitor, in Arcadia, probably for the same reason, from κλείω;[47] also Gyrton, in Thessaly, from γυρός, "round." Coroneia, in Bœotia, is similarly derived from κορώνη, a word for any curved object, unless, indeed, it comes from the other meaning of that word, and signifies "crow's town:" Corone, in Messenia, according to Pausanias,[48] was more properly called Coroneia, and received that name, in place of its earlier name, Æpeia, from the Bœotian city, in consequence of its second founder, in the time of Epaminondas, being from that place; on its coins, with a play on the name, Athena was represented holding a crow in her hand.[49] Mycenæ, if derived from μυχός, implies its remote position in the recesses of the Argive plain. Thalamæ, in Laconia, on the eastern shore of the Messenian gulf, is said by Polybius[50] to have received its name of "den," or "chamber," from its narrow and inaccessible position; and Stephanus gives a similar explanation

Enclosed situation.

[46] E. Curtius, *Pel.* i. 228.
[47] C. O. Müller, quoted by Curtius, *Pel.* i. 397. Cf. the Italian Clusium.   [48] iv. 34, § 5.
[49] Curtius, *Pel.* ii. 166.   [50] iv. 75.

of the name Megara; Glaphyræ, "hollows," in Thessaly, was probably of the same character. Delphi, from δελφύς, was called the "womb" of the earth, on account of its deep chasm;[51] in Arcadia there was a gorge called Bathos, or "gulf," and Bassæ or the "glens," the site of the famous temple of Apollo near Phigaleia, is derived from the same root;[52] Lamia, also, the town at the foot of Othrys, near the Maliac gulf, is said in the *Etym. Magn.* to signify "a chasm." Cœle was the name of one of the Attic demes, and Cœla of the pass through Othrys; and from caverns and hollows in the rocks were called Tretos, "pierced," the mountain and pass which were the abode of the Nemean lion; Antrôn, a town of Phthiotis, famous for its millstones; Cœla, the dangerous rocks on the east coast of Eubœa; and Mount Chaon in Argolis.[53]

Maritime character. The shore and harbours furnish us with the following:—Eion, or "beach," the name of the port of Amphipolis; Helice, in Achaia, from ἕλιξ, "twisted," like the Italian Sinuessa, on account of the winding line of the coast; Actium, from the ἀκτή on which it stands. Euripus is sometimes explained as "full of rushes," from ῥίψ, "a rush," Lat. *scirpus*;[54] but from its being applied to a number of other narrow channels of the sea besides that at Chalcis, it is more likely that it is from εὖ and ῥιπή, signifying the force of the cur-

[51] G. Curtius, *Gr. Et.* 420.
[52] Ibid. 416.   [53] See above, p. 57.
[54] Curtius, *Gr. Et.* 316.

rent. Halice or Halieis, in the south of Argolis, means "fishers' station;" Nauplia, from ναῦς and πλέω, means "seaport;" Dyrrhachium, from δυς and ῥαχία, is called from its dangerous breakers; Cheimerium, "stormy," is the name of another harbour on the same unsafe coast of Epirus; Panormus, "the haven safe from all winds," is found on the east coast of Attica, and near the straits at Rhium and elsewhere, as well as in Sicily; Lechæum, the port of Corinth, is named from λέχος, in the sense of "roadstead;"[55] Epidaurus Limera, in the south-east of Laconia, from its excellent harbour, Limera being an abbreviation of Limenera;[56] Hyrmina, a town and promontory of Mount Chelonatas, near the port of Cyllene in Elis, means "port," being an Æolic form of Hormina, which name, according to Strabo,[57] it also bore; Hermione in Argolis, with its important bay, has probably the same derivation, though it might come from ἕρμα, "a shoal." The derivation of Gytheium, the naval station of Sparta, from γύη, the early form of γῆ, and θέω, "the place where men run to land," "landing-place,"[58] is rather harsh, though it suits the meaning. Eleusis, "arrival," may

[55] Curtius, *Pel.* ii. 594.
[56] Ibid. ii. 328, where other possible derivations are also given.
[57] viii. 3, § 10. See Curtius, *Pel.* ii. 102, who compares Formiæ in Latium, and Strabo, v. 3, § 6, Ὁρμίαι λεγόμενον πρότερον διὰ τὸ εὔορμον. [58] Pape, *s. v.*

also, perhaps, signify "landing-place," or it may be used in the more general sense of "resting-place," "lodging."

Environs, etc.

Other places were named from their environs, soil, and similar characteristics. From their woodland character are called—Daseæ, a place in Arcadia, near Mount Lycæum, from δασύς, "bushy;"[59] Lasiôn, the mountain which contains the sources of the Ladon, from λάσιος, with the same meaning;[60] Theræ, a district on the side of Taygetus, together with the island Thera, and a number of places of the same name, signifying "chase;" Hylæ, a city in Bœotia, which gave its name to the lake Hylice, and another in Locris; Melænæ, in Arcadia, from the dark woods for which it was famous in ancient times;[61] Sciadis, a place in Arcadia, Sciathis, a mountain in the same country, the island of Sciathos, and Scione in Chalcidice, from their umbrageous character; Doriscus in Thrace, in a plain at the mouth of the Hebrus, from δόρυ, "a sapling;"[62] Daulis in Phocis, which is contracted for δάσυλις, and which Pausanias[63] rightly explains, when he says that the ancients said δαῦλα for δασέα; and, in the same way, Epidaurus stands for ἐπιδάσυρος, "overgrown with bushes;"[64] Drios, the

[59] Curtius, *Pel.* i. 338.   [60] Ibid. ii. 106.
[61] Ibid. i. 356; and compare Steph. Byz., who quotes from Rhianus πολυδρύμους τε Μελαίνας.
[62] Pape, *s. v.*   [63] x. 4, § 7.
[64] Pott, quoted by G. Curtius, *Gr. Et.* 210.

name of mountains in Achaia and Locris, signifying "thicket," and derived from δρῦς in its earlier meaning of "tree;" and perhaps also Doris, "woodland," from the same root.[65] From the profusion of flowers—Antheia in Thessaly, Achaia, Messenia, and the district of Trœzen; Anthemûs, in Macedonia; Anthedon, in Bœotia; Anthele, near Thermopylæ; Anthene or Athene, in the Thyreatis; and if Athens is to be referred to the root of ἄνθος,[66] then also Mount Athos will fall under the same head, and this is justified by its abundant flora.

The following are named from the roughness of the ground:—the city of Trachis near Thermopylæ, on the rugged slopes of Mount Œta; Scarpheia, the name of towns in Locris and Bœotia, connected with the Latin *scaber*,[67] and our *scrape*; Lepreum in Elis, from λεπρός, λεπράς, "rough;"[68] Phelleus, a mountain in Attica, the name being a word for any kind of stony soil;[69] Sciritis, the wild uplands between Sparta and Tegea, for Hesychius[70] informs us that σκιρός = σκληρός; and from the same root the rugged pass called the Scironian Way, at the foot of Mount Geraneia.

From their situation near rivers, marshy ground, and springs, the following are called:—The city of Parapotamii in Phocis on the Cephisus; Pisa on the

<small>Water.</small>

---

[65] G. Curtius, 215.   [66] See above, p. 161.
[67] E. Curtius, *Pel.* i. 271.   [68] Ibid. ii. 117.
[69] Steph. Byz., and Liddell and Scott, *s. v.*
[70] Quoted by Curtius, *Pel.* ii. 322.

Alpheius, which signifies "water-meadows," from πίνω;[71] Calydon, from καλός and ὕδωρ, the Ætolian city on the Evenus; Leibethra, the Pierian town on the flank of Olympus,[72] and Mount Leibethrium in Bœotia, from λείβω, because of their copious springs; Lebadeia, one of the best-watered sites in Greece, from the same root; Crannon in Thessaly, from κράννα, Æol. for κρήνη, a "fountain;"[73] Bryseæ, from βρύω, "to gush forth,"[74] a town in the neighbourhood of Sparta at the foot of Taygetus; and Rheiti, the salt springs in the Thriasian plain, which formed the boundary of the territories of Athens and Eleusis. Ægæ, a name of common occurrence, the most famous being the city in Achaia, perhaps means "springs," from ἀΐσσω; this was also the early name of Edessa in Macedonia, which is now called Vodena, or "place of waters;" and the name Edessa itself is said to come from the Phrygian and Macedonian word βέδυ "water,"[75] and Stephanus tells us of the city of that name in Mesopotamia, that it was called after the Macedonian city because of the force of its waters. The derivation of Nonacris, in the neighbourhood of the waterfall of the Styx, from νάω and ἄκρος, "beck-

[71] *Etymol. Magn. s. v.* Cf. Strabo, viii. 3, § 31.
[72] Curtius, *Gr. Et.* 329.   [73] Ibid. 132; and see Pape, *s. v.*
[74] Curtius, *Pel.* ii. 319.
[75] See Von Gudschmidt, in the *Symbola Philologorum Bonnensium*, p. 124, *note;* and Bergk, *Gr. Literaturgeschichte*, i. p. 42.

fell,"[76] is highly applicable to the position, though somewhat doubtful in form, but it receives some support from the statement of Hesychius that it was also called Nonapis, which perhaps means "flowing water." Helos, or "marsh," is the name of the Laconian coast town near the mouth of the Eurotas, and of places in Elis, Argolis, and Attica; Limnæa, the name of places in Acarnania and Thessaly, and Limnæ, on the confines of Laconia and Messenia, have the same meaning. The lake Pambotis in Epirus (lake of Joannina) derived its name from its fertilising waters ($\pi\tilde{\alpha}\varsigma$ and $\beta\acute{o}\sigma\varkappa\omega$); that of Xynias in the south of Thessaly, and the neighbouring town of Xynia, is probably from $\xi vv\acute{o}\varsigma$ (= $\varkappa o\iota v\acute{o}\varsigma$), as being the common receptacle of the neighbouring streams; the remark of a Scholiast,[77] that it was thought to have been so named as the common property of Thessaly and Bœotia, seems inappropriate. Copæ, the town that gave its name to the lake Copais, which Homer calls Cephisis, and lay on the northern shore of that lake, is the "place of oars."

Other names have been suggested by pasturage and tillage. By the former—Nemea, "grazing ground," in its upland plain; Nomia, a part of Mount Eira; Bucolion, a place on Mount Mænalus; Melibœa, *i.e.* "guarding oxen," in Thessaly; and Buthrotus, from $\beta o\tilde{v}\varsigma$ and $\theta\varrho\acute{\omega}\sigma\varkappa\omega$, "to leap"[78]—a derivation which

Pasturage and tillage.

[76] Pape, *s. v.* [77] Ibid.
[78] Bursian, i. 17, *note.*

reminds us of the ἱππομανὴς λειμών of Sophocles[79]—for the neighbouring districts of Epirus were celebrated for their cattle. Tillage also suggested Sparta, "the sown land;" Aroe, in Achaia, the "ploughed land;" Aroanius, a river in Arcadia, from the cultivated land on its banks, and Arantia,[80] a town in the district of Phlius, from the same derivation; Iolcos, the "furrowed," for Hesychius tells us that ἰῶλκα = αὖλακα; perhaps also Tanagra, "longlands," from ταν, root of τείνω, and ἀγρός, and Platæa, "broadlands," from πλατύς, for the derivation which Strabo[81] gives, from πλάτη, "the blade of the oar," rests upon a false supposition that this part of Bœotia was once under water. Phlius comes from φλέω, "to abound," on account of its abundant vegetation;[82] and Euryteiæ, or "wide vale," is the name of a place in Achaia.[83]

A few places are named from the nature of the soil: as Titanus, a place in Thessaly, from chalk or gypsum; Mount Pelion, and the city of Paleia (afterwards Dyme) in Achaia, which is situated in a clayey neighbourhood,[84] from πηλός, "clay;" Amathus, a river in Messenia; Amathûs, a town in Cyprus; Psamathûs, a seaport of Laconia; and Psamathe, a fountain in Bœotia, from sand. The

---

[79] *Aj.* 143.   [80] Curtius, *Pel.* ii. 581.   [81] ix. 2, § 17.
[82] ὠνόμασται παρὰ τὸ φλεῖν, ὅ ἐστιν εὐκαρπεῖν.—*Steph. Byz.*
[83] Curtius, *Pel.* i. 452.   [84] Bursian, ii. 319.

nature of the climate suggested Dysorum "tempestuous," a mountain in Macedonia, from δυς and ὥρα; Rhipæa, from ῥιπαί, "blasts of wind," the chain of northern mountains, which existed rather in the imagination of the Greeks than in any definite spot; and particularly Hysiæ, the name of towns in Bœotia and Argolis, *i.e.* "rain-town," from ὕω. A large number were derived from colour: from red (ἐρυθρός, Colour. φοῖνιξ, πυρρός) come Erythræ, the name of towns in Bœotia, in Locris near Naupactus, and in Ionia— the rock on which the acropolis of the last of these is built is a mass of red trachyte;[85] Phœnix, a stream near Thermopylæ, with a deposit of iron; and Pyrrha, a town and promontory in Phthiotis. From white or bright (λευκός, ἀργός)—Leucon Pedion, in Megaris; Leucæ, a town in Laconia; Leuctra, in Bœotia; Leuctron, in Laconia, Arcadia, and Achaia; the island of Leucas or Leucadia, so named from the white rocks of the promontory of Leucate at its southern extremity, now called Sappho's Leap; Leucasia, a river in Messenia; Leucasion, a place in Arcadia; and Leucimme, a promontory of Corcyra; Argissa, a town in Thessaly; Argolas, a height in Locris; Argûra, a place in Eubœa; Argyra, a well and town in Achaia; Argennon, a promontory in Ionia, now "the white cape" (Capo Bianco); and Arginusæ, the islands between Lesbos and Æolis. Argos, we are told by ancient authorities, signifies

[85] Smith's *Dict. Geog.* i. 852.

"a plain," especially a maritime plain,[86] and therefore must be kept distinct from these. From "black" (μέλας, πελλός)—Melangeia, a town in Arcadia; Melænæ or Melania, a district of Attica, which, perhaps, like the town of the same name in Arcadia, was called from its dark woods; and Melæna, the name of promontories in Chios and Ionia; besides several rivers called Melas: Pelinna, a town of Thessaly; Pellene, the name of towns in Achaia, Laconia, and Messenia; and the Achaian town of Pella. Whether the famous Macedonian capital belongs here is doubtful; but as the Macedonian dialect usually changed φ into π, so that in it πέλλα signified "a stone," or "stony," like φελλεύς in Attic, it was more probably derived from the roughness of the soil."[87] From yellowish (κνακός)—Mount Cnacalus in Arcadia, Mount Cnacadion in Laconia, and the river Cnaciôn in the same country. From grey-green (γλαυκός)—the river Glaucia in Bœotia, and Glaucus, a river in the west of Achaia.

Resemblances to men and animals.

We come now to a very curious and interesting class of names—viz., those which were assigned on account of the resemblance of places to objects of various kinds. In these, more than in any others, we can trace the ingenuity of the Greek mind, and the absence of conventionality in its nomenclature. Thus, to take different parts of the body—from the

[86] Curtius, *Pel.* ii. 557.
[87] See reff. in Pape; and Liddell and Scott, *s. v.* φελλός.

temples of the head is derived Corseia in Bœotia; from the brow, Mount Othrys;[88] from the beard, the harbour of Trœzen in Argolis, called Pogon,[89] probably on account of a narrow sandy promontory that projects into it (compare Mentone, "chin," from the point of land that separates the eastern and western bays); from the breast, Mount Titthium, near Epidaurus; from the elbow, Olenus, a name of towns in Ætolia and Achaia, as being in the bend of the hill or the shore, and Ancyle, one of the demes of Attica, in the same way as Ancôn, the original Greek name of Ancona; from the heart, perhaps Cardia, in the Thracian Chersonese; from the leg, Colias, a promontory and coastland in Attica; from the knee, Gonnus[90] in Thessaly; from a horn, Mount Kerata in Megaris; and from a bump or the fist (κόνδυλος), a town called Condylea, near Orchomenus in Arcadia, probably so called from being on a rising ground.

Many places were named from an apparent likeness to the forms of animals. Myrmex, a rock in the middle of the water off the Thessalian coast, from its resemblance to an ant; Chelonatas, the promontory in Elis, and Chelone, a rock below the Scironian cliff, from the shape of the tortoise; the Echinades, from their sharp outline recalling the sea-urchin; Mount Arachnæum, from the spider; Mount Geraneia, from the crane; Mount Corax,

[88] See above, p. 39.   [89] Curtius, *Pel.* ii. 444.
[90] See above, p. 54.

from the raven; Mount Corydallus, from the crested lark; Mount Oneium, from the ass, the backbone of which animal it resembled; the promontory of Onugnathus, from a likeness to its jaw; that of Leon in Euboea, from the lion; Cynosûra, or the "dog's tail," a name for several promontories; Cynoscephalæ, or the "dog's heads," heights in Thessaly; Lycosûra, or "wolf's tail," a town in Arcadia; Bucephala, the extreme promontory of Argolis; Ophis, or "snake," as a name for a winding river; and Munychia, or "single-hoof," a name descriptive of the rocky knoll which rises by the sea-shore above the Piræus, unless indeed, as some think, the place took its name from the temple of Ἄρτεμις Μουνυχία there, and not *vice versa*, and that title is contracted for Μονονυχία.[91]

Resemblances to inanimate objects.

Other names were derived from domestic implements and similar articles. From the table, as signifying position on a table-land, Trapezûs, a town in western Arcadia, as well as the more famous one on the Black Sea; from the oven, Ipnos, a place in the district of the Ozolian Locrians, and Ipni, the famous spot in Magnesia, where Xerxes' fleet was wrecked; from the poker, another place in Magnesia called Spalathron; from the frying-pan, Teganon, an island near Rhodes;[92] from the cruet, the town of Lecythus, in the peninsula of Sithonia, on a project-

---

[91] E. Curtius, *Geog. Onomatologie*, 159; and *Etymol. Magn. s. v.* Compare Preller, *Gr. Myth.* i. 236.

[92] Mentioned by Pliny, *N. H.* v. 31, 36.

ing tongue of land recalling that shape; from the ladle, Toryne, on the coast of Epirus, the modern Parga, on a similar headland. Among other implements—from the sickle many curved promontories were named, as Drepanum, a promontory of Achaia, which Strabo[93] confuses with that of Rhium; Drepanum, in the west of Sicily, the modern Trapani; Drecanum, a promontory in the island of Cos, an older form of the same name;[94] also, Drepane, the ancient name of Corcyra, which, like Κέρκυρα—connected with κυρτός, "curved," κίρκος, "a ring," and the Lat. *circum, circus,* etc.[95]—refers to the peculiarly curved form of that island; and Zancle, the old name of Messana, which town had a sickle on its coins.[96] From a wallet (κώρυκος), on account of its hollow character, are derived the Corycian cave above Delphi, and a cavern or hollow place of the same name in Cilicia,[97] together with several promontories with caverns in Asia Minor, called Corycus. From a saw a mountain in Chios gets its name of Priôn, which reminds us of the Spanish name for

[93] viii. 2, § 3.   [94] G. Curtius, *Gr. Et.* 433.   [95] Ibid. 145.

[96] Cf. Thuc. vi. 4. δρεπανοειδὲς τὴν ἰδέαν τὸ χωρίον ἐστί. The name, however, was not Greek, but, as Thucydides tells us, was given by the Sicels.

[97] Possibly the Cilician name may be derived from *carcom,* the old Semitic word for "saffron," which, according to Strabo (xiv. 5, § 5), grew very fine there. See Hehn, *Kulturpflanzen,* 175, 176.

mountain chains, Sierra. In like manner, a chisel or graving tool has suggested the name Tomeus or Τομαῖον ὄρος,[98] for a mountain in Messenia. Acontion, or "spear-head," is the name of a town in southwestern Arcadia, and of a mountain in Bœotia; Harma, or "car," represents a face of rock on Cithæron;[99] and Dirphys, *i.e.* δίφρος, "chariot" or "seat," is the title of the highest mountain in Eubœa.[100] Stephane, "chaplet," "circlet," is the name of a town in Phocis, and a mountain in Phthiotis, on account of the στεφάνωμα πύργων, or some other circular feature; in this way also the island of Samos formerly bore that name. The promontory of Zoster, *i.e.* "girdle," in Attica, is also so called, because it encircles and protects the neighbouring bay.[101] Aulôn, the name for a glen, derived from αὐλός, a "pipe or channel," is a frequently-recurring name for deep valleys and towns in their neighbourhood; as, for instance, the town on the borders of Elis and Messenia, and that in Chalcidice, near the channel by which the lake Bolbe discharges its waters into the sea;[102] the town of Aulis, in the neighbourhood of the channel of the Euripus, is probably named from the same cause. Pylæ, "the gates," is the common name for a pass; Bomi, "the altars," is the name applied to some hills

[98] See above, p. 52. [99] Ibid. [100] p. 56.
[101] Curtius, *Onomat.* 153.
[102] Thuc. iv. 103. Αὐλῶνα καὶ Βρομίσκον, ᾗ ἡ Βόλβη λίμνη ἐξίησιν ἐς θάλασσαν.

in Ætolia ; and perhaps the island of Melos is called from its resemblance to an apple, for Pliny says of it—*Hæc insularum rotundissima est ;*"[103] it also bears an apple on its coins, but this may arise from a play on the name.[104]

Another source of names was the worship of deities, which has its modern counterpart in the places called after Christian saints—a mode of nomenclature especially common in modern Greece. From Zeus were named three cities called Dium: one on the peninsula of Athos, one in Macedonia, under Olympus, and one in the north-west of Eubœa ; also Olympia, from the god in his character of Olympian Zeus; from Hera, the promontory of Heræum, which forms the western extremity of Geraneia, together with many other sites of temples; from Apollo the cities called Apollonia, in Thrace, in the north of Chalcidice, and in Illyria ; Pythium, in Bœotia, Phocis, Macedonia, and elsewhere ; and Delium, in Bœotia and Laconia ; from Athene, Athenæum in Thessaly, Arcadia, and other districts ; from Artemis, Artemisium, the mountain in Arcadia, another moun-

Worship of deities.

[103] *N. H.* iv. 12, § 23.

[104] In the case of some promontories, such as Pogon, Zoster, Zancle, Drepanum (in Sicily), and Lecythus, the correspondence of name and form is easily traceable on a good map of large scale, such as that now publishing by Mr. Murray. The sickle of Zancle is excellently given in the view of Messina, in Plate iv. of Bartlett's *Pictures from Sicily*.

tain, with a temple, in Argolis, and the famous coast and town in the north of Euboea, and also Mount Parthenium in Arcadia; from Poseidon, Poseidium, a promontory on the west of Pallene in Chalcidice; and from Potidan, or Potidas, the Doric form of the name of the god, Potidæa, on the isthmus of that peninsula, and Potidania, a castle in Ætolia; from Hermes, Hermæum, at Coroneia in Bœotia, and on the borders of Arcadia and Messenia; also Hermupolis in Arcadia; from Ares, the Areiopagus at Athens; from Aphrodite, the town of Aphrodisia in Laconia, and Aphrodisium, the name of a place in Arcadia, and of part of the harbour of the Piræus; from Hercules, the very numerous towns called Heracleia, especially those in Trachis near Thermopylæ, on the coast of Pieria, and in Lyncestis in Macedonia; from Demeter, Demetrium in Thessaly, and elsewhere; from Demeter and Cora, Potniæ in Bœotia; from Castor and Pollux, Dioscureium, near Torone in Chalcidice; from Selene, Selenæum, a mountain in Argolis; from Hestia, Hestiæa and Histiæa, names of towns in Thessaly, Eubœa, and Acarnania, and of one of the demes of Attica, though in these instances the name may possibly be derived from ἑστία in the sense of a "hearth;" from the Nymphs, Nymphæum, the southern promontory of Athos, and places in Arcadia and Laconia. This list might be vastly increased if we were to include the names of places in the Greek colonies, for this became a favourite source of nomenclature at a later time; but it is to be observed that very few places were named in this manner in the earliest period, and therefore it is very hazardous to derive such a name as that of the city of Athens from the goddess Athene.

To these we may add names which contain numerals in their composition.[105] Such are Didymi in Argolis, Didyma, hills in Thessaly, and Diope, a town in Arcadia; Tripolis, the name of six places in different parts of Greece, Triphylia, the district of Peloponnese, Triteæ in Phocis, Tritæa in Achaia, Trinasos, a haven of Laconia, from three small islands lying off the coast, Trichonis, a lake in Ætolia, Triopion, the Carian promontory, Trinacria, the name of Sicily, Tricoloni, a town in Arcadia, Tricorythus, a deme of Attica, Tricaranon, a triple-crested mountain near Phlius in Argolis, and Tricrena, a mountain in the north of Arcadia; Tetrapolis, confederations of four cities, in Doris, Attica, and other countries, and Tetraphylia in Epirus; the Attic deme of Pentele, and the Dorian Pentapolis in Asia Minor, which when Halicarnassus was included was called a Hexapolis; the river Heptaporos in Troas; Octolophus, a place on Olympus; the fountain of Enneacrounos at Athens, and Enneahodi, the original site of Amphipolis; the Syrian Decapolis; and the Hecatonnesi, off the coast of Æolia.

Names containing numerals.

Another group may be formed of the names which *Names from occupations, etc.*

[105] Pott, *Personennamen*, 461.

relate to places of industry, or occupation, or some form of usefulness. Saltworks, which, on account of the importance of that article, could hardly fail to have been numerous, gave their name to several places; two Attic demes were called respectively Halæ Araphenides, on the eastern coast, and Halæ Æxonides, on the western; also, Halæ, a coast town of the Opuntian Locrians, and very possibly the island of Halonnesus, off the south-east coast of Thessaly; from the grinding of corn were called Alesiæ, a place near Sparta, where, according to the legend, Myles, king of the Leleges, first ground corn;[106] Mylæ, a town in Thessalian Magnesia, and another in the north-east of Sicily; Mylasa,[107] a town in Caria; and Mylaon, or "mill-stream," the name of two rivers in Arcadia;[108] from bees, Melite, a deme of Attica, and Melitæa, a town in Phthiotis; from warm springs and baths, Therme, the original name of Thessalonica, Thermæ, the springs on the isthmus of Corinth, Thermopylæ, and Sermylæ, a town on the peninsula of Sithonia.[109] From copper mines we get the various places called Chalcis; from the shafts of the mines, Laureium in Attica; from pottery, the Cerameicus at Athens; from the purple-fishery, Porphyrusa, an island off the coast of Crete; from the cattle trade, Buprasium, or "cattle market,"[110] a town and district in the rich lands of Hollow Elis, though perhaps from the shortness of the

[106] Curtius, *Pel.* ii. 249.   [107] Ibid. ii. 319.   [108] Ibid. i. 309.
[109] σερμοί = θερμοί.—Hesych.   [110] Pape, *s. v.*

α in that name it may rather be derived from the leek (πράσον), so that the name would signify "horse-leek." From means of transit were named Poros, or "ford," an Attic deme; Porthmos, or "ferry," a town and harbour in Euboea, east of Eretria; and Diolcos, the place of passage for vessels over the isthmus; Gephyra, a "dam of earth," or "causeway" was the old name of Tanagra; in the earliest times this word was not used in the ordinary sense of a "bridge," but the deme of Gephyreis was said to be so called from the bridge by which the processions to Eleusis crossed the Cephisus. Naupactus obtained its name from shipbuilding, and probably also Pagasæ, at the head of the Pagasæan gulf, which was supposed by the ancients to have been so called from the building of the Argo, though Strabo prefers to derive it from πηγή, on account of the copious springs there.[111]

Some other names seem to have been suggested by political relations or events. Thus Stratus, or "camp," was the name of the chief town and meeting-place of the Acarnanians; Patræ, *i.e.* an "association of families," was the town into which the Achæans brought together their leading families from the neighbouring country;[112] Metropolis is the name of two towns in Thessaly, one in Acarnania, and one in Amphilochia, and implies that these either were formed by a συνοικισμός of other towns, or exercised some kind of hegemony over them; the Pnyx at

Political names.

[111] ix. 5, § 15.   [112] Bursian, ii. 325.

Athens, from its genitive Πυκνός, is shown to mean the "hill of assembly." The name Eleutheræ, in like manner, must have been derived from the independence of that city, owing to its position on the confines of Attica and Bœotia; Olpæ, the name of a town on the Ambracian gulf, being equivalent to ἐλπίς,[113] seems to refer to the hopes with which the place was founded; and Mantineia and Thespiæ, from μάντις and θέσπις, appear to have been so called as founded in accordance with an oracle. One place is named from a historical event—viz. Paræbasium in Arcadia, which was so called from a breach of truce on the part of Cleomenes, King of Sparta.[114]

<small>Names evidencing geographical changes.</small> In certain names we may also find evidence of a change in the ground between earlier and later times. Both in Athens and Sparta,[115] we find places called Limnæ, or "the marshes," showing that in those cities there were once undrained spots, though afterwards the name was the only evidence of this; just as in Rome the term Lacus was applied to localities where all traces of water had disappeared. Similarly, the name Piræus implies that the hill and place from which the harbour derived its name was once an island, and was reached from the mainland by a ferry; Strabo speaks of it as being regarded in his time as νησιάζοντα πρότερον καὶ πέραν τῆς ἀκτῆς κείμενον,[116] and this is probable on other grounds. Anaphe, a volcanic island

---

[113] ὄλπα· ἡ ἐλπίς.—Hesych.   [114] Paus. viii. 28, § 7.
[115] Strabo, viii. 5, § 1.   [116] i. 3, § 18.

to the east of Thera, was said by the ancients to be derived from ἀναφαίνειν, because it appeared to the Argonauts in a storm,[117] but more probably comes from ἀνάπτω, "to set on fire," from the recollection of some early volcanic phenomena. So too, now that Thermopylæ is no longer a pass, the element Pylæ in its name affords evidence of its former state. But the absence of distinctive terminations in Greek for certain classes of objects renders such changes less easy to trace than in English; thus, while the island of Lade, at the mouth of the Mæander, and some of the Echinades off the mouth of the Achelous, have become attached to the neighbouring continents, there is nothing in the names to indicate that they once were islands, as there is in English, in Battersea, Chelsea, and names of other places that have undergone a similar change.

In searching through the names of places in Greece, we meet with some, more or less alien to the Greek language, which serve as evidences of the position or the migrations of other races. The name Larissa, which is attached to four towns in Thessaly, to the citadel of Argos, and to places in Attica, Elis, and elsewhere, is pretty certainly Pelasgian; for, besides other proofs, several of these towns, according to the legend preserved in Pausanias,[118] were called after Larissa, daughter of Pelasgus. The same was pro-

Pelasgic and other names.

[117] Apollon. Rhod. *Argonaut.* iv. 1717; and Steph. Byz.
[118] ii. 23, § 9. See above, p. 293.

bably the case with two other very primitive names, Argos and Inachus—the one for a plain, and thence for a town in its neighbourhood, the other for a river; and this supposition may explain our finding both these names in Amphilochia, where Thucydides[119] states the Hellenic tongue was subsequently introduced from Ambracia, for the story of this place being an Argive colony was probably suggested by the name.[120] Again, the name Minoa, which belongs both to the island off Megaris, and to the remarkable peninsula on the east coast of Laconia, now called Monemvasia, testifies to the presence of some race, probably Carians, who were under the Cretan hegemony; for Thucydides[121] tells us that Minos expelled that race from the Cyclades, and the name of Minoa is found, not only in two places in Crete, but in Siphnos and Amorgos, and as the ancient title of the island of Paros. So, too, by means of the Dryopian name Asine, we can trace some of the migrations of that race after their expulsion from their original home in the neighbourhood of Mount Œta, for we find it in Argolis, Messenia, Cilicia, and Cyprus:[122] the foundation of one of these towns is a matter of history, for, when the Argolic Asine was razed after a siege by the Argives, the inhabitants were established by the Lacedæmonians on the

[119] ii. 68.   [120] Bursian, i. 37.   [121] i. 4.
[122] Müller, *Dor.* i. 49; Steph. Byz. *s. v.* Asine; Strabo, viii. 6, § 13.

western side of the Messenian gulf, and transferred the old name to their new abode. This place has subsequently been the scene of another transference of a name, for it is now called Coron, and there is every reason to believe that, when the site of Asine was deserted, the inhabitants of the town of Corone, which was situated further north, migrated thither and brought the name of the place with them.[123] Of the migration of a Hellenic tribe which history does not notice, we have proof in finding the names Tricca, Œchalia, Ithome, and Pamisus, together with the legend of Eurytus, and a peculiar worship of Æsculapius, both in the west of Thessaly and in Messenia.[124] The transference of the name of the mother city to colonies, according to the idea which Horace puts into the mouth of Teucer, *Ambiguam tellure nova Salamina futuram*, is found in the Messenian colony of Messana in Sicily, in the Megarian colony of Megara Hyblæa, and in the district of Chalcidice, which was colonised from Chalcis in Eubœa.

But the most important names that come from a non-Hellenic source are those which have a Phœnician origin. Here it is not a little interesting to find names that we are well acquainted with on Semitic ground reappearing under Greek auspices. The name Jordan, which means "the descender,"[125] and is applied

<small>Phœnician names.</small>

---

[123] Smith's *Dict. Geog.*, "Asine."
[124] Bursian, i. 52; Curtius, *Pel.* ii. 133.
[125] Smith's *Dictionary of the Bible*, *s.v.* Jordan.

to that river on account of the almost unparalleled rapidity of its fall, is found in Crete,[126] where Homer mentions it — 'Ιαρδάνου ἀμφὶ ῥέεθρα;[127] and Pausanias tells us that he had heard that the Acidas in Triphylia was also called Iardanus,[128] which is likely enough, as there are many evidences of the presence of Phœnicians in that district. So, too, Mount Tabor, which Greek writers call Atabyrium, is reproduced in Mount Atabyrium in Rhodes, and again in Sicily.[129] We have already noticed how the name Macaria, which occurs in many places, is derived from Makar, the Phœnician Hercules;[130] Astarte also has given her name to several places, called Astyra;[131] one near Abydos, one in the country of Atarneus opposite Lesbos[132] (and it is noticeable that Strabo[133] informs us that in the neighbourhood of both those places there were gold diggings, one of the most usual signs of Phœnician settlements); one at Potniæ in Bœotia;[134] and the place called Styra (τὰ Στύρα), near the southern extremity of Eubœa: the name Astyra is also found in Latium.[135] Samos too, which Strabo rightly explains as meaning "a height"—σάμους ἐκάλουν

[126] J. Olshausen, *Ueber phönicische Ortsnamen ausserhalb d.s semitischen Sprachgebiets;* in the *Rheinisches Museum* for 1853, p. 324.

[127] *Od.* iii. 292.   [128] v. 5, § 9.
[129] Olshausen, p. 323.   [130] See above, p. 351.
[131] Olshausen, pp. 326, 327.   [132] Paus. iv. 35, § 10.
[133] Strabo, xiii. 1, § 23; xiv. 5, § 28.
[134] Olshausen, p. 335.   [135] Steph. Byz. *s. v.* Astyra.

τὰ ὕψη[136]—is a Semitic word, and thus we can trace Phœnician settlements in the island of Samos, in Samothrace, in Cephallenia, which was formerly called Same, and in Elis at Samicon. Further, if we care to look for indirect evidence, we can find it in Byblus, or "papyrus island," which Stephanus[137] tells us was the original name of Melos; in Side and Cyparissus, names derived from Semitic words, and representing trees of Phœnician importation; in Porphyrusa, the old name of Cythera, from their purple trade; and in the harbour of Phœnicûs in the same island, and similar names. If we look to the Greek colonies we shall find others. Adramyttium in Mysia is the same name as Hadrumetum in Africa;[138] Lampsacus means "on the passage;" Lilybæum is "opposite Libya;" Catana is the "little city;" and more might be added.

Finally, the names of places furnish us with a proof that, whatever new elements have been introduced into the population of Greece between ancient and modern times, a certain part of the inhabitants have been Hellenic all along.[139] Were this not the case, it would be almost impossible to account for the permanence in the same locality of such names as Corinth, Patræ, Epidaurus, Argos, and Methone, either exactly in their old form or slightly changed in the course of ages. In other instances we find that a

Ancient names in modern Greece.

[136] viii. 3, § 19.   [137] s. v. Melos.
[138] Olshausen, p. 322.   [139] See Curtius, *Pel.* i. 88.

name has been transferred in consequence of a migration of the inhabitants to a neighbouring site, as in Corone, which we have already noticed, and Calamæ in Messenia, which is reproduced in Calamata; or that it exists in some neighbouring village, as Cleitor in the village of Clituras, and Pheneus in that of Phonia. Some ancient names also appear differently applied, and in different places from what they were originally; thus, the town, which in classical times was called Cyparissiæ, is now called Arcadia; and the name of Mantineia now belongs to a place on the east of the Messenian gulf. And, in many places which have long been deserted, traces of the classical name are found still clinging to the spot: so the Hieron of Æsculapius, near Epidaurus, is still called Hiero; the site of Cenchrea is called Cechries; that of Leuctra is now Leftra; Cardamyla on the Messenian gulf is Scardamyla; and the promontory of Scyllæum is Skyli. In all these instances there is no suspicion of a subsequent colonisation having taken place, or of the name having been reintroduced at a later period.

ETYMOLOGICAL
INDEX OF GREEK NAMES OF PLACES.

A
Acanthus, 343.
Acarnānia, 53.
Acherdus, 340.
Achradīna, 340.
Acidon, 89.
Acis, 89.
Acontium, 54, 372.
Acrăgas, 358.
Acritas, 76.
Acte, 71, 76.
Actium, 71, 76, 360.
Adramyttium, 383.
Æantium, 79.
Ægæ, 346, 364.
Ægaleos, 58, 346.
Ægialus, 264.
Ægilia, 346.
Ægīna, 346.
Ægiplanctus, 58, 346.
Ægīra, 340.
Ægium, 346.
Æneium, 79.
Æpeia, 358.
Æpy, 355.
Æthaleia, 134.
Aganippe, 346.
Agnus, 341.
Agræ, 258.
Alalcomĕnæ, 358.
Alesiæ, 376.
Alōpĕce, 345.
Alopeconnēsus, 345.
Alpheius, 91, 97, 349.
Amăthus, 366.
Ambrăcia, 356.

Ampĕlos, 79, 341.
Amphiăle, 76.
Amphilochia, 356.
Amphipăgus, 76.
Amphipŏlis, 356.
Amphissa, 356.
Anagȳrus, 343.
Anăphe, 378.
Anāpus, 92.
Anchesmus, 57, 357.
Ancon, 369.
Ancȳle, 369.
Anthēdon, 363.
Antheia, 363.
Anthēle, 363.
Anthĕmus, 363.
Anthēne, 363.
Antiphellus, 356.
Antirrhium, 356.
Antissa, 356.
Antron, 360.
Aphĕtæ, 214.
Aphrodisia, 374.
Aphrodisium, 374.
Apidănus, 92.
Apollonia, 373.
Arachnæum, 46, 347, 369.
Arachthus, 88.
Arantia, 366.
Araxus, 77.
Arcadia, 287, 345.
Arconēsus, 345.
Arctonnēsus, 345.
Arctōnŏros, 345.
Arethūsa, 91.
Argennon, 367.

Arginūsæ, 367.
Argissa, 367.
Argŏlas, 367.
Argon Pedion, 109.
Argos, 367, 380.
Argūra, 367.
Argўra, 367.
Arne, 346.
Arnissa, 346.
Aroanius, 91, 366.
Aroë, 360
Artemisium, 57, 79, 373.
Ascra, 340.
Asĭne, 380.
Asōpus, 90.
Asteria, 68.
Astўra, 382.
Atabyrium, 382.
Athēnæ, 161, 375.
Athenæum, 373.
Athēne, 363.
Athos, 363.
Attica, 71, 238.
Aulis, 238, 372.
Aulon, 283, 372.

B

Bate, 341.
Bassæ, 360.
Bathos, 360.
Boagrios, 89.
Bocăros, 90.
Bœbe, 346.
Bœotia, 346.
Boium, 346.
Bolbe, 343.
Bomi, 56, 372.
Bomūcas, 89.
Brilessus, 56.
Bruchon, 89.
Brysēæ, 364.
Bucephăla, 77, 370.
Bucephălon, 77.
Bucolion, 365.
Buphăgus, 89.
Buporthmus, 78.
Buprasium, 376.
Buthrōtus, 346, 365.
Byblus, 383.
Byzantium, 347.

C

Caiēta, 79.
Calămæ, 343.
Callirrhoë, 93.
Calўdon, 364.
Campўlus, 92.
Canastræum, 79.
Canthărus, 244.
Cardia, 369.
Carneātes, 53.
Caryæ, 340.
Castălia, 93.
Casthanæa, 342.
Catacecauměne, 10.
Catăna, 383.
Celădon, 89.
Celădos, 89.
Cenchreæ, 342.
Cephīsus, 90.
Cerameicus, 376.
Cerăta, 53, 240, 369.
Ceraunia, 50.
Chalcidice, 381.
Chalcis, 127, 376.
Chaon, 57, 360.
Charadrus, 86.
Cheimerium, 361.
Chelonātas, 58, 77, 347, 369.
Chelōne, 325, 347, 369.
Chelydŏrea, 58.
Chenæ, 347.
Cherronēsus, 76.
Chersonēsus, 76.
Chœrĕæ, 347.
Circæum, 79.
Cissūsa, 344.
Cithæron, 56.
Cleitor, 359.
Climax, 290.
Cnacadion, 56, 368.
Cnacălus, 55, 368.
Cnacion, 88, 368.
Cnemis, 52.
Coccygium, 58, 347.
Cœla, 208, 360.
Cœle, 360.
Colias, 369.
Colōnæ, 358.
Colōne, 358.
Colōnus, 358.

GREEK NAMES OF PLACES. 387

Colyergia, 77.
Comărus, 340.
Condylea, 369.
Copæ, 365.
Copāis, 365.
Corax, 55, 347, 369.
Corinthus, 53.
Corōne, 359, 381.
Coroneia, 359.
Corseia, 53, 369.
Corsiæ, 53.
Corycium, 371.
Corȳcus, 371.
Corydallus, 55, 347, 370.
Coryphasium, 76.
Cotylæum, 52.
Craneia, 340.
Craneium, 340.
Crannon, 364.
Crathis, 25, 89.
Crausindon, 89.
Cremaste, 213.
Crios, 90, 346.
Crithōte, 79, 342.
Croceæ, 343.
Crocion Pedion, 343.
Crocyleia, 343.
Crommyon, 342.
Cyclădes, 67.
Cyclobŏrus, 89.
Cyllēne, 46.
Cynoscephălæ, 346, 370.
Cynosūra, 77, 346, 370.
Cynthus, 354.
Cynuria, 346.
Cyparisseis, 160, 340.
Cyparissia, 340.
Cyparissus, 160, 340, 383.

D

Daphne, 341.
Daphnus, 341.
Daseæ, 362.
Daulis, 362.
Delium, 373.
Delphi, 360.
Demetrium, 374.
Derrhis, 76.
Didȳma, 375.
Didȳmi, 375.

Diolcos, 377.
Diŏpe, 375.
Dioscureium, 374.
Dirphys, 56, 372.
Dium, 323.
Donăcon, 343.
Doris, 363.
Doriscus, 362.
Drecănum, 371.
Drepăne, 371.
Drepănum, 371.
Drios, 362.
Drymia, 156.
Drymōdes, 155, 340.
Drymos, 156, 340.
Dryŏpis, 340.
Dryoscephălæ, 156, 240, 340.
Dyme, 357.
Dyrrhachium, 361.
Dysōrum, 367.

E

Echinădes, 55, 348, 369.
Echīnus, 348.
Edessa, 364.
Eion, 360.
Elæus, 342.
Elæussa, 342.
Elaion, 58, 341.
Elaphītis, 345.
Elaphonnēsus, 345.
Elăphus, 345.
Elateia, 340.
Elătos, 340.
Eleusis, 361.
Eleuthĕræ, 378.
Elis, 266.
Enneacrounos, 103, 375.
Enneahŏdi, 375.
Ephȳra, 51.
Epicnēmĭdii, 358.
Epidaurus, 362.
Epidaurus Limēra, 361.
Epīrus, 216.
Erasīnus, 93.
Eretria, 350.
Ericeia, 343.
Ericūsa, 343.
Eridănus, 93.
Erineos, 340.

Erymanthus, 57, 358.
Erythræ, 367.
Eryx, 77.
Eubœa, 315, 345.
Euŏras, 51, 284.
Eurīpus, 360.
Eurōtas, 87, 93.
Euryēlus, 54.
Euryteiæ, 366.

G

Gephȳra, 377.
Cephȳreis, 377.
Geraneia, 55, 347, 369.
Glaphȳræ, 360.
Glaucia, 88, 368.
Glaucus, 368.
Gomphi, 54.
Gonnus, 54, 369.
Gonussa, 54.
Gortys, 358.
Gyrton, 359.
Gytheium, 361.

H

Halæ, 376.
Halicarnassus, 53.
Halĭce, 361.
Halieis, 361.
Halonnēsus, 376.
Harma, 52, 372.
Hecatonnēsi, 375.
Helĭce, 360.
Helicon, 52.
Helisson, 91.
Helixus, 91.
Helos, 84, 365.
Heptapŏros, 375.
Heracleia, 374.
Heræum, 373.
Hermæum, 374.
Hermiŏne, 361.
Hermūpŏlis, 374.
Hestiæa, 374.
Hexapŏlis, 375.
Hippocrēne, 107, 346.
Histiæa, 374.
Hydrussa, 348.
Hylæ, 362.
Hypătos, 50.

Hyrmīna, 361.
Hysiæ, 367.

I

Iardănus, 382.
Ichthys, 77.
Ida, 58.
Ilissus, 91.
Inăchus, 380.
Iolcos, 366.
Ipni, 370.
Ipnos, 370.
Ismēnus, 93.
Itea, 340.
Ithăca, 51.
Ithōme, 51, 381.
Ithōria, 51.

L

Lacīnium, 79.
Lacmon, 52.
Laconia, 282.
Ladon, 92, 348.
Lamia, 360.
Lampeia, 50.
Lampsăcus, 383.
Lapăthus, 343.
Larissa, 293, 379.
Larissa Cremaste, 358.
Las, 358.
Lasion, 362.
Laureium, 129, 376.
Lebadeia, 364.
Lechæum, 361.
Lecȳthus, 370.
Leibēthra, 364.
Leibethrium, 57, 364.
Leon, 77, 345, 370.
Leontarne, 345.
Leontion, 345.
Lepreum, 363.
Leucadia, 367.
Leucæ, 367.
Leucasia, 367.
Leucasion, 367.
Leucāte, 78.
Leucimme, 78, 367.
Leucon Pedion, 367.
Leucopȳra, 343.
Leuctra, 367.

GREEK NAMES OF PLACES. 389

Leuctron, 367.
Libybæum, 383.
Limnæ, 357, 365, 378.
Limnæa, 365.
Lusius, 91.
Lycabettus, 57.
Lycæa, 345.
Lycæum, 58, 345.
Lycŏa, 345.
Lycōne, 345.
Lycoreia, 345.
Lycormas, 90, 345.
Lycosūra, 345, 370.
Lycuria, 345.
Lycus, 90.
Lyncestis, 345.

M

Macăria, 350, 382.
Maciston, 57.
Mænălus, 50.
Malea, 73, 355.
Malis, 346.
Manes, 89.
Mantineia, 378.
Marăthon, 343.
Marpessa, 77.
Mecōne, 344.
Megăra, 360.
Megăra Hyblæa, 381.
Melæna, 368.
Melænæ, 362, 368.
Melangeia, 368.
Melania, 368.
Melas, 87, 368.
Melibœa, 365.
Melitæa, 376.
Melīte, 376.
Melos, 373.
Mesobŏa, 357.
Mesogæa, 356.
Mesŏla, 357.
Messa, 356.
Messāna, 381.
Messēis, 357.
Messenia, 274, 356.
Methydrium, 356.
Metropŏlis, 377.
Migonium, 75.
Minōa, 380.

Minthe, 58, 344.
Munychia, 370.
Mycăle, 78.
Mycēnæ, 331, 359.
Mylæ, 376.
Mylāon, 376.
Mylăsa, 376.
Myonnēsus, 347.
Myrmex, 347, 369.
Myrrhĭnus, 341.

N

Narthācion, 58, 343.
Naupactus, 377.
Nauplia, 361.
Naxos, 67.
Neda, 89.
Nedon, 89.
Nemĕa, 365.
Nestus, 89.
Nomia, 365.
Nonăcris, 364.
Nyctĭmus, 97.
Nymphæum, 79, 374.

O

Octolŏphus, 375.
Œnĕon, 341.
Œniadæ, 341.
Œnöe, 341.
Œnophўta, 341.
Œnus, 341.
Œnussæ, 341.
Œta, 58, 346.
Œum, 346.
Olĕnus, 369.
Olmiæ, 78.
Olpæ, 378.
Olympia, 373.
Olympus, 44.
Olynthus, 342.
Oneium, 45, 347, 370.
Onugnăthus, 54, 73, 77, 347, 370.
Ophis, 92, 348, 370.
Opus, 79, 343.
Orchomĕnus, 359.
Orthe, 358.
Orthopăgus, 52.
Ortygia, 347.

390 ETYMOLOGICAL INDEX OF

Ossa, 51.
Othrys, 38, 350, 369.

P

Pagăsæ, 214, 377.
Paleia, 366.
Pambōtis, 365.
Pamīsus, 91, 381.
Pangæus, 57.
Panŏpeus, 358.
Panormus, 361.
Паræbasium, 378.
Parapotamii, 363.
Parnassus, 54.
Parnes, 54.
Parnon, 54.
Parthenium, 57, 3 4.
Patræ, 377.
Peiræum, 357.
Peiræus, 378.
Peiraice, 357.
Peirēne, 89.
Peiros, 89.
Pelăgos, 155.
Pelinna, 368.
Pelion, 56, 366.
Pella, 368.
Pellēne, 368.
Peloponnēsus, 260.
Peneius, 90.
Pentapŏlis, 375.
Pentĕle, 56, 375.
Pentelicus, 56.
Peræa, 357.
Phacion, 342.
Phacūsa, 342.
Phædriădes, 230.
Pharygium, 78.
Phegæa, 340.
Phegos, 340.
Phelleus, 363.
Phellŏë, 340.
Phlius, 366.
Phocæ, 347.
Phocæa, 347.
Phocis, 347.
Phœnīce, 342.
Phœnīcus, 383.
Phœnix, 88, 223, 367.

Phrikion, 50.
Phylăce, 359.
Pimpleia, 93.
Pindus, 56, 93.
Pisa, 363.
Pityussa, 340.
Planctæ, 69.
Platæa, 366.
Platamōdes, 76.
Platanistas, 340.
Plataniston, 340.
Platanistus, 79.
Platanius, 340.
Pleistus, 93.
Plemmyrium, 77.
Plotæ, 67.
Pnyx, 377.
Pogon, 369.
Polyægos, 346.
Pontīnus, 76.
Pŏros, 377.
Porphyrūsa, 376, 383.
Porthmos, 377.
Poseidium, 79, 374.
Potidæa, 374.
Potidania, 374.
Potniæ, 374.
Prasiæ, 342.
Prīnos, 340.
Prion, 371.
Probalinthus, 52.
Probatia, 91, 346.
Pron, 54.
Prote, 68.
Psamăthe, 366.
Psamăthus, 366.
Ptelĕa, 340.
Pteleon, 340.
Ptōum, 50.
Pylæ, 372.
Pylos, 76.
Pyrgi, 359.
Pyrrha, 78, 367.
Pythium, 373.

R

Rhamnus, 341.
Rhegium, 14, 329.
Rheiti, 364.

GREEK NAMES OF PLACES.

Rheneia, 346.
Rheteium, 77.
Rhipæa, 367.
Rhium, 76.
Rhizus, 343.
Rhodŏpe, 344.
Rhoduntia, 344.
Rhodussa, 344.
Rhus, 341.

S

Same, 383.
Samicon, 383.
Samos, 382.
Scarpheia, 363.
Schiste, 226.
Schœneus, 343.
Schœnus, 343.
Sciădis, 362.
Sciăthis, 362.
Sciăthos, 362.
Scillus, 343.
Sciōne, 362.
Scirītis, 363.
Scirōnis, 363.
Scollis, 52.
Scope, 358.
Scyllæum, 77.
Scylletium, 77.
Selenæum, 374.
Selīnus, 343.
Sepia, 348.
Sepias, 348.
Sermỹlæ, 376.
Sicyon, 342.
Side, 341, 383.
Sidus, 341.
Sidussa, 341.
Spalathron, 370.
Sparta, 284, 349, 366.
Speiræum, 77.
Spercheius, 93.
Stena, 200.
Stenyclērus, 274.
Stephăne, 372.
Stratus, 377.
Strophădes, 67.
Strūthus, 79, 347.
Strymon, 93.

Stymphālus, 358.
Styra, 382.
Sybŏta, 346.
Sycūrium, 342.
Symplēgădes, 69.
Sys, 90, 345.

T

Tænărum, 74.
Tanăgra, 366.
Taurius, 90, 346.
Taygĕtus, 44.
Tegănon, 370.
Tegĕa, 289, 358.
Teichius, 359.
Teichos, 359.
Tempe, 329.
Tetraphylia, 375.
Tetrapŏlis, 225, 375.
Teutheas, 89.
Thalămæ, 359.
Thaumasion, 50.
Thebæ, 358.
Thera, 362.
Theræ, 284, 362.
Therma, 376.
Thermæ, 376.
Thermopỹlæ, 376, 379.
Thespiæ, 378.
Thoas, 88.
Thornax, 57.
Thrius, 341.
Thryon, 343.
Thyămis, 88.
Thyrïdes, 78.
Tipha, 343.
Titănus, 55, 366.
Tithoræa, 54.
Titthium, 54, 369.
Tomæum, 52, 372.
Torȳne, 371.
Trachis, 363.
Tragos, 90, 346.
Trapezus, 370.
Tretos, 360.
Tricarānon, 375.
Trichōnis, 375.
Tricolōni, 375.
Tricorȳthus, 375.

Tricrēna, 375.
Trinacria, 375.
Trināsos, 375.
Triopion, 375.
Triphylia, 375.
Tripŏlis, 375.
Tritæa, 375.
Triteæ, 375.
Troezen, 357.
Typhrestus, 50.

X

Xynia, 365.
Xynias, 365.

Z

Zacynthus, 354.
Zancle, 371.
Zelasia, 77.
Zoster, 78, 372.

GENERAL INDEX.

A

Achaia, 264.
Achæan League, the, 194.
Achelous, river, 37, 83, 95, 311.
Acheron, the, 121.
Acontium, mount, 54, 234, 372.
Acritas, prom., 76, 273.
Acropolis, the, of Athens, 249, 252.
Acte, 76, 205.
Actium, 71, 76, 360.
Ægaleos, mount, 39, 58, 242.
Ægean Sea, the, 204, 238.
Ægialus, 264.
Ægina, island of, 70, 188.
Æsculapius, sanctuary of, 295.
Æthaleia, 134.
Ætolian mountains, 39.
Africa little known to the ancient Greeks, 21.
Agamemnon's fleet detained in the Greek seas, 65.
Aganippe, fount of, 100, 346.
Aglaurus, grotto of, 252.
Alcibiades at Olympia, 270.
Alcmæonidæ, the, 245.
Alexander of Macedon, 269.
Alexandria chosen before its time as a commercial metropolis, 5.
Alpheius, 83, 91, 97, 266, 271.
Anaphe, 378.
Animals, names derived from, 344-347.
Anthele, plain of, 223, 363.
Anthena, "the flowery," the peasants' modern name for Athens, 161.
Aous, river, 37, 83, 217.

Apesas, mount, 294.
Apidanus, river, 92, 207.
Arachnæum, or Spider Mountain, 43, 46, 347, 369,
Arachthus, river, 37, 83, 88.
Araxus, prom., 77, 264.
Arcadia, 287, 345 ; Artemis, Pan, and the Lycæan Zeus held in special honour, 288 ; the pig and the ass reared in, 288 ; its two strongholds, Tegea and Mantineia, 289 ; five great battles fought here, 289 ; character of the inhabitants, 290.
Arcadians, the, became the mercenary soldiers of the Hellenic world, 291 ; the Swiss of antiquity, 291.
Archilochus' description of the island of Thasos, 44.
Architecture, military, in ancient Greece, 48 ; in Orchomenus, 234 ; at Messene, 278 ; in Argolis, 293.
Areiopagus, the, at Athens, 252.
Argæus, Mons, 10.
Argolis, 292 ; importance of the Argive plain, 292 ; here is localised the story of Palamedes, 292 ; numerous ancient towns congregated in its small area, 293 ; the sanctuary of Æsculapius, 295.
Argon Pedion, 109.
Argos, 293, 367, 380.
Aristodemus, 274.
Aristotle, 124, 186, 192, 219.

394 GENERAL INDEX.

Aristotle on the subterranean outlets of the lakes, 111.
Aristophanes, 121, 241, 244, 249, 254.
Arne, 346.
Arnold, 243.
Aroanius, mount, 41.
Artemisium, mount, 79.
,, prom., 41, 57.
Asia Minor, geography of, 9.
Asopus, river, 90, 236.
Asteria, 68.
Athena Promachus, statue of, 249.
ATHENS, climate of, 140 ; the most central point in Greece, 246 ; the Acropolis, 248 ; the statue of Athena Promachus, 249 ; the Parthenon, 249 ; the Erechtheium, 250 ; the Long Rocks, 251 ; the Pelasgicum, 251 ; the Areiopagus, 252 ; the Grotto of Pan, 252 ; the hill of the Pnyx, 253 ; the Bema, 253 ; the Dionysiac theatre, 255 ; Temple of Olympian Zeus, 257 ; the suburb of Agræ, 258 ; the Panathenaic stadium, 258 ; the suburbs of Cœle and Cerameicus, 258.
Athos, mount, 42, 169, 363.
Attica, 71, 238, 243.
Aulis, 238, 372.
Aulon, 283, 372.
Axius, river, 80, 200.

B

BALYRAS, river, 273.
Baths of Hercules, 105.
,, of Helen, 105.
Battles, the five great, in the neighbourhood of Mantineia, 289.
Bermian mount, 204.
Bertiscus, mount, 7.
Boar, the, violence of a torrent symbolised by, 94.
Bœbe, lake, 108, 207, 346.
BŒOTIA, 192, 233, 346.
Bomi (the altars), 56, 372.

Brasidas, his masterly retreat from the Illyrians, 201, 202 ; his enthusiastic reception by the people of Scione, 269.
Bronze, 127.
Buch, Leopold von, 134.
Bull, the, or bull's head, rivers compared to, 95.
Buporthmos, prom., 78.
Buprasium, 376.
Bura, city of, destroyed by earthquake, 132.
Burnouf, M., 18.
Bursian's 'Geographie von Griechenland,' 336 n.
Buthrotus, 346, 365.
Byron's description of the aspect of modern Greece, 166.

C

CAICUS, river, 11.
Caieta, prom., 79.
Calauria, island of, 312.
Callidromus, mountain, 223, 225.
Callimachus, 69.
Callirrhoë, 93.
Cambunian range, the, 37, 206, 209.
Canastræum, prom., 79.
Cantharus, or the "Beetle," 244.
Caria, 11.
Carystus, green and white marble of, 129.
Cassandreia, 205 ; see Potidæa.
Cassotis, fount of, 232.
Castalia, fount of, 103 ; destroyed by an earthquake in 1870, 104.
Casthanæa, 342.
Catacecaumene, or the "Burnt Land," 10.
Catana, 21, 383.
Catavothras, subterranean passages for rivers and lakes, 114 ; myths of the, 322.
Catullus, 112.
Caverns—The Corycian, 115 ; of Pan, at Athens, 116 ; of the Eumenides, 117 ; of Trophonius, 117.
Cäyster, river, 11.

Cenchrea, port of, on the Saronic gulf, 263, 342.
Cephisus, river, 82, 90, 235, 242.
Cerameicus, 258, 376.
Cerata, 53, 240, 369.
Ceraunia, mountains, 50.
Chæroneia, 234.
Chalcidice, peninsula of, 204.
Chalcis, 127, 237, 376.
Chaon, mount, 57, 360.
Chaonia, 217.
Charadrus, 86.
Chelonatas, prom., 58, 77, 265, 347, 369.
Chelone, 325, 347, 369.
Cicero, 60.
Cirphis, mount, 226, 233.
Cirrha, the port of Delphi, 229.
Cithæron, mount, 39, 42, 56, 234.
Cladeus, river, 271.
Clark's 'Peloponnesus,' 108.
Classification of names, 356.
Climate of Greece, 138; its contrasts in different districts, 139; its influence on the character, 184-186; on the language, 188.
Climax, pass of, or the 'Ladder,' 290.
Cnemis, mount, 52.
Cœla, pass of, 208, 216, 360.
Cœle, 258, 360.
Coinage, the first gold, at Athens, in the time of Alexander the Great, 126.
Colonus, site of, 242, 358.
Colyergia, prom., 77.
Comedy, birthplace of, 241.
Copaic Lake, the, 108, 310; story of, 333.
Copper mines, 127.
Corax, mount, 39, 42, 55, 347, 369.
CORINTH, 262, 263; earthquake at, 133; the fitting centre of commercial enterprise, 183.
Corinthian gulf, the, 238.
Corn largely imported into Greece, 125.
Corone, 359, 381.
Coroneia, 234, 359.
Corycian cave, 116, 371.
Corydallus, 55, 347, 370.

Coryphasium, 76, 280.
Cotton, 125.
Cranaë, island of, 74.
Crathis, torrent, 25, 89.
Crios, river, 90, 346.
Crissa, the guardian city of Delphi, 229.
Crissa, bay of, 226.
Crissæan gulf, the, 229.
Crithote, prom., 79, 342.
Curtius, E., 'Peloponnesos,' 284, 335 n., 336.
Curtius, 'G., Grundzüge der Griechischen Etymologie,' 335 n.
Cyllene, mount, 41, 266.
Cynoscephalæ, 213, 346, 370.
Cynosura, prom., 77, 346, 370.
Cynthus, 354.
Cyparisseis, 160, 340.
Cyparissus, 160, 340, 383.
Cythera, island of, 74; occupied by the Athenians during the Peloponnesian war, 69; also by Conon, 69.

D

DANAIDES, legend of, 317.
Deianeira, 95.
Deities, haunts of, 304; lofty mountain summits specially dedicated to Zeus and Helios, 308; the springs and promontories associated with, 309; names derived from worship of, 373.
DELPHI, 182, 360; its influence, 227; the focus of information, 228; its remarkable position, 228; climate of, 233.
Delos, island of, 68.
Demetrias, 214, 215.
Demosthenes, 225, 254.
Devol, river, 37.
Diacrii, the, or Hyperacrii, 246.
Diolcos, 262, 377.
Dionysiac, the, theatre, site of, 255.
Dirce, river, 236.
Dirphe, mount, 42, 56.
Dodona, site of, 217, 218.

Doris, 223, 225, 363.
Drainage of the plains, 109.
Drymæa, 156, 340.
Drymodes, 155, 340.
Drymos, 156, 340.
Dryoscephalæ, 156, 240, 340.
Dyme, 357.
Dyrrhachium, 361.

E

EARTHQUAKES in antiquity, 129-132; in modern times, 132-134.
Echinades, islands, 55, 348, 369.
Edessa, the ancient capital of Macedonia, 202, 364.
Eetionia, 243.
Egnatian Way, the, 202.
Eira, peak of, associated with the name of Aristomenes, 274.
Eleusis, plain of, 242, 361.
Elevation of mountains, 42.
ELIS, its triple division, 265; not easily defended, 267; first cause of prosperity was the fertility of the soil, 267; second cause of prosperity the Olympian festival, 268.
Enipeus, river, 207, 213.
Enneacrounos, fount of, 103, 375.
Epaminondas, 277; the scene of his death, 290.
Ephyra, 51.
Epicnemidii, the, 224.
Epidaurus, 295, 296, 362.
Epidaurus Limera, harbour of, 361.
Epirus, 'the continent,' 216.
Eratosthenes, 11, 17, 24.
Erechtheium, the, at Athens, 250.
Eretria, 350.
Eridanus, river, 93.
Erigon, river, 201.
Eruptions in historic times, 135; in Methana, 135; in the islands of Thera and Therasia, 137.
Erymanthus, mount, 41, 57, 266, 358.
Etymological myths, 330.
Etymology of Greek river names, 88.
Eubœa, island of, 70, 237.

Euboic Sea, the, 239.
Eumenides, the, 117, 252, 256.
Euripides, 238, 275.
Euripus, 360; spanned by a stone bridge towards Bœotia, 237; by a wooden bridge towards Chalcis, 238; extraordinary changes of tide take place in, 238.
Euroclydon, wind, 150.
Eurotas, river, 83, 87, 93, 283.
Eva, mount, 41, 274.
Evenus, river, 90, 96.
Explorers, modern, 32.

F

FESTIVAL, *the Olympian*, 268; cause of wealth to Elis, 269; from it arose the true Pan-Hellenic feeling, 269; a thoroughly national celebration, 270.
Flax, 125.
Flowers of Greece, 161; see Vegetation.
Forchhammer's 'Hellenica,' 317.
Forests of Greece, 154; see Vegetation.
Fountains, a determining element in the choice of a site, 102; their appearance in antiquity, 102; at the present day, 103; legends connected with, 106; sacredness of, 100.
Fountains—Cassotis, 232; ·Castalia, 103, 104; Aganippe, 100; Hippocrene, 107, 346; Messeis, 357.

G

GELA, 21.
Geography, of Asia Minor, 9; of the Iliad and the Odyssey, 16; of Greece, ancient authorities on, 22; the sea the determining element of, 58.
Geography, Greek, 190; its influence on character, 191.
Geraneia, mount, 39, 43, 55, 347, 369.
Glaucia, river, 58, 88, 368.
Gold mines, 126.

Gomphi, pass of, 54, 216.
Gonnus, 54, 215, 369.
Gorges, the Acheron, 120 ; vale of Tempe, 122.
GREECE, ancient, the smallness of its area, 3 ; its central position, 4 ; it occupied a position in many respects similar to that of England at the present time, 5 ; its most characteristic feature the mountains, 35 ; scenery of, equal if not superior to that of any country in Europe, 164 ; classical character of the landscape, 165 ; Byron's description of, in the 'Giaour,' 166 ; symmetry of the component parts, 168 ; the combination of snow peaks with southern vegetation, 168 ; the presence of the sea, 169 ; the charm of brilliant colouring, 170 ; influence on the Hellenic mind, 180.
GREEKS, maritime character of the, 61 ; hardihood and caution, 65.
Grisebach's 'Reise durch Rumelien,' 7.
Grote, 201, 269.
Grottoes, Pan, 252 ; Aglaurus, 252.
Gulf, the Crissæan, 229.

H

HALÆ, 376.
Haliacmon, river, 37, 204.
Haliartus, 234.
Hahn's, Von, 'Reise von Belgrad nach Salonik,' 7.
Halys, river, 10.
Hæmus, the, or Balkan Mountains, 6, 8.
Hebrus, river, 80.
Helen, Baths of, 105.
Helice, 360 ; destroyed by earthquake, 131, 133.
Helicon, 52, 183, 234.
Helicon, river, 98.
Helisson, river, 91.
Hellene, traces of the name in Hellopia and Helli, 219.

Helos, 84, 365.
Helots, the, 286.
Heracleia, 223, 374.
Hercules, 94, 95, 96, 135.
,, Baths of, 105.
Hermione, 361 ; purple-fisheries at, 75.
Hermus, river, 11.
Herodotus, 9, 38, 74, 88, 93, 119, 120, 201, 223, 224.
Hesiod, 119.
Hestiæotis, 212.
Hettner's 'Athens and the Peloponnese,' 167.
Hippobotæ, the, 124.
Hippocrene, fount of, 107, 346.
Hollow Elis, 266.
Homer, 81, 103, 118, 120 ; description of the torrents, 85.
Homeric epithets, 43, 44, 45, 47, 61.
Honey, 126.
Horologium, or Temple of the Winds, 146.
Horse, the aristocratic character of, 124.
Humboldt, 20.
Hyampeia, mount, 231.
Hydarnes, 223, 224.
Hylice, lake, 114.
Hymettus, mount, 39, 43, 242 ; blue marble of, 129.
Hypatos, mount, 50.

I

IARDANUS, river, 382.
Ichthys, prom., 77, 265.
Iliad, the, 55, 86, 267 ; the geography of, its careful description, 17.
Ilissus, river, 82, 91.
Illyria, 216.
Iolcos, 214, 366.
Ion of Euripides, 251 ; description of the Phædriades or the 'gleaming peaks,' 231.
Iris, river, 10.
Iron, 127.
Islands of Greece, 66 ; ideas sug-

gested by, 67 ; served as a base for offensive operations, 69.
Ismenus, river, 93, 236.
Isthmus of Corinth, 261.
Italy and Greece, comparison of, 12 ; difference also forcibly marked, 13 ; their relative position, 15.
Ithome, mountain, 41, 51.

J

JOANNINA, lake, 108.

K

KELADON, torrent, 89.
Kelados, torrent, 89.
Kerata, mount, 53, 240, 369.

L

LACMON, mount, 37, 52, 207.
Laconia, 282 ; its valley-plain, 282.
Ladon, river, 92, 310, 348.
Lakes in Greece.—Lychnitis, 107 ; Ascuris, 108 ; Bœbe, 108, 207 ; Copaic, 108 ; Hylice, 114 ; Pambotis, 108, 218 ; Nessonis, 207, 208 ; Ochrida, 107 ; Pheneus, 108 ; Stymphalus, 108.
Lamia, 208, 360.
Lampeia, mountain, 50.
Language, effect of the climate on the, 188.
Laphystium, mount, 135.
Larissa, 293, 379.
,, Cremaste, 213, 358.
,, plain of, 207.
Laureium, 129, 376 ; silver mines of, 128.
Leake, William Martin, 24, 32.
Lebadeia, 364.
Lechæum, port of, 361.
Lecture I. 1.
,, II. 35.
,, III. 80.
,, IV. 123.
,, V. 164.
,, VI. 199.
,, VII. 221.
,, VIII. 259.

Lecture IX. 298.
,, X. 335.
Legend of the Copaic lake, 333 ; of the Danaides, 317 ; Lernean hydra, 320 ; of Selemnus and Argyra, 319 ; of Theseus, 324.
Legends, suggested by rivers, 94 ; by their tendency to disappear underground, 97 ; connected with fountains, 106.
Leibethrium, mount, 57, 364.
Leontini, 21.
Lepreum, 363.
Lernean hydra, fable of, 320.
Lesche at Delphi, 233.
Leucate, prom., 78.
Leucimme, prom., 78, 367.
Limnæ, 257, 365, 378.
Liubatrin peak, or the "Lovely Thorn," 36.
Livy, 209, 215, 238 ; description of Thaumaci, 208.
Locrians, the Epicnemidian, 224 ; the Locri Ozolæ, 225 ; the Opuntian, 224.
Long Walls, the, 244.
Lycabettus, mountain, 57.
Lycæum, mount, 43, 50, 58, 273.
Lydia, 11.
Lydias, river, 204.
Lyncestis, 201, 345.

M

MACARIA, 350, 382.
Macedonia, 200.
Mæander, river, 11.
Mænalus, 41, 42, 50.
Malea, prom., 71, 73, 355.
Malis, 208, 346.
Mantineia, 289, 378.
,, plain of, 109.
Marathon, 343.
,, field of, 245.
Marbles, 129 ; Pentelicus, 129 ; Paros, 129 ; Hymettus, 129 ; Carystus, 129.
Maritime character of the Greeks, 61.
Marpessa, prom., 77.

GENERAL INDEX. 399

Mediterranean, the, western peninsulas of, 11; the three basins of, 20.
Megalopolis, founded by Epaminondas, 291.
Megara, 240, 360; its importance and early prosperity, 240; its numerous colonies, 241; its policy, 241; the birthplace of comedy, 241.
Megara Hyblea, 21, 241.
Melas, river, 235.
Melibœa, 215, 365.
Melos, island of, 373.
Mesogæa, 245.
Messene, city of, 278; the famous walls, 278.
MESSENIA, 273; its two plains, 273; the famous plain of Stenyclerus, 274; its climate the softest and warmest in Greece, 275; the extraordinary fertility of its soil, 275; subdued but not denationalised, 277; contrast between, and Laconia, 275; possesses the two harbours of Methone and Pylos, 278.
Messenians, the, called the Poles of antiquity, 277; restored by Epaminondas to their native country, 278.
Methana, mountain, 135.
Methone, harbour of, 278.
Military architecture in ancient Greece, 48; in Orchomenus, 234; the finest specimen at Messene, 278; in Argolis, 293.
Minerals, 126.
Mines—Copper, 127; gold, 126; iron, 127; silver, 127.
Minoa, island of, 241, 380.
Minyas, treasury of, 235.
Molottis, 217.
Mommsen, 14, 20.
MOUNTAINS—Acontium, 54, 234, 372; Ægaleos, 39, 58, 346; Ægiplanctus, 58, 346; Ætolian, 39; Anchesmus, 57, 357; Apesas, 294; Arachnæum, 43, 46, 347, 369; Aroanius, 41, 91, 366;

Artemisium, 41, 57, 79, 373; Athos, 42, 169, 363; Bertiscus, 7; Brilessus, 56; Cambunian, 37, 206, 209; Ceraunia, 37, 50; Chaon, 57, 360; Chelydorea, 58; Cirphis, 226; Cithæron, 39, 42, 56, 234; Cnacalus, 55, 368; Cnemis, 52; Coccygium, 58, 347; Corax, 39, 42, 55, 347, 370; Craneia, 340; Cotylæum, 52; Cyllene, 41, 46; Dirphys, 42, 56, 372; Eira, 274; Elaïon, 58, 341; Erymanthus, 41, 57, 358; Eva, 41, 274; Geraneia, 39, 43, 55, 347, 369; Hæmus, 6, 8; Helicon, 39, 42, 52, 234; Hymettus, 39, 43; Hypatos, 50; Ithome, 41, 51, 381; Lampeia, 50; Laphystium, 135; Leibethrium, 57, 364; Liubatrin, 36; Lycabettus, 57; Lycæum, 43, 50, 58, 273, 345; Maciston, 57; Mænalus, 41, 42, 50; Minthe, 58, 344; Narthakion, 58, 343; Œta, 39, 42, 58, 346; Olympus, 38, 42, 44; Oneian, 40, 45, 347, 370; Orbelus, 8; Ossa, 38, 42, 51, 206; Othrys, 38, 42, 206, 350, 369; Pangæus, 57; Parnassus, 39, 42, 54, 226; Panachaicum, 42; Parnes, 39, 42, 54, 234; Parnon, 41, 42, 54; Parthenium, 41, 43, 57, 374; Pelion, 38, 42, 56, 206, 366; Pentelicus, 39, 43, 52, 56, 169; Phrikion, 50; Pierian, 38; Pindus, 36, 56, 93, 206; Ptoum, 50; Rhodope, 344; Scardus, 7, 36; Scollis, 52; Taygetus, 41, 42, 44, 51, 284; Thaumasion, 50; Thornax, 57; Titanus, 55, 366; Tymphe, 37; Typhrestus, 36, 38, 42, 50.
Mountains of Greece, 35; main chain of Northern, 36; Cambunian range, 37; central chains of, 38; the Peloponnese, 40; general elevation of, 42; distinguishing characteristics of, 44;

sharp outlines, 44; results of their rocky character, 47; descriptive nomenclature of, 49.
Müller, C. O., 61, 329.
„ Max, 61.
Munychia, hill of, 243; harbour of, 243.
Mycenæ, 293, 331, 359.
Mysia, 10.
Myths, origin of Greek, 298; in a few instances can be traced the correspondence of myths in Sanscrit and Greek, 299; connected with geography, 302; Strabo's interpretation of, 303; Pausanias' explanation of the story of Narcissus, 304; local, of Thessaly, 304; sacred centres of, 306; of the nymph Syrinx, 310; genealogical, 313-317; descent derived from river-gods, 315; suggested by water, 317; of the catavothras, 322; local legends of Theseus, 324; of observation, 326; etymological, 330; ancient legends in modern Greece, 331.

N

NAMES derived from vegetation, 339-344; animals, 344-347; birds, insects, reptiles, 347-350; non-Hellenic, 350-352; vagueness of Greek terminations, 352-354; peculiarities of form, 354-356; from relative position, 356; elevated position, 357-359; inclosed situation, 359; maritime character, 360-362; the environs, 362; water, 363-365; pasturage and tillage, 365; nature of soil, 366; colour, 367; resemblance to men and animals, 368-370; resemblance to inanimate objects, 370-373; worship of deities, 373-375; containing numerals, 375; from occupations, 375-377; political, 377; evidencing geographical changes, 378; Pelasgian and other, 379-381; Phœnician, 381-383; ancient, in modern Greece, 383-384.
Naupactus, 377.
Nauplia, 292, 361.
Navarino, harbour of, 278.
Naxos, island of, 21, 67.
Neda, river, 89, 272.
Nemea, 294, 365; the scene of one of the four festivals, 294; described by Pindar, 294.
Nereids, the, 332.
Nessonis, lake, 207, 208.
Nestus, river, 80, 89.
Niebuhr, 256.
Nisæa, its position, 241.
Nomenclature, descriptive, of Greek mountains, 49; of promontories, 76; derived from vegetation, 339.
Nonacris, or Nonapis, 364.
Nymphæum, 79, 374.

O

OBSERVATION, myths of, 327; markings on rocks, 328.
Ochrida, lake, 107.
Odyssey, the, 63, 69, 72, 267; the geography of, a region of fable, 17.
Œta, mount, 39, 42, 58.
Oil, 124.
Olive, the, 242.
Olympia, 271, 373.
Olympian Zeus, temple of the, 271.
Olympus, mount, 38, 42, 203, 206.
Oneian mountains, 40, 45, 47, 262, 370.
Onochonus, river, 207.
Onugnathus, prom., 54, 73, 77, 347, 370.
Ophis, river, 92, 348, 370.
Orbelus, mount, 8.
Orchomenus, 359; characteristic specimen of military architecture, 234.
Orpheus, legends of, 99, 100.
Ossa, mount, 38, 42, 51, 206.

Othrys, mount, the 'Brow,' 38, 42, 350, 369.
Ovid, 136.
Oxeiæ islands, the, 55.
Ozolæ, the, explanation of name by Pausanias, 28.

P

PAGASÆ, 214, 377.
Pagasæus Sinus (Gulf of Volo), 212 ; the cradle of Greek navigation, 214.
Palamedes, 292.
Pallene, peninsula of, 205.
Pambotis, lake, 108, 218, 365.
Pamisus, river, 84, 91, 207, 273.
Pan, grotto of, 252.
Pan-Hellenic feeling, the true, arose from the Olympian games, 269.
Panachaicum, mount, 42.
Panormus, 361.
Pape's 'Wörterbuch der griechischen Eigennamen,' 335 n.
Paræbasium, 378.
Parali, the, 246.
Paralia, 245.
Parnassus, mount, 39, 42, 54, 226.
Parnes, mount, 39, 42, 234.
Parnon, mount, 41, 42, 54, 282.
Paros, white marble of, 129.
Parthenium, mount, 41, 43, 57, 288.
Passes—Climax, 290 ; Cœla, 216 ; Dryoscephalæ, 240 ; Gomphi, 216 ; Phyle, 240 ; Prinos, 290 ; Thermopylæ, 222.
Patræ, 377.
Pausanias, 97, 98, 99, 104, 105, 106, 110, 119, 120, 132, 140, 235, 249, 268, 294 ; the great geographer of Greece, 25 ; a thorough archæologist, 26 ; great power of observation, 27 ; unrivalled in describing cities, 29 ; his explanation of the story of Narcissus, 304.
Pedieis, the, 246.
Peiraice, 357.
Peiros, torrent, 89.

Pelagonia, 201.
Pelasgiotis, 212.
Pelion, mount, 38, 42, 52, 206.
Pella, the later capital of Macedonia, 203, 368.
Peloponnesus, geography of the, 259 ; compared to the leaf of the plane by Strabo, 259 ; has always contained fragments of a variety of races, 260 ; called the fortress of Greece by Strabo, 260 ; its name first occurs in the Homeric hymn to the Pythian Apollo, 260 ; the isthmus, 261 ; an attempt made by Nero to cut a canal from sea to sea, 261 ; the true line of defence formed by the Oneian mountains, 262.
Pelops, the reputed founder of the Olympian games, 260.
Peneius, river, 37, 83, 86, 90, 122, 206, 208, 266.
Penestæ, the, 210.
Peninsulas, western, of the Mediterranean, 11.
Pentapolis, 375.
Pentedactylon, 284 ; see Taygetus mountain.
Pentele, 56, 375.
Pentelicus, mount, 39, 43, 52, 169.
„ white marble of, 129.
Peparethus, island of, 135.
Perdiccas, 201, 205.
Pericles, 125.
Periœci, the, 286.
Phædriades, or the 'gleaming peaks,' 230.
Phalerum, 243.
Pharsalus, 213.
Phelleus, 363.
Phelloë, 340.
Pheneus, lake, 108, 112.
Pheidippides, 290.
Phocæa, 347.
Phocis, 226, 347.
Phœnice, 342.
Phœnix, river, 88, 223.
Pholoe, mount, 266.
Phthiotis, 212.

Phyle, pass of, 240.
Physical conditions of the country, 123.
Pierian, the, mountains, 38.
Pindus, chain of, 36, 56, 206.
,, river, 93.
Piræus, harbour of, 243.
Pisa, 272, 363.
Pisatis, 266.
Platæa, 234, 366.
Plato's Critias, 45.
Pleistus, river, 93, 226, 230.
Plotæ, islands of, 67.
Pnyx, hill of the, 253, 378.
Pogon, harbour of, 357, 369.
'Politics' of Aristotle, 192.
,, Greek, affected by the geographical position, 190 ; opposition generated by proximity, 194 ; balance of power, 195 ; rude beginnings of international law, 195 ; varied forms of civic life, 196.
Political parties in Attica—the Diacrii or Hyperacrii, the Pedieis, and the Parali, 246.
Polybius, 13.
Polygnotus, pictures of, 233.
Polytheism, Greece specially adapted to the development of, 300.
Pontinus, prom., 76.
Poseidon, worship of, 311 ; the Peloponnesus the focus of the, 311 ; had a high position at Nauplia and Trœzen, 312 ; and at several places on the coast of Elis, 312 ; worshipped under the name of Prosclystius, 313.
Potidæa, 205, 374.
Pott's, Prof. 'Personennamen,' 353.
Prinos, pass of, 290, 340.
Products, the chief, of Greece, 124.
PROMONTORIES :—Classification of their names. — *Headland or similar idea.* — Acritas, 76 ; Acte, 76 ; Actium, 76 ; Chersonesus, 76 ; Coryphasium, 76 ; Derrhis, 76 ; Malea, 73 ; Rhium, 76 ; Tænarum, 74. *From their position.*—Amphiale, 76 ; Amphipagus, 76 ; Platamodes, 76 ; Pylos, 76. *From the dangers they cause to navigation.*— Araxus, 77 ; Colyergia, 77 ; Eryx, 77 ; Marpessa, 77 ; Plemmyrium, 77 ; Rhœteium, 77 ; Scyllæum, 77 ; Scylletium, 77. *From their shape.*—Bucephala, 77 ; Bucephalon, 77 ; Buporthmos, 78 ; Chelonatas, 77 ; Colias, 369 ; Cynosura, 77 ; Ichthys, 77 ; Leon, 77 ; Mycale, 78 ; Onugnathus, 77 ; Speiræum, 77. *From their resemblance to inanimate objects.*— Drecanon, 371 ; Drepanum, 78 ; Zancle, 78 ; Zoster, 78. *From their colour.* —Argennon, 367 ; Leucate, 78 ; Leucimme, 78 ; Pyrrha, 78. *From caves and hollows.*— Caieta, 79 ; Canastræum, 79 ; Lacinium, 79 ; Olmiæ, 78 ; Pharygium, 78 ; Thyrides, 78. *From the vegetation and animals.*—Ampelos, 79 ; Circæum, 79 ; Crithote, 79 ; Opus, 79 ; Platanistus, 79 ; Struthus, 79. *From places of worship erected on them.* —Æantium, 79 ; Artemisium, 79 ; Heræum, 373 ; Nymphæum, 79 ; Œneium, 79 ; Poseidium, 79.
Promontories, the, of Greece, 71 ; their influence on history, 72 ; as points of contact with foreigners, 73 ; their nomenclature, 76.
Psamathe, fount of, 366.
Psamathus, port of, 366.
Pylos, harbour of, 278.
Pythian games, the, 230.
Purple-fishing, 74, 75.

R

REEDS of the Copaic lake, 110.
Rheiti, 364.
Rheneia, island of, 346.
Rhium, prom., 76.
,, straits of, 264.
Rhœteium, prom., 77.
RIVERS.—Acidon, 89 ; Achelous,

37, 83, 95, 311; Acheron, 120; Alpheius, 83, 91, 97, 266, 271, 349; Anapus, 92; Aous, 37, 83, 217; Apidanus, 92, 207; Arachthus, 37, 83, 88; Arethusa, 91; Aroanius, 91, 366; Asopus, 90, 236; Axius, 80, 200, 204; Balyras, 273; Boagrios, 89; Bocaros, 90; Bomucas, 89; Bruchon, 89; Buphagus, 89; Caicus, 11; Callirrhoë, 93; Campylus, 92; Cayster, 11; Cephisus, 82, 90, 235, 242; Cladeus, 271; Cnacion, 88, 368; Crathis, 25, 89; Crausindon, 89; Crios, 90, 346; Cycloborus, 89; Dirce, 236; Enipeus, 206, 208; Erasinus, 93; Eridanus, 93; Eurotas, 83, 87, 93, 283; Evenus, 90, 96; Glaucia, 88, 368; Haliacmon, 37, 204; Halys, 10; Hebrus, 80; Helicon, 52, 98; Helisson, 91; Helixus, 91; Hermus, 11; Ilissus, 82, 91; Iris, 10; Ismenus, 93, 236; Keladon, 89; Kelados, 89; Ladon, 92, 310, 348; Lusius, 91; Lydias, 204; Mæander, 11; Melas, 87, 235, 368; Neda, 89; Nedon, 89; Nestos, 80, 89; Onochonus, 207; Ophis, 92, 348, 370; Pamisus, 84, 91, 207, 273, 381; Peiros, 89; Peneius, 37, 83, 86, 90, 122, 206, 208, 266; Pleistus, 93, 226, 230; Pimpleia, 93; Pindus, 56, 93; Phœnix, 88, 223, 367; Probatia, 91, 346; Sangarius, 10; Scamander, 86; Schœneus, 343; Selemnus, 319; Selinus, 133, 344; Spercheius, 36, 81, 93, 222; Strymon, 80, 93; Styx, 33, 92, 310; Sys, 90, 345; Taurius, 90, 346; Thoas, 88; Thyamis, 88; Titaresius, 87, 208; Tragos, 90, 346.
River-gods, myths of the, 315.
Rivers, Greek, of two kinds, perennial streams and torrents, 81; features of the large rivers, 82; character of the water, 86; legends suggested by, 94.
Ruskin's 'Stones of Venice,' 96 *n*.

S

SAMICON, 312, 383.
Samos, 383.
Saronic gulf, the, 238.
Scamander, river, 86.
Scardus, mountains, 7, 36.
Schar, the, 8; *see* Scardus.
Sciritis, 282, 363.
Scironian rocks, the, 239.
Scollis, mount, 52.
Scopadæ, the, 210.
Seas, the Greek, dangers of the, 62; navigation difficult in, 65.
Selinus, river, 133, 343.
Sellasia, where the Spartans met with their greatest and final defeat, 285.
Seriphus, island of, 127.
Sicyon, 264, 342.
Side, 341, 383.
Silver mines at Laureium, 128.
Sithonia, peninsula of, 205.
Soil of Greece, the, its influence on the character, 187; nature of, 123.
Sophocles, 82, 96, 230, 251.
Sparta, 283, 349, 366; the hegemony of, a natural one, 285; few antiquities in, 286.
Spercheius, river, 36, 81, 93; alluvium of the, 222.
Sphacteria, island of, 70, 279.
Springs, warm, 104; in Thermopylæ, 104; at Ædepsus, 105; baths of Helen, 105; sacred, extraordinary number of, 332.
Stanley on Greek topography, 171.
Statius, 50.
Strabo, 82, 84, 87, 113, 135, 184, 187, 196, 205, 207, 227, 259, 260, 272.
„ on the mountains of Greece, 6, 7; on Spain, 12; on the geography of Greece, 22, 58; on the dangers of the Greek seas, 63, 65; on the Achelous, 95.

Stratus, 377.
Strophades, the islands, 67.
Strymon, river, 80.
Stymphalus, lake, 108, 112, 358.
Styx, river, 92, 310; discovery of, by W. M. Leake, 33; waterfall of, 117.
Symplegades, the, 69.
Syracuse, 21.
Sys, river, 90, 345.

T

TÆNARUM, prom., 74.
Tanagra, 234, 366.
Taygetus, mount, 41, 42, 51, 284.
Taylor's, Mr., 'Words and Places,' 353.
Tegea, 289, 358.
Tempe, vale of, 38, 122, 206, 214.
Temple of the Winds at Athens, 149; of Olympian Zeus, 257, 271; of Zeus at Nemea, 295.
Tetrapolis, 225, 375.
Thaumaci, Livy's description of, 208.
Theatre, the Dionysiac, 255.
Thebes, 236.
Theocritus, 294.
Theogony, the, 306.
Thera, island of, 137, 362.
Theræ, 284, 362.
Therasia, island of, 137.
Thermopylæ, 376; pass of, 222.
Theseus, local legends of, 324.
Thespiæ, 234, 378.
Thesprotia, 217.
Thessaliotis, 212.
Thessalonica, 204.
Thessaly, 206; upper and lower, 207; character of its subdivisions, 207; divided into four districts, 212; passes leading into, 214.
Thrasybulus, 240.
Thriasian plain, 242.
Thucydides, 16, 64, 123, 200, 205, 213, 242, 243, 251, 280, 286.
Thyamis, cascade of, 117.
    ,,   river, 88.

Thyia, altar erected to the winds at, 143.
Thyrides, prom., 78.
Tiryns, ruins of, 48, 293.
Titaresius, river, 87, 208.
Torrents, Homer's description of the, 85.
Torrents, 84; *see* Rivers.
Toryne, 371.
Trachis, 363; where Xerxes established his camp, 223.
Trees, important, in antiquity, 157; the pine of Isthmus, 157; the date-palm, 158; the pomegranate, 158; the fig, 159.
Triodos, or meeting of the three roads, where Œdipus slew his father, 226.
Triphylia, 266, 375.
Tripolis, 375.
Trophonius, cave of, 117.
Tylor's 'Primitive History of Mankind,' 326.
Tymphe, chain of, 37.
Typhrestus, mount, or Tymphrestus, 36, 38, 42, 50.
Tyre, 5.
Tzaconians, the, 260.

V

VALLEY-PLAINS, inland, peculiar character of their climatic influences, 141.
Vegetation, the, of Greece, 152. *Forests*, 154; the pine of the Isthmus, 157; the plane, 157; the date-palm, 158; the pomegranate, 158; the fig, 159; the chestnut, 159. *Shrubs*—The myrtle, 159; the tamarisk, 160; the juniper, 160; the cytisus, and judas tree, 160; the cypress, 160. *Flowers*—Anemones, gum cistus, narcissus, cyclamen, gladiolus, asphodel, violet, daphne, crocus, 162; their importance to mythology, 163.
Vegetation, names derived from, 339-344.

GENERAL INDEX.

Virgil, 69, 110.
Volcanic island upheaved in 1831, 20.
Volcanoes, extinct, 10.
Vostitza, earthquake in, 133, 134.

W

WATERFALLS—Styx, 117 ; Thyamis, 117.
Welcker's, Prof., 'Kleine Schriften,' 19.
Western countries, the—Illyria, Epirus, Acarnania, and Ætolia, 216.
Winds, their general character, 64 ;
altar erected to the, at Thyia, 143 ; Homer only acquainted with four, 143 ; their subsequent nomenclature, 145 ; character of the several, 147 ; temple of the, at Athens, 149.

X

XERXES, 215, 223.
Xynias, 208, 365.

Z

ZEA, harbour of, 243.
Zoster, prom., 78, 244, 372.

THE END.